Mr. Young explores every area of a monumental problem and shows how and why the gap must be closed now—and closed by intensive efforts on the part of our more favored citizens. Negro equality will benefit all citizens, the author explains, providing new markets for business, a new supply of manpower for industry, a decreasing need for welfare funds, and, accordingly, lower taxes.

Among the topics Mr. Young discusses are hard-core unemployment and the ways and means of combating it through retraining and education. He deals with housing problems, and the fact that federal and local administrations have actually implemented inequalities. He discusses the necessity giving qualified Negroes more experience in responsible political, educational, and business positions, if the inevitable Negro breakthrough is not to force the inexperienced and untrained into positions where they cannot function effectively.

Whitney M. Young, Jr. became Executive Director of the National Urban League on October 1, 1961. He was formerly Dean of the Atlanta University School of Social Work. Mr. Young is a product of Kentucky, Minnesota, Nebraska—and the Urban League. His undergraduate work was at Kentucky State College; his graduate work at Massachusetts Institute of Technology and the University of Minnesota, at which latter institution he received his Master's Degree in social work in 1947. During the academic year 1960-1961 he was a visiting scholar at Harvard under a special Rockefeller grant. Mr. Young is a member of the National Advisory Council of the U.S. Office of Economic Opportunity; the Commission on Technology, Automation and Economic Progress; the Commission on Law Enforcement and Administration of Justice; and served on the special Presidential Task Force on Urban Affairs. He has received many awards and honorary degrees. Articles and addresses by Whitney Young have appeared in professional journals and other periodicals. Mr. Young has been married to the former Margaret Buckner since 1944, and is the father of two daughters.

To Be Equal
Whitney M. Young, Jr.

McGraw-Hill Book Company
New York Toronto London Sydney

TO BE EQUAL

To Margaret, Marcia, and Lauren

I am particularly anxious to acknowledge the invaluable and essential role of Lester J. Brooks, who unselfishly bore the major editorial responsibility for this book.

In addition, all my professional colleagues at the National Urban League in some way—whether through the sharing of ideas or the review of work in progress—made important contributions. A special note of appreciation is due to Mrs. Enid Baird, my administrative assistant.

Finally, I am deeply grateful to my father and sisters, Arnita and Eleanor, for their early encouragement, and to my wife Margaret, whose understanding and interest in this project helped make its completion a final reality.

Contents

Introduction

This book will have meaning and value for you, the reader, only if you recognize certain basic facts:

First—The conditions and grievances to which Negro citizens are addressing themselves are real. It is a fact that a wide economic, social, and educational gap separates the majority of Negro citizens from other Americans. In all the major urban centers of the nation Negro citizens are consigned and confined, but not resigned. They are consigned to minimal jobs, inadequate education, health, and welfare facilities; they are confined to urban ghettos where their housing is substandard and they are exposed to vicious antisocial influences. But the Negro citizen in 1964 is definitely not resigned to accepting these conditions.

Second—Most Americans now recognize that this is no longer a regional problem.

10

Today the challenge of civil rights exists not only in Alabama and Mississippi, Arkansas and Georgia, but in every major urban center in the nation. It is acute in each and every Harlem in our land, whether in New York, Chicago, Detroit, Cleveland, Los Angeles, or scores of other cities both north and south. In unemployment, housing, schooling, availability and adequacy of health and welfare services, the Negro family suffers drastically and out of proportion to its numbers.

In northern ghettos hundreds of thousands of Negro citizens are struggling beneath the burden of unemployment and the mounting penalties imposed by automation; they are wrestling with the grinding, stunting effects of overcrowding in their incarceration. And they are subjected to the amorphous, gnawing attrition of subtle discrimination. Weekly their condition grows progressively worse because of continued Negro crowding into the urban centers, white flight to the suburbs, and intensification rather than alleviation of their difficulties. They are reaching the breaking point.

Third—The drive for civil rights is determined; it is dedicated; it is deep-rooted, and it is nationwide.

Negro citizens have demonstrated their determination to change their condition. They will be free. This national ferment gives evidence that the Negro must be given his complete freedom or he must be reenslaved. There is no middle ground. Negroes will claim for themselves first-class citizenship. They will persist in their efforts to correct the intolerable situation in which they find themselves a century after the Emancipation Proclamation. The March on Washington was just a beginning, and the Freedom Rides, sit-ins, kneel-ins and pray-ins thus far have been only a rumble of thunder on the horizon signaling the storm that will surely engulf all of us if tangible, meaningful results are not achieved with speed and sincerity.

Fourth—It is clear that the Negro can no longer be ignored. For all Americans have been confronted wherever they are—not just in the South, but all across our land. The test of our concern is no longer a reaction of horror to a lynching in Mississippi, but our understanding and the decisions we make about integration in our own neighborhoods, our own schools, our own places of employment. A true test is whether we grow more exercised about such methods as school boycotts, rent strikes and the temporary blockade by human bodies of a bridge than we are about the tragic inequities that these dramatic efforts are attempting to focus upon. If 1963 was the year of confrontation in racial relations, then 1964 will surely be the year of decision-making for all Americans. Race relations is no longer a spectator sport.

A determination that is universal among Negroes has emerged out of the year 1963, a year that has been called by several names— the year of decision, the moment of truth, or more popularly, the year of the Negro Revolution. Yet some other things have emerged: it should be clear to all that this is truly a grass-roots movement; it is a ferment that is present wherever Negro citizens are living, and it is a revolution that is not stimulated by any particular organization or by professional agitators. So it is deceptive to believe that the accelerated thrust is the direct result of the Negro leadership organizations or of leaders arousing people.

In fact, if all of the Negro leaders had gotten together in 1962 and tried to predict where the areas of greatest tension and conflict would be in 1963, none of us would have foreseen Cambridge, Maryland, Lexington, North Carolina, or Danville, Virginia.

In this same connection, it is well to mention a psychological phenomenon called "relative deprivation": an observed behavior pattern in which human beings display impatience rather than patience as they approach their goals. As goals come closer to attainment, especially a goal such as freedom, people tend not to think about what they have won nor how far they have come, but rather what they have yet to win. This is definitely not to say that the goal of true freedom for Negroes is within easy reach, even though obvious progress has been made.

Concerning present activity in civil rights, it is naïve for people to say that the new thrust is due to the Kennedy and Johnson administrations. Such a statement certainly fails to credit sufficiently the efforts of Negro citizens. One who is suffering does not need to be told, either by his next door neighbor, or by representatives of the administration in Washington, that he is in pain. The Negro knows full well. And the protests result from his own awareness of his relative condition compared to that of other Americans. If anything, the Kennedy and Johnson administrations have intelligently reacted to the pressures and the just demands of Negro citizens. But certainly Negro citizens do not believe that the present administration has yet gone far enough.

The truth is that any administrations in power during this period would have faced the same situation. If these administrations had not taken the steps that they did, the problem would have been much worse. These administrations have simply responded to the facts of life; they found themselves in power at the moment that the revolution built toward its crisis.

People constantly ask about this Revolution, "Why 'sixty-three?" There are a number of reasons. One, it was the Emancipation centennial year. This fact brought home dramatically that one hundred years after the Emancipation Proclamation we still have tragic problems. But this is just a minor reason.

A second is that we have today more Negroes who have had more and better education than ever before, and they provide better trained leadership. These college graduates, in most cases, have not been absorbed and given a vested interest by the community's power structure as was the case when we had so few college-educated Negroes that they were all made school teachers or given positions that made it difficult for them to protest.

Third, we cannot overestimate the profound effect of World War II on Negro servicemen who found themselves involuntarily transplanted into other countries and other societies where, for the first time, they experienced freedom and a sense of dignity. Over and over again they were told how they were risking their lives to preserve world freedom and democracy. These same servicemen returned to find that the freedom they had fought to preserve abroad was far from being won in their own communities. These disillusioned veterans are today, understandably, to be found among the leaders of our struggle in this country.

Fourth is the fact that in the last several years we have seen the well-publicized emergence of African nations into independence. This development has been important. It has given American Negroes a new sense of pride, a new awareness, and a new self-respect to see Africans accorded equal positions at the United Nations, to see the heads of African states received with dignity and respect by our government, to hear and to read about their speeches. All of this makes it abundantly clear that no race has a monopoly on intelligence, energy, creativity, and dedication.

But if I had to single out one incident that, more than anything else, triggered this Revolution, I think it was the action—or rather the inaction—of Rosa Parks in Montgomery, Alabama. There, on December 1, 1955, for whatever reasons—even she cannot explain— Rosa Parks decided not to move to the back of the bus. All the previous years she had. On this occasion she was not seated in a place reserved for whites. But the law was that as whites filled the bus Negroes must move to the rear, and she refused to move.

If it hadn't been for that episode, there would have been no Montgomery and no Tuskegee crises. But Montgomery and Tuskegee, the sit-ins and freedom rides, all these have given the Negro a new dignity, a new pride, a new sense of confidence in his power and destiny.

There has been a great deal of discussion about "hardening of attitudes" in the north. But essentially it is not so much a matter of hardening of attitudes as it is confrontation and awareness for the first time. In the past, 80 percent of the public was not really aware of, nor confronted by, "the Negro problem." Prior to the 1960's, probably no more than 10 percent of Americans reflected sincere concern or goodwill; perhaps another 10 percent reflected active bigotry or ill will. The remaining large segment of white America reflected congenital apathy or no will. Race relations was a matter of mass indifference—an issue about which few individuals had to make a personal decision.

Now the whole society has been confronted; today, it is necessary for people to take sides. And, as one might expect, polarization is taking place. The white person who has been ignoring the Negro is now confronted, and his real attitudes are revealed. This person faces a choice between identifying himself with those who place states rights and property rights above human rights or with those who honestly face up to historic and present inequities and are willing to right a traditional wrong, even at the cost of inconvenience and pain. Civil rights, therefore, has become a clear test for Americans as individuals, for our beliefs in our Judaeo-Christian teachings, and for our democratic ideals.

We American Negro citizens are no longer looking at our friends as people who are friends up to a point. Now they are with us all the way, or they are on the other side. From here on out, therefore, it will not be a struggle between white and black, but a struggle between right and wrong as far as we are concerned. It is a struggle between people who care and people who are callous.

I feel that there are two major problems that stand in our way at this time. The first is a problem difficult to write about because it deals with a state of mind. Most decent American citizens now understandably feel guilty about the problems of race relations. They also want to believe that they live in a truly open and free society where race is no barrier. Therefore, there is at present a great danger that people will quickly and easily read into the establishment of new civil rights laws and into the removal of signs and symbols that so disturb them the conclusion that the problem is solved and all is well. How wonderful if we could erase so rapidly and painlessly the problems accumulated over the centuries!

We now live in a period where it is no longer popular or respectable to articulate crude and primitive prejudices. Few people speak openly about a return to slavery. Only an ignorant handful publicly admit a belief in constitutional inferiority or differences in blood or body odor. Very few people, except in a moment of anger or regression, speak of or use the word "nigger." Even the Southerner, though he hasn't completely corrected his pronunciation and it usually comes out "nigra," is at least trying with "all deliberate speed."

Yet the real danger is that people may mistake what is basically a change of vocabulary for a change in behavior, practices, and attitudes. While practically all Americans have learned to talk inoffensively, not enough have learned to think differently, or what is more important, to act positively. Unfortunately, most people have simply adopted a new system of rationalization.

In this supposedly logical rationale the white person starts out saying "I like Negroes, but . . ." or "I'm a liberal, but . . ." He then goes on to talk about how property values depreciate when Negroes move into a neighborhood, how school standards deteriorate when Negro children come in, and so on.

I contend that it makes little difference whether people are saying they don't want Negroes to move next door or into their schools because "the blood is different" or whether they say "the child might be lonely" or "the property values might go down." The end result is the same: the individual Negro does not move in. Now this is a real danger and poses a real problem, because as long as people are motivated by language rather than by action, as long as their consciences are being salved without actual, measurable progress being made, then we are in trouble. The question is, therefore, how do we get Americans to treat the *substance*, not the symbols, to address themselves to the real act of injustice instead of the externals that disturb their consciences. How do we get white Americans to concentrate on the inequity and not just the methods of protest?

The second major barrier has been created by *generations of deprivation*. The Negro, if he fails to recognize his deprivation or acts as though it doesn't exist, is guilty of stupid chauvinism. And the white person who ignores this reality or acts as though it doesn't exist is guilty of dishonesty.

The scars resulting from generations of deprivation do exist in Negro citizens unless you assume, as the Black Muslims do, that the Negro is a superior human being. But any group that has been denied for well over three hundred years the barest minimum in health and welfare, in cultural and educational opportunities, is bound to bear the scars of those generations of deprivation. These are facts of life that I think maturity on the part of the Negro and honesty on the part of the white person require be faced.

But this presents difficulties because most people don't want to face up to these facts. To do so is embarrassing both to the middle-class Negro and to the average white person. The middle-class Negro does not want to be reminded of scars that he believes he himself does not possess, scars that will stigmatize him and suggest some kind of inferiority. The white person does not want to be reminded because, although he may not believe that he is directly responsible, he certainly knows that his forefathers cannot escape responsibility.

Given these factors and the existing climate, discussed earlier, what constructive and positive approaches can and must be taken?

Above all, there is the necessity to face up to the fact that we have a problem. The major hurdle in many sections of the country, particularly the North, is unwillingness to admit that there is a problem. This avoidance of reality is also true of many professional people: social workers, for instance, may claim that there is no integration problem in the social work profession; teachers, lawyers, and doctors rationalize similarly with respect to their professions. Another important step is to adopt proper criteria. This is where many people fall short, because most people use criteria that are not valid. They usually measure their position in race relations progress relative to somebody or something else, or to some other place. New York, for instance, feels morally superior and therefore complacent when it compares itself to Chicago. Chicago feels superior because it compares itself to Atlanta; Atlanta feels fine when it compares itself to Birmingham and Dallas. And the mayor of Jackson recently spoke of his city as "the closest place to heaven" for Negroes, because he was obviously comparing it to Johannesburg, South Africa.

The truth is that there is nothing noble in being superior to somebody else. The only real nobility is in being superior to your former self. One other criterion that has validity, and that we so rarely use, is the criterion of justice. We should look at our cities, at our professions, at ourselves and ask: "Are we, in fact, examples of true equality and justice? And is the United States a place where a human being can reach the maximum level of his potential based solely on his own abilities without color as a factor?"

Every step in race relations really measures two distances: how far we've come and how far we have yet to go. To see a person like Dr. Robert C. Weaver in an important subcabinet position in Washington as head of the Housing and Home Finance Agency is a measure of how far we've come. But to see anything unusual in it is an indication of how far we have yet to go. Here is a man who has his bachelor's, his master's, and his Ph.D. degrees with honors from Harvard University; and who has had twenty-five years' experience in housing and in administration. The most unusual thing about it is the fact that this job has never had in it a man with such outstanding qualifications.

Still another key to progress is to recognize that there is no unilateral or monolithic solution to this problem. To believe otherwise is a trap into which many people fall. It is dangerous for two reasons: the person who identifies a single facet as the solution is usually identifying the thing farthest removed from his own responsibility. The real estate man or the builder says the problem is economic;

business, or the employer, says the problem is education; and the educators say that the problem is a matter of housing.

The other reason this search for a single cause is dangerous is that none of these so-called causes is guilty alone. The true cause is a combination of many factors. I go to the employer and ask him to employ Negroes, and he says, "It's a matter of education. I would hire your people if they were educated." Then I go to the educators, and they say, "If Negro people lived in good neighborhoods and had more intelligent dialogue in their families, more encyclopedias in their homes, more opportunity to travel, and a stronger family life, then we could do a better job of educating them." And when I go to the builder he says, "If they had the money, I would sell them the houses"—and I'm back at the employer's door again, where I started to begin with. So instead of everybody pointing to somebody else "over there," in reality everyone can and should intervene wherever he may be in this cycle.

This matter of seeing integration as an overwhelmingly complex, delicate, or revolutionary kind of thing must be overcome. In reality, integration is concerned most properly and urgently with the simple, elementary fundamentals of everyday life. For example, most of the civil rights legislation proposed or enacted is being cited as the most comprehensive, the most revolutionary, the most radical legislation ever. Yet, in fact, all of its provisions are rights that all Americans other than Negro citizens take for granted as really routine: the right to a job, the right to a house, the right to vote, the right to a mediocre hot dog in a five-and ten cent store, the right to go into any movie house, the right to relieve hunger or fatigue, and to enjoy recreation facilities without fear of humiliation—these are all fundamentals. There is nothing revolutionary or complicated about rights such as these. But that they are thought of as such is one of our difficulties.

Still another hindrance to progress is the American tendency to view everything in terms of problems; we are a problem-oriented society. Rather than look at something in terms of the idea behind it or its rationale, we immediately view it as a problem. I contend that integration presents an opportunity, and that we will make great strides when we begin to see it this way.

It is an obvious opportunity for Negro citizens to get better houses, better jobs, better education. Most people can see this. But most people fail to understand that it is a great opportunity for white citizens. It offers them an avenue to rid themselves of the drab sameness that is so stagnating, so self-defeating. Integration provides an opportunity for white citizens to help prepare their children in a natural, diversified kind of setting for the world they're going to have to live in.

Today only hopelessly insecure, tragically immature people need to surround themselves with sameness. People today who are secure and mature, people who are sophisticated, want diversity. One doesn't grow, one cannot be creative, one cannot develop by living and associating with, going to school and church only with people who look like oneself, have the same backgrounds, the same religion, the same interests.

It seems to me that today anyone who wants to be at all fair to his children should fight for integration, fight for the right for his children to have a more cosmopolitan exposure. We live in a world where it is fifteen minutes from Cape Kennedy to Africa. For a youngster to grow up today with a notion of superiority based on his white race or with an uncomfortable feeling in the presence of people of another color—when two-thirds of the world's population is non-white—will be a terrific handicap. Unless he overcomes or outgrows these hindrances, this youngster will not be able to work for any enlightened major corporation. He won't be able to work for the State Department or for the United Nations. He will not qualify for a $75 a month job with the Peace Corps. I doubt that he will any longer be acceptable as a minister.

What I'm saying is not that we can change the practice of conformity or status-seeking in this country. I'm simply suggesting that we change the norms to which people conform and the status symbols. Instead of conforming to exclusiveness, people ought to conform to inclusiveness. I hope that we will be able to create the kind of society wherein people will have to apologize for sameness—for an all-white school or neighborhood or church—because this would be an indication of their immaturity, their lack of sophistication and security. We want a society in which people will boast of diversity and the fact that their churches, their businesses, their schools, and their neighborhoods are like little United Nations. This will be an indication that they are mature and secure human beings.

I know that there are some white people, many in the South and a few in the North, who have no claim to fame other than some myth that they are superior to the Negro. If you took this myth away, they'd be lost. I'm not talking about people who have to have this kind of crutch. I am suggesting, though, that the large majority of Americans no longer need this kind of myth and certainly not at the sacrifice of their youngsters.

We, therefore, must work toward making the norm inclusiveness, which is creative, and eliminating the norm of exclusiveness, which is self-destructive. Show me a person who is full of prejudice, and I will show you a sick, unhappy, fearful individual, who is not going anywhere and who is not growing. People don't shut other people out; they fence themselves in. Show me, on the other hand, an individual who is free of prejudice, and I will show you an exciting, creative, developing human being, who is both secure and mature, and who will certainly relate in a well-adjusted fashion to the society in which we live.

It has become necessary for me to face realistically the true state of America's development as it seeks to make operational, and give honest meaning to, its creed of equal opportunity and justice for all. Like most human beings and certainly most Americans, I seek the beautiful, the positive, and the pleasant while avoiding that which is ugly, negative, and sad.

This is especially true when my own responsibility is clear, and when honest introspection arouses guilt. But there comes a time when the alternatives to facing ourselves frankly and seeing our roles clearly are so tragic, so dangerous, so foolish, and so irresponsible that even the most insensitive, the most blasé, or the most adept at rationalizing among us must stop and analyze both his attitudes and his actions or inactions. For me this moment has come, and I fervently hope that what I say in the next few chapters will cause some of you to do likewise.

> The only thing necessary
> For the triumph of evil
> is for good men to do nothing.
> Edmund Burke

1
Needed Now: A Special Effort

To most white Americans the headlines, reporting the crescendo of victories against discriminatory practices, are clear evidence that the Negro citizen is on the threshold of equal participation in American life. This observation is, unfortunately, inaccurate. For at this moment in history, if the United States honestly drops legal, practical, and subtle racial barriers to employment, housing, education, public accommodations, health and welfare facilities and services, the American Negro still will not achieve full equality in our lifetime.

The reason is that the "discrimination gap" caused by more than three centuries of abuse, humiliation, segregation, and bias has burdened the Negro with a handicap that will not automatically slip from his shoulders as discriminatory laws and practices are abandoned. The situation is much like that of two men running the mile in a track meet. One is well-equipped, wears track shoes and runs on cinders. The other is barefoot and runs in sand. Seeing that one runner is outdistancing the other with ease, you then put track shoes on the second fellow and place him on the cinder track also. Seconds later it should surprise no one to see that the second runner is still yards behind and will never catch up unless something else is done to even the contest.

The discrimination gap is real and is explosive. It must be recognized that our Negro citizens, after only grudgingly receiving the barest minimum in health, education, welfare, housing, economic, and cultural opportunities cannot conceivably compete equally for, or share in, the full rewards and responsibilities of our society simply by an announcement, with impressive flourishes, that now a state of equal opportunity exists. Equal opportunity, if it is to be more than a hollow mockery, must also mean the opportunity to be equal; to be given a fair chance to achieve equality. Anything less is simply the exercise by the white majority of a concern that all too clearly is only skin deep. For the individual it represents a shallow attempt to salve one's conscience and remove the symbols that disturb.

There are pressing evidences of the discrimination gap between Negro and white citizens. The gap is indexed neatly in a few paragraphs of sordid statistics that convey tragically little of the crippling, grim actualities from which they stem. What are the Negro American's chances today in this "affluent society"? Here is a statistical profile:

The Negro citizen begins life with higher odds against him. He is more likely to die in infancy than the white baby. In fact, the death rate in 1958 was 92 percent above that for white infants—a rise from 66 percent above that in 1950. This is largely because Negro women receive less prenatal care, more Negro babies are born prematurely or without hospital care and are more likely to be delivered by midwives rather than doctors.

If the Negro baby lives, the chances of losing his mother in childbirth are relatively high—the maternal mortality rate was four times as high as for white mothers in 1958.

The Negro baby comes into a family that lives in the city (72 percent of the Negro population does) in the Negro ghetto. It is a family that is larger than the white counterpart (4.4 persons vs. 3.6) and is jammed into housing that is dilapidated—quarters structurally

23

unsound or unable to keep out cold, rain, snow, wind, rats, or pests. In other words, housing that is a danger to life or limb. Half of all Negro rented dwellings are dilapidated or lack adequate plumbing. In owned housing, every sixth Negro home is dilapidated, a rate five times the white proportion.

With more mouths to feed, more bodies to clothe and more needs to satisfy, the Negro family is forced to exist on a median income of $62 per week, just 55 percent of white family income. This proportion has actually slipped since 1952 when Negro family income was 57 percent of the white family's.

Negro men now earn 60 percent as much as white men, and Negro women earn only slightly more than half as much as white women. One reason for this is that three out of four urban Negroes work in low skill jobs, those that are at the bottom of the pay scale, the type that automation is gobbling up at the rate of 35,000 per week. Only one out of three white workers is in this category. Another limitation is that one out of ten Negro workers is illiterate—four times the rate among whites.

But if the breadwinner is working, the Negro youngster is truly fortunate, for in every fourth Negro home the worker is jobless, compared with about one white worker out of twenty. In Detroit, 60 percent of the unemployed are Negroes. So it often happens that the Negro family has to depend on welfare. In many major urban centers the welfare roles consist largely of Negroes. In Chicago, where welfare costs the city more than $16 million annually, Negroes constitute 85 percent of those supported; every fourth Negro family is on relief—some for the third generation!

When the Negro youngster goes to school he starts down a path that has proven no avenue to adequate living, much less to fame or fortune. He averages three and a half years less education than white children. And because Negro children are generally taught in slum schools with inferior teachers, equipment, and facilities, the real gap is closer to five or six years. (In Chicago and New York, 90 percent of the teachers in "Negro schools" are new, "problem" or probationary teachers.) Across the nation, only 7 percent of high school graduates are Negroes.

So, the Negro youth is likely to be a dropout or a "pushout"—

out of school, out of work, out of the home and without a future. On street corners and in alleys in cities across the country, one million youths are idling away their time. Half of these youths are Negroes, more than three times as many as there should be, relative to population.

Historically, in the matriarchal Negro society, mothers made sure that if one of their children had a chance for higher education the daughter was the one to pursue it. Twice as many Negro girls as boys are in college, just the reverse of the situation among Jews in the United States. But if the Negro completes his college work, what can he anticipate? His lifetime income will be less than that of a white who has finished the 8th grade. Finally, when all other factors are accounted for and all the facts are in, the Negro dies seven years earlier than his white counterpart.

What I have described in barest outline is a study in inhumanity. In the economic area, it is a disaster—and not just for the Negroes. For the Negro, the situation is far worse than a recession—it constitutes a condition paralleling the Great Depression of the thirties in its pervasive impact. If these conditions affected most Americans to a similar degree, we would be witnessing not peaceful protests but a shooting revolution.

The basic issue here is one of simple logic and fairness. The scales of justice have been heavily weighted against the Negro for over three hundred years and will not suddenly in 1964 balance themselves by applying equal weights. In this sense, the Negro is educationally and economically malnourished and anemic. It is not "preferential treatment" but simple decency to provide him for a brief period with special vitamins, additional food, and blood transfusions.

This is a situation which clearly calls for emergency action on a broad scale in urban communities across the land. Fact-finding committees, pilot projects, tokenism and halfhearted, one-dimensional small-scale efforts will not suffice. This nation and the world need a demonstration that we can bridge the social, economic and educational gap that separates American Negroes from their fellow citizens. It is mandatory that a broad-spectrum, intensive program be launched in the United States, a program that will bring the majority of American Negroes to the point at which they can compete on an equal basis in the nation's increasingly complex and fast-moving industrial economy.

That is why the National Urban League and I, together, have called for an unprecedented domestic "Marshall Plan" approach to these problems. We urgently recommend cooperative *special efforts* by private, public, and voluntary organizations in a massive "crash" attack on the complete range of economic and social ills involved.

Once before, a century ago, this nation focused the attention of the world on its effort to change the status of the Negro. The hopes and expectations of that time were cynically bartered away in political and economic deals. The world, with other events to occupy its attention, took little notice. Negroes, with no education, no economic power, few leaders equipped to cope with the conditions, were powerless to prevent their exploitation.

Today, conditions are radically different. The justified impatience of the Negro must be met with responsible action from the entire white community.

This *special effort* program that we recommend should phase out as need for it diminishes over the next decade. It will not be cheap. But it will prove to be an invaluable investment that will reap great returns. Its cost must be viewed in the same terms as programs of preventive medicine. What were the savings from smallpox vaccine? From polio shots? Or from economic infusions such as the Marshall Plan and our other foreign aid projects? Although the Marshall Plan cost us more than $17 billion, what price can we honestly put on saving Western Europe from being overrun by Communism, on building healthy economies across a war-ravaged continent and strengthening nations in other corners of the world?

We have long given special emergency aid to the oppressed, the sick, the handicapped and the deprived. In recent years we have seen this concept applied through our aid—in employment, education, and welfare—to Hungarian and Cuban refugees. We see it annually carried out in the form of emergency help to "depressed" and "disaster" areas, suffering from joblessness or devastation by hurricanes, drought, and other misfortunes.

The "GI Bill of Rights" after World War II and the Korean

26

War was a comprehensive approach to meeting the special needs of our veterans who had been out of the mainstream of American life during their military service. The Servicemen's Readjustment Act of 1944 helped construct needed hospital facilities, established regional, branch, and local veterans facilities, provided generous retraining and education benefits, guaranteed loans for houses and established inspection facilities to prevent GIs from throwing their money away on overpriced housing, made available loan guarantees for purchase of farmland, buildings, livestock, machinery, and business needs, established a veterans placement service that put a representative in each state and provided readjustment allowances for unemployed vets.

The American Negro has been out of the mainstream for more than three centuries and a special effort must be made to bring him into the central action of our society. The effects of more than three centuries of oppression cannot be obliterated by doing business as usual. In today's complex, technological society, a sound mind, a strong back, and a will to succeed are no longer sufficient to break the bonds of deprivation as was the case with minority groups in the past.

A comparable effort must also be made for millions of other Americans of minority groups—the Mexican-Americans, Puerto Ricans, and others—so that these millions will also benefit. I am confining my remarks to Negroes, because I am more expert on the problems of my own people, and because their plight is worse than that of any other minority (except perhaps for our seven hundred thousand Indians). However, I ought to make it clear that I do not believe in extraordinary measures to help more Negroes progress and become self-supporting simply because they are Negro. I believe we must receive assistance until we can make use of equal opportunities now opening to us because we are Americans, and no Americans ought to be deprived or disenfranchised economically, politically, or socially.

Thus our call for an immediate, dramatic, and tangible domestic Marshall Plan is aimed at closing the intolerable economic, social, and educational gap that separates the vast majority of us Negro citizens from other Americans. Unless this is done, the results of the

27

current heroic efforts in the civil rights movement will be only an illusion, and the struggle will continue, with perhaps tragic consequences.

In our plea for such a domestic Marshall Plan, we are asking for *special effort*, not for special privileges. Our program is designed to reverse economic and social deterioration of urban families and communities and to help develop the tools and understanding that will prevent such deterioration in the future. Here is the proposed *special effort* program:

1. Our basic definition of equal opportunity must include recognition of the need for special effort to overcome serious disabilities resulting from historic handicaps. When you find a man in the wilderness dying from malnutrition you don't just bring him to civilization and turn him loose with a pat on the back saying, "We've saved you, now you're on your own; lots of luck!" He is on the point of starvation. He requires special attention, careful diet and rest, and psychological and physical aid to readjust to civilization.

The Negro has been starving, not in the wilderness, but in the midst of the world's richest nation in the period of its greatest prosperity in history. He has been sighted, but whether his true condition has been "diagnosed" accurately and will be corrected by the majority is yet to be seen.

2. America must recognize and assess at a higher value than ever before the human potential of its Negro citizens, and then our society must move positively to develop that potential.

It is no accident that the U.S. Department of Labor and economists such as Gunnar Myrdal, Eli Ginzberg and others agree that the Negro population is America's greatest undeveloped natural resource. The extraordinary contributions to America of those Negro citizens who have overcome incredible handicaps merely hint at the tremendous benefits that will be ours when Negroes can participate freely in our society.

3. The best schools and the best teachers are needed:
—to instill in Negro children and other educationally disadvantaged youth a desire for excellence;
—to motivate them to achieve and prepare them to advance up the economic ladder with full understanding of the rewards they will receive.

We do not need more examples of school boards treating ghetto schools as the Siberias of their systems, relegating to them largely the problem teachers, probational teachers, neophyte teachers on a "make or break" basis. We need insight, courage, understanding, and an educational value system which parallels that of the medical profession, where doctors and nurses who selflessly devote themselves to combatting an epidemic, for example, earn greater prestige than those who dispense pills for allergies and colds in the suburbs.

4. A conscious, planned effort must be made to bring qualified Negroes into "entrance jobs" in all types of employment, to upgrade them and aid them to qualify for advancement, and to place them in positions of responsibility, including the full range of management positions. The day is past when token integration and pilot placement of Negroes in business and industry, labor and government can be considered solutions. These devices never were acceptable nor adequate, except to white Americans.

For employers the special effort, domestic Marshall Plan approach means exercising the same creative zeal and imagination to include Negro workers at all levels that management has used throughout the years in excluding them. And incorporating Negroes into the work force will not happen automatically by taking down a sign, pasting up a poster, or autographing the President's Plans for Progress Program—a statement of fair-hiring practices. It means honest, realistic seeking out of workers, for fillable jobs, not just positions for which industry can't find whites—such as nuclear physicists, or secretaries who look like Lena Horne and can type 120 words per minute.

Special effort means not hiding behind lame excuses. Any employer who does not want to hire can find excuses. This approach suggests that if a business has never hired Negroes in its offices or plants and two equally qualified people apply, it should hire the Negro to redress the injustice previously visited upon him. Such action has double virtue: it gives Negro youth a new role model and promotes the image of a truly American company.

5. Effective, positive action must be taken to destroy the racial ghetto and to open housing opportunities of all types on the basis of need and ability to buy or rent. Too long the cancerous sore of the ghetto has festered in our urban communities, spewing forth human wreckage and the major portion of criminal offenders; draining our body politic of treasure; robbing us of the meaningful contributions of hundreds of thousands of citizens whose lives and ambitions have been thwarted and truncated.

6. Health and welfare agencies, both public and private, must bring to the ghettoized population their best services and most

competent personnel. Needed are trained workers who understand the myriad ills that afflict ghetto dwellers—unstable family patterns, illegitimate births, the direct relationship between low socio-economic status and social problems—and how to rehabilitate urban Negro families.

7. Qualified Negroes should be sought and named to all public and private boards and commissions, particularly those that shape policy in the areas of employment, housing, education, and health and welfare services. These are the key areas in which the racial differential is greatest and the need for dramatic change—meaning the inclusion of Negro citizens in decision-making—is most urgent.

To achieve this, strong leadership within the Negro community must be encouraged and developed. This leadership will then be ready to step into the vanguard of the teamwork effort so imperative in resolving the smoldering problems of civil rights. The experiences of 1963 should have made clear, if it was not evident before, that the era of paternalistic handling by whites of the needs and ambitions of Negro citizens is gone. American Negroes are done with being "done for"; they demand the right to participate, to do for themselves and determine their own destiny.

8. Every opportunity to acquire education and technical skills must be utilized to the fullest. Every means of strengthening the social and economic fabric of the Negro community must be employed.

Negro citizens, adults as well as young people, must maintain and even accelerate the sense of urgency that now characterizes the drive for first-class citizenship.

9. It is vital that government at all levels, philanthropic foundations, labor, business, and industry reassess their financial support of, and cooperation with, established organizations committed to securing equal opportunity for Negro citizens to share in the fundamental privileges and rights of American democracy.

It is imperative that all of these major sources of support increase substantially their contributions, both financial and non-financial, to the preventive and remedial programs carried on by responsible Negro leadership organizations. These agencies aid Negroes to help themselves by staying in school, registering and voting, making use of adult education classes and retraining centers. For far too long the agencies that have seen the needs and attempted unspectacularly but effectively to meet them have suffered from a crippling anemia of finances, caused by the acute myopia of government, philanthropy, business, and labor.

10. Negro citizens must exert themselves energetically in constructive efforts to carry their full share of responsibilities and to participate in a meaningful way in every phase of community life. It is not enough to man the machinery of protest. Equally important today and twice as important tomorrow is participation in the responsibilities and opportunities of full citizenship in our democracy. This means Negroes moving not only onto the picket lines but also into PTA meetings, moving not only into lunch counters but also into libraries, moving into both community facilities and committee rooms, into both public accommodations and public hearings, and, finally, moving onto the commissions and boards to exercise their rights and insure their fair share.

The *special effort* program outlined above represents a mature, realistic, broad-front attack on the existing problems, a program through which significant breakthroughs of sufficient scale and extent can be accomplished. The program has a simple, practical aim: to provide the Negro citizen with the leadership, education, jobs, motivation and opportunities which will permit him to help himself. It is not a plea to exempt him from the independence and initiative demanded by our free, competitive society. Just the opposite. It is a program crafted to transform the dependent man into the independent man. It makes practical economic sense as a measure to reduce unemployment and welfare costs and to increase our productivity and national income by including Negro citizens in the benefits of our rich society. The President's economic advisers estimate that our Gross National Product could be raised 2.5 percent if the Negro worker's earnings were commensurate with the nation's average.

This program makes historical sense as a rehabilitation of the damage inflicted upon the Negro by generations of injustice and neglect. He, too, has given his blood, sweat, and tears to build our country. Yet, where the labor and initiative of other minority groups have been rewarded by assimilation into the society, the black American has been isolated and rejected.

There are profound moral and religious justifications in this domestic Marshall Plan. Our country is in sharp jeopardy as long as it has within its body politic a socially and economically deprived group of citizens, whether they are actually enslaved or denied the full benefits of equality and freedom by an insidious economic and

31

psychological slavery. In this sense, the crash program proposed is not an effort to impose the guilt and sins of a past generation on our present white community. This is rather an appeal for all Americans, working together, to rid present-day America of its sickening disease, its moral shame.

This is what *special effort* means. It is this kind of *inclusion*, selection, and "preference" which responsible Negro leadership advocates. The nation should not be misled by sloganeers of dubious motivation who conjure up fright phantoms by waving trigger phrases such as "preferential treatment," "reverse discrimination," "indemnification," and "reparation" before unsuspecting, unthinking, and uninformed Americans.

Some ask, why single out the Negro, since there are whites who have been disadvantaged. Yet nobody complained when Helen Keller, for example, spoke out for the blind and said the people who have this handicap need new facilities, new resources, and new assistance in their particular difficulty. Further, she said, where they qualify they should be given special consideration.

With infantile paralysis Franklin D. Roosevelt made a similar effort. There are millions more Americans with cancer, heart trouble, or diabetes. But nobody bothered to ask why he singled out polio for his attention because everyone recognized the truth of the assertions and the special qualifications of Roosevelt as an advocate to speak on this matter.

My basic contention here is that Negroes are subjected to all of the hazards that other Americans face—they may be mentally retarded, have heart trouble, cancer, be lazy or brilliant or lame—but the additional fact of color complicates and aggravates every other hazard. This is why the Negro requires special attention and special effort.

The concept of special effort for Negro citizens may be difficult for the majority of white citizens to accept for three reasons: first, to accept the need for such programs means necessarily to admit that there has existed deliberate or unconscious discrimination in this country. Second, to accept the concept is to admit that the whites themselves have been beneficiaries of a preferential system—and nobody really wants to admit this. Finally, it is extremely difficult for a society that has only recently begun to adjust itself to affording equal opportunity for all its citizens to find itself suddenly called upon to offer special treatment as well.

As in the case of the GI Bill of Rights, the Marshall Plan in Europe, and the use of preventive medicine, this crash program should be seen as an investment rather than a give-away program. It constitutes an investment in human resources, and it will pay off— just as the Marshall Plan paid off in a prosperous Western Europe of strong and friendly allies; just as the GI Bill paid off in better-educated Americans, a revitalized housing industry, etc. The hundreds of millions of dollars poured into medical research through our National Institutes of Health do not disappear into the sand. They have an economic payoff in increasing longevity, improving the level of health and making possible more years of productivity by millions of our citizens. These additional productive years and reduced public payments for medical rehabilitation yield tax revenues which more than offset the federal funds committed.

Finally, and most important, it provides a meaningful and constructive alternative to continuing demonstrations, unrest, despair, tension, and outright racial conflict.

The Negro is in revolt today not to destroy the fabric of our society nor to seek an insulated compartment in it, but to enter into full partnership in that society. We have the material and spiritual resources as a country to meet the challenge and to accomplish the urgent task ahead. All we need is the will to act and the spirit of decency and sacrifice that abounds in our land.

It is true that the ultimate solution will not be found in laws, but in the dark places of men's minds and hearts. But it is also true that laws are the manifest of the national purpose, and when government is unwilling, or unable, to provide them, there is no standard to which the wise and just may repair.

Harry S. Ashmore,
Look Magazine,
July 16, 1963

2
A Nation
Governed
by Law

The determined, peaceful civil rights protests in various communities of this nation are actions to secure effective protection of law. American Negroes are not flaunting the law, nor taunting their oppressors. Impartial evaluation of the tactics employed and the incidents which have occurred will show that in 99 percent of the cases extraordinary discipline has been maintained by Negro demonstrators and that lawlessness, if any, has been hurled against, rather than used by, them.

This is consistent with the purposes of the Negro revolution. The drive is not to destroy public respect for law and order. Far from it. The goal is to gain effective protection by the law. In the South, this requires elimination of segregationist regulations and statutes which deprive Negro citizens of their Constitutional rights. In the North, the primary emphasis is to bring to bear laws that will eliminate discrimination in housing, education, employment, and other areas of life.

The use of law as a method of assisting the Negro in his struggle for equal rights has been the subject of continuing debate. Most frequently those uncommitted to civil rights—and certainly the enemies of civil rights, as well as some well-intentioned but naïve friends—are falling victim to the argument that you can't legislate morality, that you cannot instill brotherly love by edict. Such people miss the fundamental point that the purpose of legislation is not to alter the *attitudes* of people initially, but to influence their *behavior*.

Certainly no law can make one person respect or love another. But there should be laws that prevent one person from acting out his disrespect and hate by denying or withholding basic rights that are Constitutionally guaranteed and God-given. Advocates of civil rights legislation are not attempting to force people to take into their private homes guests that they don't want, or even to speak to people whom they don't wish to. The thrust of the current effort is to make certain that people, in acting out their hostilities toward other people, do not deny them such basic rights as voting, education, housing, and employment.

It is frequently argued that we learned through the unfortunate attempt to prohibit liquor in the country under the Eighteenth Amendment that you can't change attitudes, that you cannot force people to change their habits. Those who seize on this illustration fail to note the vast difference. Prohibition attempted to dictate to citizens what they could not do to *themselves*—i.e., that they could not drink beer or bourbon or anything in between—by making it "impossible" to sell or to purchase liquor.

The fair employment laws and other civil rights measures describe what one citizen cannot do to *another*. There is, of course, a tremendous difference between the social and economic self-inflicted harm done to the individual who drinks and the inescapable damage to millions of people who are denied basic rights because of race or color.

It will be a great step forward when people understand that the Negro is not too much concerned with whether or not he is loved. He just doesn't want to be lynched. And too many people are being lynched daily—psychologically and economically. Economic injustice is sometimes more painful, and certainly affects thousands more of our citizens, than the quick way out via the end of a rope. Legislation can and must provide the basic framework for change in this condition.

One of the most important benefits of legislation is that it adds the full force of law to the support of many people who wanted to do the right thing but never felt strong enough to risk either the real or imagined consequences. They went along with the status quo and did nothing; in many cases such inaction meant denying jobs and denying services. When laws are put on the books these people are given the necessary protection and excuse for taking positive action. Many people needed and wanted to take advantage of the work skills of Negroes, wanted to open up their restaurants and hotels to additional customers, even though the official posture of the various business groups through their lobbyists was to oppose passage of a law that would make it possible.

The truth of the matter is that many, perhaps most, individual businessmen preferred that such laws be passed. Many told me this recently when I was on tour for the President's Committee on Equal Opportunity in the Armed Forces. A large number of the businessmen in southern cities said they would like nothing better than for the commander of the local armed forces base to issue an order that put off limits any establishment that refused to serve all troops. They wanted such action because they could then open up their places and get additional business without running the risk of having other customers complain. Such a move lifts from the proprietor and the employees the responsibility for making a decision which might be unpopular with some people. The blame can be placed impersonally on government or its representatives.

In the absence of statutes, invariably the practices of people at the community level tend either to cling to the status quo or to be more influenced by the small but highly vocal minority of racists than by the large majority of people who would be indifferent or who would welcome changes. Historically, society sets its legal expectations below its highest moral values. We see that in our society most of our practices settle downward to our minimum conception of human response. They seldom rise above the minimum and rarely equate with the highest ideals and the moral thinking of the majority of people. The millenium will not arrive automatically, therefore, when all men simply observe the laws.

All of our experience has shown that attempts to determine public reaction to a law prior to its enactment are never valid, because people are generally inclined to be afraid of change. People usually favor what they feel is most comfortable and avoid anything that they think might lead to disorder. Random queries, public opinion polls, and attitude studies are invalid, because people are asked about conditions with which they have had no real experience.

I recall one study where, in a number of cities, people were asked: "Do you mind having a Negro drive your bus?" Many persons said they would mind. Then Negro drivers actually were put on the buses, and the survey was repeated. The results showed that most of the people didn't even realize that there were Negro drivers, nor did they have any objection. They had been asked previously about something that they had never experienced and so had no basis on which to make a valid judgment.

Attitudes invariably change after the law causes behavior to be modified. This is why laws should never be dependent upon attitude studies before enactment. Given the condition under the law, people do, when placed in contact with other people, lose some of their stereotypes; some of the pictures in their mind change.

The difficult part, of course, is getting laws on the books. The Negro has had a severe handicap in trying to secure statutory relief by legislative action. Legislators are usually white, generally of middle-class origin, afflicted by all the fears and insecurities characteristic of the bourgeoisie. And because the legislator is up for election so often, he has even more insecurities about job tenure than many of his nonlegislative peers. I have found that anybody who is basically insecure is not likely to be rational on interracial matters.

In addition, the legislator has come from a white neighborhood, has probably been educated in an all-white school, and most likely has had extremely limited contact with Negroes. His reactions, therefore, are almost purely subjective, reflecting the prejudice of his white environment; seldom if ever do they stem from deep commitment based on personal experience or knowledge. And, of course, he is always subjected to pressures that are usually strongest and best organized from the conservative, far right, and racist groups. It seems to be much more difficult to organize liberals. Perhaps if they could be organized they wouldn't be liberals. Anyway, they tend to be much more individual and independent in their thinking, but they seldom lay it on the line with their legislators. In addition, the great mass of white voters have been indifferent on the subject of civil rights, and many Negroes still do not or cannot vote.

Thus, a legislator sensitive to the prevailing winds is more likely to be swayed by the militant conservatives. And as voters we have not distinguished ourselves by choosing many people for the legislatures who could qualify for the label "statesman." The Negro, therefore, has been at a real disadvantage in leaving his destiny to persons who neither knew nor understood him or his needs. Because the legislator's major goal is survival, i.e., reelection, only rarely has one of them espoused the relatively unpopular cause of civil rights.

There are, lamentably, few notable examples of candidates who have recognized the deep psychological and practical possibilities of using their campaigns to educate and mold public opinion on this subject. One such legislator is Senator Hubert Humphrey of Minnesota, a state having a Negro population of less than 1 percent. There certainly were no pressing political reasons for him to go after the "Negro vote," but he stumped the state, educating the people on the racial question. Earlier, as mayor of Minneapolis, he had made it a matter of civic pride that the city enact a fair employment practices law and other, liberal statutes. He so impressed the voters with this philosophy that the public reaction was: "Anyone who speaks out for the Negro, the least of our citizens, must be a good man." Humphrey successfully identified himself in this way with a minority group and captured the sympathies of the majority.

Here is practical statesmanship of a high order as well as sound political strategy to which more legislators should give serious consideration. A voter who may know nothing of a candidate's economic philosophy or how he voted on wheat allotments can readily appreciate one who fights for the underdog.

For the Negro there are three possible avenues to achieve legal protection. Changes can be brought about by executive, judicial, or legislative action. In the long run, legislative action is preferable because of the vulnerability of executive action and the lengthy process of using the courts. What the executive does is not permanent and can be wiped out by the Congress or the courts or the whim of another executive. Further, executive action is hazardous because it has been established only indirectly by the representative process.

I am convinced that no local, state, or federal official has ever used his executive powers to the fullest for civil rights. The most significant action an executive can take, whether mayor or governor, is to set the example in his own department. All of his executive leadership should be used to establish the interracial attitude in relationships with other governmental bodies, with business organizations, labor, and the public. After all, the businessman takes the position, with some justification, that if the heads of government, who are not risking their own capital, are afraid to hire Negroes and place them in responsible positions then by what right do these officials expect businessmen to invest money and effort to do so?

On this point, there was a feeling among Negroes that President Kennedy had by executive order done more than any previous President and that these efforts were largely the result of his own initiative. He was committed, after his 1960 election, to making good many campaign pledges for legislation and other programs. Finding himself without a clear mandate, President Kennedy determined to accomplish as much as possible by executive order rather than by new legislation. For some time, he relied heavily upon the effectiveness of this technique, the U.S. Civil Rights Commission, and persuasion. His Executive Order No. 10925 on March 6, 1961, established a President's Committee on Equal Employment Opportunities and outlawed discrimination by corporations holding defense contracts and by federal agencies. Another stride forward was made on November 27, 1962, with the enactment of his Executive Order No. 11063 banning bias in federally aided housing developments. The president also used the influence of his office to persuade companies not holding defense contracts to end job discrimination in a series of off-the-record White House conferences with top business executives. At the same time, the then Vice-President Lyndon B. Johnson pressed the Plans for Progress program intended to elicit written statements of fair play by business in hiring and promotion.

It is true that the Negro community felt that President Kennedy had done more than any other president in the area of civil rights. Still, few Negroes thought that his actions were completely the result of his own initiative. It was clear in our minds that he was reacting intelligently to the increased pressure generated by the street demonstrations and the mounting impatience of Negroes. But given this motivation, we felt that he reacted with courage and compassion once it became clear that this problem could not be wished away. In his special message to Congress, on February 28, 1963—in the first such address devoted exclusively to civil rights by a chief executive— he urged enactment of wide-ranging new legislation to help cure what he termed "the cruel disease of discrimination." In a series of speeches throughout 1963, President Kennedy left no doubt in the public mind that the enactment of his proposals was a crucial necessity. He had become the first president to put civil rights in its true moral context.

Now the administration's so-called omnibus civil rights bill has had an extraordinary history. Originally called the "Civil Rights Act of 1963," it was first proposed by President Kennedy as a "strong" bill to deal with urgent needs. It contained eight sections: voting; public accommodations; school desegregation; the establishment of a Community Relations Service to mediate racial friction; the extension of the Commission on Civil Rights for four years; statutory authority for the existing President's Committee on Equal Employment Opportunity to operate as a commission; authorization to withhold federal funds from any programs supported by federal assistance directly or indirectly in which discrimination was practiced; and a miscellaneous section.

First to be pruned off in committee was the Community Relations Service. The proposal dealing with discrimination in employment—hiring, upgrading, training, etc.—was left in the framework of the Committee on Equal Opportunity. This meant that it affected only federal offices and government contractors, when what was and still is needed is a broad authority similar to the Fair Employment Practices (FEP) order issued by President Roosevelt during World War II. It outlawed discrimination in employment and set up a commission to insure nondiscrimination in all aspects of employment, across the board. Still needed today are strong enforcement provisions to make it clear that the government means business.

The bill as presented by President Kennedy was at best a minimum measure in terms of the needs with which it deals. At one point the bill came out of a subcommittee so strengthened that the President and Attorney General feared its very strength would insure its defeat in the House and Senate. Therefore they recommended changes that weakened it substantially. One of these limited Justice Department action in voting, school and public accommodations cases. It allowed intervention only when an individual initiated a suit claiming denial of equal protection under the law.

The rewritten bill, taking away the Attorney General's power to initiate action, removed an essential element. By this change the impoverished, vulnerable Negro in lonely rural areas of the South was made responsible for initiating his own complaints. This would reduce, for obvious, practical reasons, the number of complaints filed. This revision was the most unfortunate change made in the bill.

Taking the FEP portion of the bill and putting enforcing powers in the courts was a similar restricting action. Implementation ought to be the Labor Department's responsibility. Placing this in the courts puts it in the hands of local political appointees and elected officials who reflect the prejudices of their constituents in areas where the Negro is effectively disenfranchised. Such officials are generally committed to existing discrimination patterns.

The House, aware of these weakening aspects, reinstated some of the bill's original protection and added sections on public facilities, voting statistics and court appeals. And, though the "Dirksen amendments" were considered damaging, their net effect was largely to permit the states and communities more time to correct abuses before the Justice Department moved in. The danger in the Civil Rights bill is that it will mislead Americans into thinking that protection has been guaranteed which, in terms of practical enforcement, is severely limited.

As bitter experience showed in implementing the school desegregation decision, every tiny technical detail has to be carried to the Supreme Court in an agonizingly time-consuming, expensive process. Only above the state level are decisions likely to escape

43

discriminatory influences. Further, overburdened local legal machinery is historically slow. The individual who presses suit may wait a year—if it goes to a higher court it will be longer—and this is simply impractical. So, for the really dedicated discriminator, this legislation presents no hindrance.

Another dilution of the bill came in the voting provisions. These were modified to apply to federal rather than local elections. The protection of the right to register and vote in federal but not local elections seems to indicate more concern for the election of the President than for correcting local conditions.

Unless a man can vote for his councilman and his mayor he is not able to correct local conditions, nor to have much impact in the party organization. The interesting thing about this particular provision is that the same people who cried so loudly in favor of local control, decentralization of authority, and states' rights are the ones who this time advocated taking control of local conditions out of the hands of the individual.

The exemption of small businesses from the public accommodations section was an obvious compromise to try to eliminate the opposition of these groups. But it raises questions about the morality of the act. One can be just as effectively discriminated against by small businesses as large ones. It's like saying that there are different degrees of murder—that it is all right to go out and slaughter until you commit a certain number of killings. It's all right for small businesses to discriminate but wrong for large businesses.

However, the most important weakness in the Civil Rights Act is that it deals with minimums, in terms of needs, urgency, and problems. The fact is that we have had FEP laws for years, in many states —thirty of them—and the major northern cities already had legislation that is much stronger than the supposedly revolutionary Civil Rights Act. Many of the senators who opposed the public accommodations section have similar or stronger accommodations statutes in their own states. Take Ohio: Senator Lausche opposed the public accommodation section, but Ohio has a law that dwarfs the national proposal.

We have learned the hard way that laws without enforcement powers are no more than good advice. And we all know how eagerly people seek and abide by good advice. All such laws do is to salve people's consciences by giving them the feeling of having done something without actually inconveniencing them in any substantial way. We also have found that failure to finance and staff the enforcement machinery adequately invariably undermines its effectiveness. You will observe in the staffing of these agencies that even today, almost without exception, the chief staff person is white. Now he may have had limited experience and training in this field, but he has been appointed (usually) because it is believed that the businessmen—white of course—will reveal their prejudices more freely to a white person, that the white staff chief will understand and be more reasonable. So the practice is to have the second in command a Negro, though often he is better trained and much more experienced. Such an arrangement often leads to tension on the staff. And it indicates that even for these agencies there is still a great deal of condescension and failure to equate on an equal basis the training and skills of candidates. So the white person is usually made the director, not because he's better qualified, but because he is white.

Now it is true that FEP laws have their limitations. Actually, the law does not state that people cannot discriminate. It says that if they discriminate they're doing so illegally. But this has never been sufficient to stop most Americans from doing what they want to do. As a result, many people find devices to get around the law by setting up other criteria or using subjective tests such as personal interviews or by filling their job needs only through private employment agencies. So, in many cases the availability of jobs never becomes known to the Negro.

On the plus side, FEP laws can have positive effects in their communities. The best have commissions and boards that are vigilant in their determination to see that the Negro really gets an even break. They are not set up simply to maintain the status quo. In order to be effective they must be adequately staffed, have the power of subpoena and the right to initiate complaints. The best FEP agencies have aggressive educational programs designed to inform the Negro of his rights and to make the law understandable to him. Furthermore, the services of the Fair Employment Practices Commission must be designed to minimize delays between filing of complaints and adjudication. Some of these cases take six months or longer and the job-seeker becomes discouraged. Word gets around that it takes a long time to get action and those having legitimate complaints don't bother to file them.

To be effective with the majority group the FEP Commission has to advertise aggressively the fact that there is such a board, that there are laws on the books making discrimination illegal, and that the individual violates the law by doing a), b), and c).

We have found that far more benefit is derived from placing the laws on the books than from actual complaints and adjudicated cases. This is because there are very few actual complaints and even fewer adjudicated cases decided in favor of complainants. What has happened, however, is that when many of these FEP regulations went into effect there were people who welcomed them because they wanted to take advantage of the skills of Negro workers and the buying power of Negro consumers. The big shift comes when the laws are passed.

Looking at the basic effects of legal changes, the law doesn't force people to hire Negroes. It just says you cannot refuse to hire a qualified Negro because he is a Negro. It doesn't say you have to sell your house to a Negro. It says you cannot refuse to sell to him simply because of his color. You can think up some other basis for not selling—hundreds of thousands have and, perhaps, will. So law is no guarantee of a job or a house. It is only a guarantee that a man cannot be refused because of race.

The law, therefore, is simply a means to eliminate one of the barriers. There are still many more to be overcome—lack of skills, training, education, social services, health facilities, counseling, housing, financing, and others. One of the great hypocrisies of our time is that so many states and cities have passed FEP laws but have then proceeded to maintain inadequate vocational schools and educational facilities. As long as this situation obtains, the law really doesn't achieve much, because without skills or knowledge you don't qualify for the jobs.

So, when we consider the federal Civil Rights Act and its probable impact, we can conclude that it deals with minimum needs in a minimal way. It is supposed to meet overwhelmingly urgent wants, and reflection on the agonizing months required to pass it gives wry insight into the responsiveness of our legislative system to urgent calls.

Our whole legislative system is antiquated and ineffective in meeting modern problems. It has proved itself unworkable and increasingly unresponsive in recent years. It is in the actions of Congress that we feel the dead weight of the seniority system in its most highly evolved condition. Because of the one party system in the South, power is concentrated in the hands of people who represent the smallest number of voters in the country. The rest of the United States literally gives this prize concession—control of the machinery of Congress—to the most reactionary, unresponsive bigots in the nation. It hands this precious gift to the finest wrong-headed minds of the South by tolerating the disenfranchisement of the Negro.

This act of robbing the Negro of the vote, causing him to live a subjugated life without recourse to the machinery of consent, is the root cause of the one-party system in the South; it delivers the federal governmental machinery into the hands of these long-lived, short-sighted perennial Congressional committee chairmen who run the engine rooms of the American ship of state. These men have almost invariably proved themselves narrowly parochial in their outlook. They often are most limited in their experience and background, coming from places that are less developed economically, where most of the elements that characterize the best in our lively society—modern cultural and educational experiences—are nonexistent. Yet these museum specimens of nineteenth-century thought control the direction of the most powerful nation in this twentieth century world. This relative handful of dedicated, willful, contrary men can delay and hold up an action that the whole country wants and sorely needs, effectively proving that representative democracy, as practiced here, has a prominent Achilles heel.

One other observation is pertinent. The fact that eighty senators can be completely stymied by twenty says to me that those twenty believe in what they are fighting for. They care a great deal about segregation and all its trappings. And they are willing to do everything possible to retain this system. The eighty, therefore, obviously do not care enough. They must not really believe deeply in justice, Constitutional rights, and integration. Proof? We saw on the government's Communications Satellite Corporation bill that, when most senators wanted to pass it and a few did not, the majority shut off a filibuster and all other delaying tactics and rammed it through.

This, of course, wasn't related to race or justice; this was simply something in which they were deeply interested.

Most of the men in Congress are lawyers. Their ethics in Congress and out bear analysis. Many lawyers become judges; many more aspire to the bench. Most successful lawyers have a hand on or near the levers of power in their communities. What do they do with their expertise, their counsel?

Every profession, it seems to me, has to be weighed against its basic philosophy. What is the basic commitment of the profession? What commitments are inherent in it? By such standards, lawyers should be expected to cherish civil rights and civil liberties, to respect the Constitution and the courts, and to conduct themselves by highly ethical codes of behavior. And because lawyers are usually the most ambitious in terms of political careers and public service and are articulate in their strategic roles, they could render great service.

But invariably lawyers have pushed into the background their ethical and professional commitments and have used their talents like lesser mortals to perpetuate the status quo and to exploit it as much as possible to their own advantage. Their great heritage and the basic framework in which they practice should so influence them that they, most of all, should understand the tragedy, the great danger, inherent in denial of consent, denial of civil rights. In this context, the scales of justice find them wanting.

The fact is that the lawyer takes on the coloration of his region far faster than he reflects his professional orientation. So lawyers are found in the South defending segregation and fighting justice, helping the oppressors to find loopholes in, and avenues around, the Constitution, and actively participating in and promoting defiance and discredit of the Supreme Court and the courts generally. Thus they weaken their own profession.

Some people, of course, do not know any better and cannot be held responsible. Lawyers, however, do know the facts of life, and they know when they are in the wrong. Their failure to educate or to share with their fellow citizens what they know to be right is, to me, the greatest indictment against them. During this period when they should have been providing civil rights leadership they have failed lamentably.

It is only recently that some lawyers have begun to speak up. A number of them have begun to challenge their fellow lawyers to set standards for adherence to, and support of, the law in their communities. Of course, such actions may be short cuts to publicity and leadership. I don't discount that. Civil rights is *the* area today, and the lawyer who becomes active in the movement gets a lot of publicity that he normally cannot solicit without being considered unethical. What better way to establish yourself than to fight for the underdog by taking civil rights cases?

It is interesting, I think, to note the reversal taking place as the nation is confronted by the Negro revolution. There was a time when legal action was considered radical and controversial, and the National Association for the Advancement of Colored People was considered an extremist organization. Now, as direct action has increased, legal action has become refreshingly respectable. Increasingly, responsible leaders in the nation say to the Negro: Go ahead and fight, but take it out of the streets and put the protest in the courts. Yet only ten years ago to carry the fight into the courts caused real riots.

The legal profession can help tremendously if its members sincerely wish to involve themselves. On some massive national basis, with units in every local community, there ought to be a Civil Rights Society. Since it appears that we are going to have to continue with this burden of the victim proving that he has been discriminated against, I believe that lawyers ought to volunteer in great numbers to form legal aid pools through which they can freely offer their services to seek out cases of abuse under the Civil Rights Act, since the Attorney General can't initiate action. Volunteer lawyers should initiate complaints on behalf of victimized people. And those who participate in this effort should be given status, prestige, and rewards within the legal profession.

President Kennedy in mid 1963 called a White House conference of lawyers to consider what the legal profession could do to help assure equal rights. The result was the formation of a national Lawyers' Committee on Civil Rights Under Law by one hundred leading white and Negro barristers. It and other state and local groups of lawyers can have real and important impact if they pursue actively their stated purpose: "To stimulate, supervise and participate in various activities helpful to a solution of the problems in the field of civil rights under law."

Some positive signs are: The enlistment of volunteer lawyers in New Hampshire for volunteer counsel service in southern states where local legal counsel is not available; the formation of biracial committees of lawyers on civil rights in New York; enrollment of volunteer attorneys of the Metropolitan Council of the American Jewish Congress in New York City to work with leading civil rights groups in providing counsel for those arrested in demonstrations and to help establish broad legal principles on which such cases can be argued.

Lawyers should volunteer for such activity not only to help people who are incapable of such action or who cannot afford counsel themselves, but also to uphold the majesty of the law itself. To the extent that the rights of people are being denied them, the law does not have its full meaning, effectiveness, and respect. Law still lies in that shady area of unequal service. It works and renders justice for some people but not for others. The lawyer has an enlightened self-interest as well as a grave responsibility to see that the law applies equally and that it works. Thus, the law will give meaning to his noble profession and adherence to it will yet put the ring of truth into that noble sentiment that ours is a nation governed by laws, not by men.

Among the purposes of a society
should be to try to arrange for
a continuous supply of work at
all times and seasons.
Pope Leo XIII,
Encyclical on
the Condition of Labor,
May 15, 1891

3
Help
Wanted:
New
Jobs
for
Negroes

Not long ago President Johnson asked me to visit him at the White House. We talked about the urgent need for new jobs for Negro citizens and about various methods of tackling this supremely important matter. One possibility we discussed was a broad program of works at the community level across the nation, a program of slum clearance and rehabilitation to take millions of families off breadlines and put them in pay lines. The President asked for a memorandum outlining my suggestions.

For the Negro, the opportunity to be equal means not only the right to an equal chance for available jobs, but equality in unemployment as well. Some of you will remember that back in 1933 the nation was virtually prostrate. The national income was $39 billion, half what it had been in 1929. Millions of Americans were existing on a standard of living typical of 1913. Throughout the country in the soup lines, the jerry-built shacks known as Hoovervilles, outside the shut-down factories, fourteen million unemployed—one out of every four persons in the work force—sat numbly, beaten by forces they did not understand, could not cope with, and could not reverse by their own efforts.

There are many who believe that this country was on the brink of a shooting revolution at that moment in history. Certainly the ingredients of upheaval were abundantly present. I cite this history to make one point: unemployment in 1933 was at the calamity level for the nation as a whole. Today, a generation later, that same condition—one out of four workers unemployed—prevails among America's Negro population. Unemployment in the nation was 5.7 percent of the labor force in 1963. Among Negroes it was officially reported by the Labor Department as 10.9 percent. But the figures indicate only those who are *actively* seeking work through the facilities of the employment services. They do not count the hundreds of thousands—white and Negro—who have given up after fruitless efforts to find jobs. They do not count the thousands who are on relief and the thousands who have not qualified for, or who for one reason or another are not receiving, public aid. My best estimate, based on reports from Urban Leagues in sixty-five cities, is that one million Negroes—one out of every four Negro workers—are unemployed, compared with one out of twenty whites.

This constitutes a disaster situation for Negro citizens and for our country. When disaster strikes, emergency action has traditionally been the American response. When the recent earthquake struck Alaska, voluntary organizations such as the Red Cross, the neighboring communities, the county, state, and federal government came to its aid. Alaska was declared a disaster area, and we brought to bear the whole arsenal of available aid weapons to help the people of that state get back on their feet.

I say that for a century Negroes have borne a disproportionate burden of unemployment, that now it is of disaster proportions, and that emergency aid is needed. Not tomorrow, but *now*. Not when "full employment" is achieved—for there is no evidence that we will have full employment in the foreseeable future unless extraordinary, emergency action is taken—but *now*.

That is why, in full cooperation with the Urban League, I have called for special effort in employment as well as in education, housing, health, and welfare. These are the crucial areas of concern in making equality a meaningful reality for Negroes. As President Kennedy put it, "Employment opportunities play a major role in determining whether civil rights are meaningful. There is little value in a Negro's obtaining the right to be admitted to hotels and restaurants if he has no cash in his pocket and no job."

We must have jobs available to us that are commensurate with our education, ability, and interests. We must have the right to study, to worship, to travel, to live, and to work alongside our white countrymen. Then, and only then, can we walk with dignity as citizens of the modern world.

We must have all these things not just because it is right and just, but because every time they are denied us the whole American ideal is betrayed. One cannot expect the world to accept America as a free land where all enjoy equal rights and equal opportunity when we deny both to every tenth American.

We all know this is easier said than done. To simplify matters, the core of the civil rights problem is the matter of achieving equal opportunity for Negroes in the labor market. For it stands to reason that all our other rights depend on that one for fulfillment. We cannot afford better education for our children, better housing, or medical care unless we have jobs.

Let us look at the Negro citizen's economic situation: About 45 percent of the Negroes and 40 percent of the whites in the United States work. The median income of Negro families in 1960 was $3,233. In other words, half of them just made it across the $3,000 "poverty line" in wages. White-family median income was $5,385.

In the white-collar-and-jacket occupations—the professional, technical, and managerial—fully 23 percent of white workers are to be found. Only 6.7 percent of Negroes are so employed, and almost all of them by Negro schools, businesses, or construction.

But Negroes are very big in the "handle" trades—semiskilled, service, and unskilled workers wielding hoe, broom, shovel, door, and occasionally wrench or brake handles—where fully 80 percent of them are employed, versus 40 percent of white workers.

In the "key" occupations, those white and light-blue collar jobs where typewriter, cash register, computer, and motorized machine keys are pushed, only 13 percent of Negroes work; 36 percent of white workers are in these categories. It is for these jobs that more Negroes must be educated, trained, and retrained, for this is the area where significant numbers of new jobs are expected.

In general, Negroes are employed fewer hours per week than whites, and Negro men earn only 60 percent as much as white men. This low income scale forces more Negro women to work—41 percent of them do. Negro women earn just over half as much as white women.

Negroes are underemployed. For instance, only 43 percent of working Negroes used their training in their jobs in 1963, compared with 60 percent of all workers. Furthermore, one out of five Negro women who have some college training or have completed high school are domestic workers; among white women with similar background only 2 percent are domestics.

Unemployment rates for Negro men have consistently run more than twice as high as for white men since 1951; for Negro women, the rate of unemployment has been between 66 percent and 100 percent higher than the rate for white women.

More than half of all unskilled Negro workers have been unemployed for lengthy periods during the past six years. Current trends indicate that the unskilled Negro who is over forty-four years of age and out of a job will never work again unless something drastic is done.

Today our unemployment rate is four times that of whites. Negroes have less protection under unemployment insurance programs and, because we are concentrated in low-paid jobs, we receive smaller benefits than unemployed whites. In addition, many Negroes remain in those occupations that are not covered by unemployment compensation and social security.

In places such as Detroit, 60 percent of the unemployed are Negroes, though they constitute only 22 percent of the population. In Chicago, every fourth Negro family is on public assistance.

As a footnote, perhaps one of the most discouraging aspects for the future is that only 1.69 percent of all the apprentices in the nation in 1960 were Negroes.

But enough of statistics. They are equally dreary up and down the land. The question is, what can be done about this?

Since the vast majority of Negro workers are unskilled laborers, the problems of this group are the most pressing. The unskilled man is doomed in our society. Equal opportunity will not give him the skills he lacks. To expect him to compete for better jobs without training is like expecting me to speak Spanish without having learned it. Barring a miracle, it cannot be done.

The real solution to the problem of unskilled labor is to teach each man a skill. And that takes more than good will. It takes long-range planning. It will take the combined efforts of business and industry, organized labor, government, Negro organizations, and the cooperation of the worker himself. It will take an all-out crash program to get the Negro moving up to skilled jobs. It will require a training program for youth and a retraining program for adults.

Business can help by actively recruiting Negroes to fill jobs in every job category and by grooming outstanding prospects for top jobs. It can initiate training programs to help the new employees acquire new skills that will help them to move up the ladder.

Organized labor can help by actively recruiting Negroes into the unions and by opening up apprenticeships to young Negroes in all the trades. It can protect the Negro from discrimination and see to it that he gets promotions when he deserves them.

The government can help by expanding its training program which presently does not touch the "hard core" unemployed. Government can underwrite some of the expense and provide incentives for industry on-the-job training programs. I suggest a special effort, a massive program, along the lines of the GI Bill of Rights for veterans after World War II.

Other organizations—churches, foundations, service clubs, and fraternal groups—and individuals can help by supporting programs of hiring, training, and education of Negroes. They can also take the initiative in hiring, training, and paying living wages to Negro workers.

None of these measures should be thought of in terms of a handout. Rather, they are to give a hand up—a helping hand to rescue the Negro from economic disaster; to give him a foundation for a normal middle-class American life.

How can the Negro secure his share of jobs in America? There is no magic key to this problem. We cannot put our finger on one barrier and say, "Remove that and the problem is solved." The effort to help the Negro citizen earn his bread and pay his way must be multidimensional and simultaneous across a broad front. Here is a list of urgent needs:

- Vocational training—the best.
- On-the-job training, the finest industry has to offer.
- Informed, up-to-date vocational counseling.
- Education of the most inspiring type, using modern techniques and facilities.
- Special help with school dropouts, with young people out of school and out of work.
- Entrance jobs by the hundreds of thousands.
- Personnel people who apply realistic standards that are meaningful and fair to Negro applicants.
- More Negroes in personnel work—on the hiring line.
- Enlightened managements that will earnestly and wholeheartedly adopt the principles of advancement on merit and train Negroes for supervisory and executive posts.
- Unions that will abandon archaic membership rules and bring in qualified Negroes.
- Union apprenticeship programs which recruit rather then exclude Negroes.
- Prompt government enforcement of equal employment regulations to insure hiring and promotion on an equal basis.
- Equal training opportunities and unbiased employment services through government agencies and employment offices.
- Government action to create more jobs open to Negroes.
- Voluntary agency, public service, union, and industry people who understand the reasons for, and employ the techniques for overcoming, the inertia of potential Negro workers.

These are some of the major requisites of any concerted attack on the problem of Negro unemployment. They are interrelated and interdependent. The needs are so vast, the situation so complex, that a coordinated, highly organized program encompassing all these elements is most unlikely. However, this in no way relieves any of the individuals and groups concerned from responsibility for appropriate, vigorous action.

Business
Consider the role of business in the process of integration. Busi-

ness has the know-how, the leverage and the resources to do the job. And since the law of the land calls for equality of opportunity, civil rights groups will increasingly direct their efforts at management in business and industry rather than at legislators. The business community can set the tone and style of a new acceptance of the Negro on all levels of life. Many have called for an end to token integration and pilot placements in industry and business as well as in labor and government. These are not enough. They never were; but in earlier times, when prejudice was so widespread, they served to prove that Negroes were capable of working in the "white" world.

The Urban League, for example, welcomed the pilot placement of Negroes because it helped to convince industry that Negroes could do the jobs, that hiring them did not disrupt production. Further, we needed the role models—the proof to Negro youth that there was a reason for studying and training. And we needed the jobs. Generally those Negroes who were pilot placements were vastly overqualified for the positions they were given: we had men with doctorates going in as junior chemists and electronic technicians. Industry was usually well pleased with them—it should have been, for it was getting bargains when the wages of similarly qualified whites were compared.

Industry frequently said, "When you find another man with these qualifications we may be interested." Ten years ago we didn't have many Negroes who were so overqualified; we didn't have too many Negroes with college degrees other than in teaching and theology, so there was no danger of flooding a corporation with well-trained persons.

We spent untold man-years in finding Negroes for pilot placements, negotiating with industry, "opening doors" for each man placed. At that time recruiting by business at Negro colleges was unheard of and unthinkable—to business. So we did what we could within the framework of the pilot placement program. But all too often the pilot turned out to be the total crew and was also management's showpiece every time it was asked about integration of its work force. "Sure we're integrated," they would say. "There's our Negro over there."

Thus, in an earlier era, pilot placement and token integration were frequently identical. However, in the past few years, with greater pressure from public opinion as well as from civil rights groups, many corporations have frantically gone out and hired a handful of Negroes, often in high-visibility jobs such as guards, or receptionists, to whom they can point when the inevitable question of integration of work force is raised. Though the hiring of any Negro is welcome, this approach fools no one and is increasingly unacceptable because of its blatant condescension.

What is needed is a conscious, planned effort by management to find and place qualified Negroes in positions of responsibility as well as in entrance jobs. Businessmen who have begun to open jobs to Negroes at levels which were formerly closed repeatedly say to us, "This person must be better than the average white. He's got to be 'Exhibit A.'" Management must now accept the qualified average Negro as it has accepted the qualified average white for so long. In fact, management must give us some jobs of the type that it has set aside for the less bright whites. We have some Negroes who are not the brightest people in the world, and we need work for them as well as for our outstanding individuals.

The major need today is for management to intervene on behalf of the vast majority of Negro workers. They need entrance jobs in clerical, construction, industrial, sales and service industry (such as communications) work. Even though the industrial community is changing, it still seeks Negroes primarily for jobs that it cannot find white people to fill. We receive all kinds of calls for chemists and physicists, first-rate stenographers, engineers and technicians.

But the real test is not that you want Negroes for these jobs because you can't find whites for these posts. The real pay-off is when you hire Negroes in those jobs where there is an obvious, large pool of white people available. This includes apprenticeships in unions also. The young fellow who has finished college with a liberal arts education, if he is white and shows promise, can probably start in a management trainee program at some retail store. There is no shortage of whites for such positions. Thus, we have very few calls for Negroes for jobs requiring only a general background such as this.

There is no question in my mind that business can do wonders in putting Negroes to work if it sets its mind to it. One look at the history of business accomplishment in this country gives convincing proof that when business determines to do something it has the creativity, the organizational imagination, and the resources to do it. There were those who scoffed when President Roosevelt during World War II announced that we were going to produce fifty thousand planes a year. Within a couple of years we were manufacturing one hundred thousand annually. The production of the atomic bomb was an unparalleled marshaling of industrial and scientific know-how. And since then we have seen the development of space exploration, lasers, masers, subminiaturization, computer technology and wonder drugs.

Industry spends billions of dollars on research—the managers are very adventurous in this regard. But they often hesitate to take a chance in recruiting, hiring, training, and promoting Negroes. In fact, businessmen are very proud of their rugged individualism and rail at government controls which, they say, encroach on and sap the initiative from free enterprise. But when it comes to race relations business says, "I'll move if everybody else will, but not until."

Often people come to me and say, "You know, Mr. Young, it was wonderful that at the particular moment in history when baseball was ready to hire Negroes you had an intelligent and gifted athlete such as Jackie Robinson to take advantage of this opportunity." And I say nonsense!

We had intelligent Negroes playing baseball as well as Jackie Robinson forty years before. The significant difference was that at that particular moment we had a Branch Rickey. We never had one of those before. Here was a man who said to himself, "This is supposed to be the all-American game but it is closed to one-tenth of our citizens. I refuse to perpetuate this lie." And so he took a stand, based on the courage of his convictions. Because what he did was right, nobody could publicly disagree with him. Subsequent events proved that the utilization of Negroes in baseball was not only fair and just but also economically successful, as was later proven true in other professional sports.

Now I am suggesting that what we need today in the United States are hundreds and thousands of Branch Rickeys, not just in sports but also in manufacturing, communications, banking, finance, research and service industries, in real estate, religion, education, welfare, and government. We need Branch Rickeys everywhere who will make a special effort to place Negroes.

As between a Negro and a white worker, both *equally qualified*, I make no apology for urging that businessmen hire the Negro in an area where no Negro has been previously employed. One of the reasons for this is that we need *role models* in order to encourage young Negroes to stay in school and prepare for careers. We need role models right away; we can't encourage Negro children to stay in school and go to college in a vacuum. We didn't even have intercollegiate baseball in Negro colleges until Jackie Robinson. And we had very few Negroes majoring in political science until Ralph Bunche. You can't motivate people in the abstract; you can only spark their initiative to the extent that they can see the possibility of reward for their efforts. You don't have to hire the unqualified, but if two equally qualified people present themselves, then give the job to the Negro. After all, for decades you never even let him get through the door.

Now it is not so simple as it might appear at first glance to determine whether or not a Negro is qualified for a job. It is not merely a matter of running the candidate through your personnel department and deciding on the basis of objective scoring on aptitude tests and subjective evaluation by your professional interviewers. Unfortunately, because of prejudice and segregation and their effects, and because present-day personnel tools and methods are poorly suited to Negro applicants, the evaluations may be wide of the mark.

For a rough parallel, consider how well you would be likely to score on the examinations, and how adequately your background would be evaluated by the trained personnel interviewers if you applied for the British Foreign Service. Your American background, excellent as it might be, would handicap you on exams designed to measure the products of British society, of its public schools, and the framework of knowledge applicable to the British Commonwealth. Your interviewer would be interested not only in your experience and knowledge, but in your Old School Tie, and the way in which your accent and diction placed you in the social structure.

Personnel people will tell you that U.S. aptitude tests are designed by academicians as the result of experiments and evaluations with Northern, white, urban, middle-class respondents. They measure applicants from a similar background with relative accuracy. But they are scarcely valid for the young men and women I am referring to you.

As Prof. Eli Ginzberg, director of the Conservation of Human Resources Project at Columbia University, points out:

most Negro parents have had to work hard most of their lives at jobs which command little esteem, are often extremely unpleasant, and provide no more than a subsistence wage. Many Negroes are likely to feel embittered or resigned about their work, and these attitudes will eventually carry over to their children. The Negro child, moveover, is also likely to respond to the attitudes of the dominant white population toward the work role of his race. Seeing his elders holding down poor jobs and sensing that the white community takes this for granted, the Negro child is not likely to develop high aspirations for himself. Only as increasing numbers of their own race rise in the world of work will more young Negroes develop the motivation necessary to prepare themselves properly to compete for the better jobs.[1]

Prof. Ginzberg also states that . . .

a major disability of the young Negro in the world of work is his lack of intimate knowledge of the values and behavior of the white population. . . . His ability to cope with the problems presented by working with whites depends largely on the opportunities he has had in his formative years to live in close association with members of the white race.[2]

And, as we know, the ghetto background, the de facto segregated schools and recreational facilities effectively isolate most Negro youngsters from opportunities for playing, learning, and working with whites.

It must be clear that the Negro's achievement on job aptitude tests and interviews is dependent upon his previous vocational and educational experience. Such experience is dependent in turn upon his high school which usually has been an inferior, segregated one; and achievement in high school has stemmed directly from the elementary school where segregated, inferior instruction has been the rule. Further, and fundamentally, these four built-in failure factors

[1] Eli Ginzberg, The Negro Potential, Columbia University Press, New York, 1946, p. 99.
[2] Ibid., p. 1–4.

are operative on the Negro child from birth: poverty, segregation, unstable family life, and inferior, second- or third-class citizenship. This is the causal chain which begins in deprivation and ends at the desk of your employment officer.

I will never forget one day when I was executive secretary of the Urban League in Omaha. A young man came in to ask my help in finding work. He had just graduated with honors from the Graduate School of Business Administration at Harvard. He had seen all of his white classmates hired by the recruiting teams from various blue chip corporations. He too had been hired for several excellent junior executive positions by telephone, only to be rejected when he appeared in person.

He sat across the desk from me and said, "Mr. Young, if they do this because I'm dirty I can take a bath. If it is because I lack culture I can read and go to operas and museums and acquire culture. If it is because I don't have sufficient education I can go back to school. But when they do this to me because I'm black, I am helpless, because God made me black." This was a case of a career stillborn at the desk of a professional personnel man.

In most cases, of course, the qualifications of the applicant may not be so outstanding as was the case with this lad. It is at this point that I contend that a Negro candidate who makes 115 on an aptitude test is likely to be just as bright if not a whole lot smarter than the white fellow who scores 125. When you consider the inferior education, deprived cultural background, and negative socioeconomic conditions operating on the Negro candidate, such a score represents a real triumph.

Furthermore, another element often overlooked by personnel people is this: the Negro will usually value the job more than his white counterpart because his opportunities are fewer. Where the white fellow may be taking the job as a stopgap until he can find something better, this may be the best job the Negro ever dreamed he could land. He will value it accordingly and work hard in it. Many enlightened companies have learned this by experience. What I am suggesting here is a sensible review of hiring procedures to insure that they do not actually or unwittingly discriminate against Negro applicants.

Today it is not enough for the businessman simply to take down the FOR WHITE ONLY sign or drop this phrase from his want ads and consider that he has, therefore, opened his hiring to Negroes. It is not sufficient to post the President's executive order on equal employment outside the hiring office door. Even statements that the company will employ any qualified man may not be enough, nor will the sentence "equal opportunity employer" in his ads be sufficient.

It is not enough to do these things today, when you have established for generations in the mind of the Negro that your company is a place that doesn't want him. You don't erase that impression simply by taking down the signs. You can only erase this ingrained, experience-taught attitude by aggressively going to the community and saying, "We've changed," and by hiring some real human symbols who will go out and witness to the fact that you have changed. This is one kind of *special effort* that is necessary. You don't have to do this in the white community, but you do have to in the Negro community. And unless you make the effort you will not have Negro applicants. After all, who wants to invite rejection?

There is no magic formula for bringing Negro applicants to your employment office. But there are sensible techniques which have no mystery. First, you let the Negro community know that you are seriously seeking Negro workers; you talk to leaders of the community and ask their counsel on spreading the word. You let the Urban League know of your needs and talk to all the employment agencies, both public and private in your area. You beat the bushes by recruiting at the colleges and high schools, by advertising through the Negro media—the newspapers and radio stations. And in some places companies give time preference to Negroes by actively seeking a Negro to fill a position one week before opening it to all applicants.

But there are other, built-in business practices that operate to the detriment of the Negro applicant. The prerequisite for a regional sales representative in one corporation, for example, was ten years of experience with the firm. Since the firm had never employed Negroes before, this automatically placed a ten-year minimum waiting period for any Negro hoping to qualify for the regional sales post. Certainly, sales ability and administrative ability can be determined in a shorter time. The company thinks so, too, and has developed different criteria.

Since Negroes have had scant opportunity to acquire the work history and training normally required of white job applicants, it makes sense to revise hiring policies so as to give the Negro a fair chance. He may have equivalent skills or experience, but they may have been acquired in ways unfamiliar to a personnel man, unless he happens to be a Negro. There are at least two ways, therefore, to equalize the situation: staff the personnel department with qualified Negroes as well as whites; offer Negroes the chance to compete on the basis of demonstrated skills, measured by appropriate tests, rather than on experience or job history typical only of qualified white applicants.

At some point, the company that seriously sets out to integrate its work force is likely to find that it has run out of qualified Negro applicants. This becomes the watershed, separating the conscientious from the superficial, for this is the point at which training programs, refresher courses, and on-the-job training can make the difference. This is the sensitive point at which special effort is called for. Enlightened businessmen, with vision freed from parochial blinders, will take the next step. Many of them already have.

In a secretarial retraining program cosponsored by several major corporations, the Urban League, and New York University, groups of young women are being helped. They all flunked Civil Service or business performance exams by small margins—typing thirty-five words per minute instead of forty, for instance. Though many of them were graduates of commercial schools and most had high school diplomas, all believed that they were destined to continue as domestic workers. And they would have been, if this program had not been instituted. We set up a special secretarial refresher course and put the women through eleven weeks of training.

Beyond the formal work skills that needed brushing up, other pointers such as help with poise, grooming, and good speech were built into the curriculum. But most important, these women received something invaluable—confidence. They were freed of their anxiety and some of their suspicion. They realized that industry really wanted them and was not just going through the motions because it feared boycotts.

Some of these women had taken very few tests and were test-ignorant or test-frightened. In the tests for jobs they had been in situations that had made them highly apprehensive. The course, with understanding, professional help, made it possible for them to bring their skills and confidence up to the point where they could successfully compete for jobs. The course was free, incidentally, and included whites as well as Negroes, in the ratio of one to eight.

Obviously business can swing its weight behind sensible vocational guidance and training programs to produce more qualified Negro workers. Since 30 percent of Negro youngsters never complete high school and 30 percent never go beyond it, vocational education at the early secondary level is extremely important. If, as has been the case in some communities, business and industry have little regard for the products of their local vocational schools, it is up to businessmen to see that changes are made.

As it now stands, vocational courses for high school students are available to fewer than 20 percent of high school students in the large cities and fewer still in small towns. Here again prejudice is obvious: vocational schools for Negroes generally offer instruction and experience only in traditional, low-rated jobs. A quick glance at the curricula tells the story. In Atlanta, three programs in technology are offered at the white vocational school; none, at the Negro school. In Baltimore, the all-Negro school gives courses in dry cleaning and pressing, shoe repair, painting, etc.; the white school offers airplane mechanics, electronics, mechanical drawing, and so on.

Too often enrollment in vocational courses has been based partially on the student's chance of securing employment in the occupation for which he is preparing. This practice freezes the employment pattern and makes it impossible for Negroes to qualify for jobs newly opened to minority groups. And, of course, it helps confine Negroes to jobs which are rapidly being taken over by machines. Businessmen can change these conditions if they decide to do so.

Industry can aid in many other ways. For instance, it can be helpful to Negro job applicants by a little extra effort. Often Negro youths are naïve about job opportunities and believe that they have been turned down for a job because of discrimination when the real reason may be lack of training or preparation for the work. Employment officers can combine candor with sound advice in turning down the Negro applicant. Furthermore, industry can participate in career guidance institutes and clinics to help Negro youth secure the appropriate training.

Actually, I am confident that America's prime-mover corporations, those business and industrial giants noted for progressive policies, have adopted or will soon adopt affirmative action programs to integrate their work forces. Increasingly, big business in this nation in 1964 is not trying to segregate with more sophistication or to discriminate with increased subtlety. It is becoming more enlightened and is beginning to see the need as well as the ultimate potential in adding Negroes to its staff and production forces.

The reasons for integrating the work force are compelling and sound:

• Prejudice costs the nation an estimated $28 billion every year, directly in unrealized production and indirectly in welfare costs.

• Business cannot function in a climate of tension, conflict, and discord. And until integration of work forces is accomplished we are going to have this kind of climate. Even at the local retailer's level this has impact: people stay home rather than go shopping.

• There are now nineteen million Negro citizens—more than the population of Canada—with a total purchasing power of $20 billion annually. Unquestionably this is a fertile market for consumer goods.

• Here also is a potentially rich labor supply of people whose skills have never been put to their fullest use. We have been satisfied to allow well-educated Negro citizens to waste their training and serve as waiters, railroad porters, post office workers, and such. In Atlanta, for instance, the post office used to employ more Negro college graduates than whites of any type.

• The offices and plants of most businesses are still in the central cities around the nation and promise to be so for some time. These core areas are increasingly populated with Negroes; therefore, the work force on which business will draw increasingly is bound to be Negro as well.

• The Negro community is sensitive to hiring practices and knows well which firms do and do not give equal job opportunities. Brand loyalties are built by such knowledge.

• Management can view integration positively and see it as an opportunity to make its own corporation reflect the American dream, with the diversity of an integrated work force seen as a healthy, stimulating condition to be proud of.

• Finally, business can not avoid coming to grips with integration without damaging itself. This is not just a question of humaneness or morality. We are faced with a critical situation. The alternative to the Marshall Plan approach is to accept an identifiable, visible group in our society, a group that will be chronically, permanently dependent.

• The economists tell us that in our free-enterprise system we are going to have a pool of unemployed amounting to 3 percent to 4 percent of the labor force. Will it be all-Negro as the trend indicates? The significance of such unemployment will not be lost on the 80 percent of the world's population that is nonwhite, particularly in those new nations that are shopping around for both an economic and a political way of life. The colored races of the world are not likely to view with favor, nor to adopt willingly, a system that obviously works beautifully for white people but somehow slips a cog on every tenth revolution, leaving the Negro out. Our free enterprise system is, therefore, on trial.

Truly big business in America has begun to turn a corner. Sometimes there is a problem of communication—the word has not filtered down completely in all ways from the top to the lower levels. But it is becoming ever clearer that those who are really moving ahead in business today are those who have a global grasp of conditions, including the importance of sound treatment of minority groups. It is those men who are knowledgeable and progressive in the area of human rights who are being tapped for advancement.

So interested in seeing to it that "the word" permeates its entire organization is Western Electric that for a year or more they have been carrying on a comprehensive orientation program for their people. With top, middle, and community-level management, they have conducted seminars thoroughly going into the subject of integration, its ramifications and background. Other corporations have sent their key men to regional seminars held under the aegis of industry associations, chambers of commerce, trade groups, biracial committees, and the Urban League. Unquestionably, business is undertaking initial efforts to redress ancient wrongs, but this must be just a start. The real work has not even begun.

Labor

Where does organized labor fit into this picture? The industrial unions historically led the way, not only in their statements of policy but in their practices and in their identification with the Negro worker. This was true not just in employment but in public welfare, social security, education, public housing, and minimum wages. In these it was the industrial unions that were on the side of the Negro pushing for welfare legislation.

Granted that the union efforts are traditionally focused on benefits for the lower economic groups in general, whether black or white, since the Negro is disproportionately represented in these groups, these measures necessarily help him. But while business has moved in terms of its specific problems of discrimination in employment, it still actively opposes broad welfare and educational legislation which would inevitably help Negroes to qualify for new employment opportunities.

With regard to bringing Negroes into the work force, management has begun to catch up with labor and in some cases is running neck and neck with it. Certainly industry is way ahead of the craft unions. These antediluvian organizations have excluded not only Negroes but other qualified people who are not relatives of union members. The craft unions have deliberately kept the number of qualified journeymen so small that such unions have become practically family organizations.

In 1963, in New York, the State Commission for Human Rights ruled that Local 28 of the Sheet Metal Workers International Association had "automatically excluded" Negroes for seventy-six years. The commission had been in operation for eighteen years, ever since the state Fair Employment Practices law went into effect in 1945. And yet, this lily-white union with its thirty-three hundred members had blithely carried on its hoary traditions of discrimination, bias and exclusion with no flicker of interest from the anti-discrimination machinery until 1963 when waves of pickets protesting just this kind of union bias hit construction sites in New York City. Only then did the commission find that a situation existed which warranted examination, though this and many other craft unions, especially, have practiced discrimination in notorious fashion since their inception.

The hearings on this case were called after the state attorney general charged that the union and a union–contractor committee had discriminated in the selection of apprentices. Specifically, the apprenticeship committee had turned down a qualified Negro who had learned the sheet-metal trade in the Air Force and applied for apprenticeship in March, 1962. He was passed over for three subsequent training programs. For two years he worked at odd jobs and as a maintenance mechanic; every time he was needed for the hearings he had to take time off from work, without pay. For two years he and his family did not receive even welfare assistance. Finally, the Commission found the local guilty of having systematically barred Negroes from its ranks and ordered it to "cease and desist." On March 23, 1964, the local was given 60 days to do away with its old apprenticeship list. Meanwhile, the New York Urban League appealed to city, state, and federal officials to cancel their contracts with any construction companies which followed policies of hiring members of a union that discriminates against Negroes.

In these United States 18 out of 70 million workers are union members or are covered by collective bargaining. But in the twentieth century, so far as apprenticeship, membership, and job referrals are concerned, the practices of most craft unions are best described as medieval. They hark back to the guilds and often restrict eligibility for membership to sons or close relatives of current or past members. They regularly exclude Negroes from membership and apprenticeship, even, as in the case of the trained sheet-metal worker where management sits on apprenticeship selection committees. Management seldom tries to dictate to the union which men will be chosen for apprenticeship for this would "stir up the pot," and cause the union to retaliate.

In all too many unions the negotiations with management on terms and conditions of employment—not only wages and hours but also training, transfers, and promotions—exclude the Negro purposely or relegate him to the status of an afterthought. Among the notable exceptions are the United Packinghouse Workers, the United Automobile Workers, and the Textile Workers Union.

AFL–CIO president George Meany has stated that "the strongest single force behind every civil-rights proposal is the AFL–CIO. In education, in housing, in public accommodations, on voting rights —all the way down the line, on every front—we spearhead the fight for equal justice for all." This is true and we can salute organized labor's top echelons for their unswerving devotion to progressive social legislation. And in the upper reaches, at the parent, or international union level, discrimination has been largely erased from the books. Only one of the internationals has a bias clause in its constitution; a few years ago many of them did. And most of them are reviewing their practices in order to eliminate discrimination.

But at the local affiliate level, exclusion is practiced all too successfully. And at the rank-and-file level, the AFL–CIO and the international unions themselves have great difficulty in bringing about change. In fact, it is because they lack leverage that George Meany testified before Congressional committees in favor of federal fair employment legislation with sanctions against offending unions as well as employers. However, the history of union bias in states with fair employment laws and commissions and the fact that the National Labor Relations Board and federal labor laws have made no headway against local union discrimination are discouraging.

The construction industry unions are the classic examples. Bricklayers, electricians, plumbers, and heavy equipment operators are among America's highest-paid workers. Almost none of the union locals in these fields admits Negroes; some have admitted a token handful. The most qualified Negro worker has practically no hope of finding a job without a union card in thousands of communities and hundreds of occupational categories as the Chicago statistics given later in this chapter amply demonstrate. Federal law for years has stated that a worker cannot be denied initial employment because of his inability to join a union. But until the executive order establishing the President's Committee on Equal Employment Opportunities, there was no federal prohibition against a union keeping qualified workers from membership on the basis of race, creed, or national origin.

Bias against the Negro has been flagrant. As Edwin C. Berry, Executive Director of the Chicago Urban League, remarked, "Exclusion in the craft unions is so complete that segregation would be a step forward." In fact, so rank were practices in New York state that in the summer of 1963 the state's advisory committee of the U.S. Commission on Civil Rights warned the building trades unions that if they continued their biased membership practices a "civil service" form of membership selection would have to be instituted by a government agency. To add weight to its report the committee recommended that the federal government withhold funds from jim-crow apprenticeship programs and building projects supported by federal money.

The Secretary of Labor reported last winter to the Building and Construction Trades Department of the AFL–CIO that a survey of fifty cities showed that on most federal projects no Negroes were employed, either as journeymen or as apprentices, in a majority of the skilled trades. Even as he spoke, one thousand union plumbers from outside the city were working in New York on jobs which the thirty-three hundred members of the all-white Local 2 of the Plumbers and Steamfitters were unable to handle. The New York state advisory committee report cited above found that "out-of-town workers commute over one hundred miles daily to jobs in New York City, while local Negroes and Puerto Ricans are denied employment and entry to union-dominated apprenticeship programs."

In New York, because of union policies, Negroes almost never enter apprenticeship programs. Back in 1950, 1.4 percent of the apprentices were Negroes. At that time the population of the city was 13 percent Negro. By 1960, Negroes constituted 2 percent of the apprentices and 22 percent of the city's residents. At this rate of increase, it would be the year 2000 before we would hit the 5 percent level in apprenticeship programs. Hopefully, this pattern of exclusion is changing—Local 3 of the Electrical Workers in New York, for instance, has initiated a recruiting program which admitted two hundred Negroes and Puerto Ricans out of one thousand apprentices last year.

Of course it takes from two to four years of apprenticeship, depending on the trade, before a man qualifies as journeyman and receives his union membership card. This is a long, hard struggle, at best. But when, as the committee reported in the case of one New York local, " eighty to eighty-five percent of those admitted to membership are sons or nephews of . . . members," it is no wonder that the fewest skilled Negroes on any defense contract or construction job in the nation were at a site in Brooklyn, New York, last summer —the proportion was 3 percent.

The significance that the observant will spy in all this is that if the conditions were this bad in a state which has had a Fair Employment Practice law for eighteen years, with an aggressive antidiscrimination commission in its Labor Department (and both are "models"), and in a city which has FEP ordinances and antidiscrimination committees also, what realistic hope is there that the federal civil rights law will have widespread effect in any brief time span?

There has not been the gradual increase one would have hoped for in union membership by Negroes. In some cases the Negro has definitely lost ground. Census and Labor Department statistics actually show that there were proportionately fewer Negroes in carpentry in 1960 than there were half a century before. In fact, the percentage of all employed union Negro carpenters dropped from 3.85 percent in 1950 to 3:53 percent in 1960. Of course, almost never any more does a local union have racially restrictive clauses in its constitution or bylaws. Instead, the obvious pattern of exclusion is built by tacit agreement of the local's members. This is easily accomplished, because the membership votes directly on the acceptance of new members.

The following table showing the proportion of Negro to white workers in representative trades (Chicago area) illustrates the power of the unions to exclude Negroes:

Excerpts from U.S. Census Bureau Report, Chicago, 1960.

Type of Worker	Total Number	Number of Negroes	%
Painter Paperhanger Glazier	13,986	1,310	9.4
Machinist Job Fitter	29,041	1,059	3.3
Carpenter	22,239	603	2.8
Electrician	14,050	322	2.3
Plumber Pipefitter	11,249	270	⊠

Excerpts from *U. S. Census Bureau Report, Chicago, 1960* (Cont.).

Type of Worker	Total Number	Number of Negroes	%
Printing Craftsmen (Excluding: compositor typesetter)	11,742	252	☒
Structural Metal Worker	2,264	62	☒
Airplane Mechanic	1,371	50	☒
Tinsmith Coppersmith Sheet Metal Worker	5,969	48	☒
Locomotive Fireman	1,553	21	☒
Locomotive Engineer	2,416	4	☒
Boilermakers	1,039	34	☒

☒ Less than 1%

It used to be said that there was more work for Negroes in the South than the North because in the North they could not get union cards whereas in the South they could join Jim-Crow union locals. To some extent this statement may be true, but the situation is vastly exaggerated. In Atlanta, for instance, Negro locals are sometimes called upon to provide token Negro workers for government projects where equal-opportunity hiring is enforced. But most of the time they are completely out in the cold, because contractors hire through white unions locals. Often, whites from locals in other cities have been brought in to avoid using Negroes on jobs. And the U.S. Commission on Civil Rights' 1961 report on employment states that "the competition between Atlanta's white and Negro locals has hit the Negro locals so hard that one has become virtually extinct; members of the other have been forced to seek work below union rates, because of their inability to find jobs on union construction." [3]

The commission describes one situation, in the District of Columbia, as follows:

With respect to Local 26 [IBEW; 900 white journeymen, no Negroes], Negroes have been seeking entry to apprenticeship

[3] *Report of the U.S. Commission on Civil Rights, 1961, III, 131.*

training and union membership for several years without success. The barrier to Negro employment was finally overcome for the first time in 1960 when a Negro member of an IBEW local in Detroit was referred to work by Local 26. But even this breakthrough took months to accomplish and occurred only after the intervention of the President's Committee on Government Contracts, the international union, AFL–CIO leadership, and local community groups. Although this one Negro 'union' electrician is still working in the District, he has not [as of 1961] become a member of Local 26.[4]

In 1964 this situation was still unchanged.

In the industrial unions the situation is altogether different. Industrial unions include both the skilled and unskilled in the same organization, so there is a better chance for Negroes and whites to belong to the same union local and to share many of the benefits of membership. Unlike the bargaining agreements in the construction field, contracts in manufacturing industries are explicit down to minute points. Disputes are resolved by agreed-upon grievance procedure. Seniority is defined and assured by agreement, and it is vital. It usually controls layoffs, recall rights, promotion, transfer, demotion, vacations, welfare plans; it determines who gets overtime, and who works what shifts. Because it negotiates and administers collective-bargaining agreements, the union is practically omnipotent in its control of the fate of each worker in a plant.

However, the industrial unions generally don't control hiring at a plant or admission to apprenticeship training. They usually allow Negroes to join the union, but it is at this point that the difference in skin color puts the brakes on opportunity. For example, though the U.S. Commission on Civil Rights reported in 1961 that Negroes and whites in Detroit and Baltimore were doing similar work for similar wages and that the union was willing to enforce bargaining contracts on behalf of Negro employees, it contrasted these conditions with those in Altanta. There, Negro employees were relegated to unskilled classifications, mostly janitorial and common labor specialties. Seniority provisions written into the contract have frozen discrimination into the system. "Clearly," said the commission, "if Negroes traditionally have been assigned to unskilled jobs in non-

4 *Ibid.*, p. 133.

production departments, their chances of advancement to better work are hampered by such seniority systems."[5]

In another plant in Atlanta the commission found 250 of the company's 1,000 employees to be Negroes. All were covered by the basic nondiscriminatory collective bargaining agreement and have been for twenty years. Yet no Negroes work in clerical, supervisory, or professional positions there. Segregation in the plant was "total" in 1961; Negroes are in the least-skilled, lowest-paying jobs and are confined to a separate "line of promotion" which permits advancement only to semiskilled jobs. The white promotion line opens to all skilled jobs, of course.

With a scale of pay grades ranging from 1 to 26, no Negro has ever worked above GS-8, and half are at GS-4 or lower; no white in the department has ever worked at a rate lower than GS-4. Negroes perform the same jobs as whites but are classified differently and paid lower wages. Ku Klux Klan literature was on the desks of some of the foremen, and a Klan membership solicitation was posted on the bulletin board in one department.

The management denied any discrimination but said later that, if any did exist in the company, it was the union's responsibility to eliminate it through collective bargaining! The commission notes:

> Resistance to change in seniority apparently springs in part from racial prejudice, but it is reinforced by the threat to the jobs of white employees. A change might enable senior Negro employees to compete for the higher rated jobs now held by junior white employees. . . . Bound as it is to the will of the majority of its members, union leadership can hardly move more rapidly than union membership. Membership hostility coupled with employer apathy makes it highly doubtful that the union will be able to provide the necessary drive to eliminate discrimination.[6]

Abdication on the part of management is the crux of the matter. Many studies, dating as far back as 1946, have indicated time and again that a firm stand by management to eradicate discrimination often enlists the support of union leadership even though the membership may be opposed. Such a policy takes from the union leaders the burden of making and executing an unpopular decision; it also

[5] *Ibid.*, p. 136.
[6] *Ibid.*, p. 138.

makes clear that management does not mean to fan an internal union conflict that might weaken it at the bargaining table. Is there any real hope of rooting out discrimination in the unions? I think so. The unions themselves are more concerned than ever before. National attention is focused upon them as never before, and the increasing use of picketing and pressure by civil rights groups at the local level has stirred up dozing local union leadership and served notice on local employers and on rank-and-file as well. The unions themselves have made progress.

There are 1,500,000 Negro members of the AFL–CIO out of a total membership of 13,000,000, and the leaders of the organization are increasingly aware of the significance of this. The AFL–CIO has, for example, established machinery to deal with discrimination; a national civil rights committee, regional advisory committee, and civil rights committees set up by more than twenty state and many city central bodies. Last year George Meany directed local and state central bodies to help form biracial committees to end discrimination in jobs and other fields.

Though the AFL–CIO national civil rights committee releases no information, we know that it has caused some recalcitrant locals to open doors to Negroes. And some of the major international unions have taken strong stands. The United Auto Workers, for instance, put one of its southern locals in trusteeship as a means of enforcing a nonbias policy. Many AFL–CIO affiliates have established civil rights committees. But as of this date, only a few have assigned staff members to them, and very few building trades unions have established any civil rights machinery.

A key role in pushing civil rights progress within the union movement has been played by that superb statesman, A. Philip Randolph, head of the Brotherhood of Sleeping Car Porters. This stalwart has for a generation goaded the conscience of organized labor about its shortcomings in the field of race relations. It was he who established the Negro American Labor Council in 1960 to pressure the AFL–CIO to eliminate prejudice in the labor movement. It was he who organized the march of Negro labor on Washington during World War II which succeeded in triggering President Roosevelt's issuance of the original federal Fair Employment Practices executive order and establishment of a committee charged with executive powers in

1941. It was he who served as field marshal of the March on Washington, in 1963, and wisely directed its positive orientation to a "March for Jobs and Freedom."

Phil Randolph's NALC sent to the AFL-CIO in 1961 a "code of fair racial trade union practice" with the recommendation that it be adopted. Among other things it called for abolition of segregated local unions; elimination from contracts of provisions that limit Negro workers' training and promotion opportunities; creation of an AFL-CIO Apprenticeship Program Board to insure opportunities "without regard to nepotism, cronyism or race." How far these recommendations will get in the AFL-CIO, both as to adoption and execution, it is too early to judge.

On the federal level, there had been no effective avenues to deal with union discrimination until President Eisenhower's executive order, establishing the Committee on Government Contracts in 1953 and President Kennedy's establishing the President's Committee on Equal Employment Opportunity in 1961. The Railway Labor Act, the Labor-Management Relations Act, and the Labor-Management Reporting and Disclosure Act of 1959 were not designed to provide relief from racial discrimination. However, the National Labor Relations Board, which administers the LMRA, has on several occasions threatened to revoke a union's certification for failure to represent racial minorities fairly.

The NLRB has, however, denied that a union's past history of discrimination is enough to disqualify it for participation in an election which might lead to certification. If the NLRB were to reverse its stand it would put new teeth into the drive to eliminate discrimination, for it would make impossible the expansion to new plants and work forces of any union whose past practices were patently discriminatory. It was the finding of historical discrimination on the part of Local 28 of the Sheet Metal Workers in New York by the state Commission on Human Rights that was a new breakthrough. If this principle can be moved into NLRB activities it will provide a strong though admittedly limited new weapon against bias in unions. The law says simply that the employer must bargain collectively with representatives designated by the majority of employees in a unit appropriate for such purposes, and this designation does not have to

78

have NLRB certification. Nevertheless, many cases per year affecting thousands of workers are certified by NLRB.

The Committee on Government Contracts empowered the government to cut off federal funds at any construction project where there was discrimination against Negroes. This could have been interpreted to cover hiring and employment on the job, and, had it been vigorously enforced, it could have been very helpful.

The President's Committee on Equal Employment Opportunity was established in 1961 and now has legislative authorization under the Civil Rights Act. It has jurisdiction over labor unions in connection with employment under government contracts. Among other things, the presidential order directed the committee to "use its best efforts . . . to cause any labor union . . . to cooperate with, and to comply in the implementation of, the purposes of this order." The committee was empowered to hold public or private hearings concerning union practices and to submit reports to the President concerning discriminatory practices and policies of any labor organization. It could publish the names of unions failing to comply and could even recommend to the Department of Justice proceedings to enforce nondiscrimination provisions.

Under the committee these powers were never employed aggressively against union bias. The Civil Rights Act gives the Equal Employment Opportunity Committee power to investigate and settle complaints against employers, unions, and employment agencies whose activities affect interstate commerce. If they fail to settle, the commission would file suit in federal courts to enforce nondiscrimination. This coverage is limited this year to employers and unions with one hundred or more employees. This minimum declines by stages until it levels off at twenty-five workers, after 1967.

But the government, through the Health, Education and Welfare and Labor Departments, has many other avenues of affecting union performance. One of the most effective is the purse string control of apprenticeship programs. A little over a year ago the Labor Department issued standards that were designed to wipe out racial discrimination in apprenticeship programs registered with the federal government. Both unions and management in the construction industry protested and the Department changed its standards to the voluntary plan the industry had advanced. Under this revision, enforcement was placed in the Bureau of Apprenticeship and Training, which has proven itself spineless in matters of bias.

And yet, when all factors are considered, we cannot view labor unions as the most critical factor in the job hunt for Negroes. Though the picketing of foot-dragging construction unions will continue and perhaps intensify, and the news media will play up the discriminatory practices of labor, the job potential must be seen in perspective. It is not labor that generates jobs; it is business, non-profit organizations, and government at all levels. Unions play an important role in determining whether the Negro will or will not work in the hundreds of thousands of jobs covered by collective bargaining. But so far as work for Negroes is concerned, the unions have a veto power rather than a positive, job-creating power. If all unions dropped their Jim-Crow practices tomorrow, the result would be a few thousand Negroes enabled to work at their trades. Important? Yes, but limited in impact when the need is a million jobs for Negroes.

Government

In 1946 the Congress passed Public Law 304. This declared the federal government's intent to use:

> all practicable means consistent with its needs and obligations and other essential considerations of national policy, with the assistance and cooperation of industry, agriculture, labor, and State and local governments, to coordinate and utilize all its plans, functions, and resources for the purpose of creating and maintaining, in a manner calculated to foster and promote free competitive enterprise and the general welfare, conditions under which there will be afforded useful employment opportunities, including self-employment, for those able, willing and seeking to work, and to promote maximum employment, production, and purchasing power.

This typically long-winded statement is the declaration of policy of the Law, which has been labeled the "full employment act of 1946."

From this, one would logically conclude that government could and should exert itself to put people to work and keep them employed. Further, for those who have been deprived of a livelihood, such as our Negro citizens, this law seemingly provides a mandate to do something to reverse generations of systematic neglect in the employment area.

And, regardless of the chronic complaint by business against government encroachment on free enterprise, the truth of the matter is that only by massive action on the part of government are we likely to put any substantial number of jobless Negroes to work in a short time. Government's position and leverage in the economy makes this unavoidable. Uncle Sam is the nation's number one employer. There are six million persons working in the Civil Service and Armed Forces. Ten million more are employed by the one hundred largest defense contractors and subcontractors. Additional millions of individuals work for government contractors or organizations with federal grants-in-aid which totaled nearly $40 billion in fiscal 1961.

But the most devastating evidence that business and labor combined can have relatively little impact in providing one million new jobs necessary for out-of-work Negroes lies in the statistics of the Labor Department: Secretary Wirtz stated last winter that in the seven years since 1957, 4,300,000 new jobs had been created in the United States. However, he pointed out that only 800,000 of these were provided by private industry and only 200,000 of these were full time. The remaining 3,500,000 jobs were in government at all levels, or in programs that are created, sponsored, or underwritten by the government.

It is at this point that Secretary Wirtz, President Johnson, his economic advisers, business, and labor leaders chant in unison that job opportunities for Negroes can be achieved only by "full" or "fuller employment" of the national work force. President Kennedy also had endorsed this analysis and cited it, as did President Johnson, in placing the highest possible priority on passage of the tax cut bill.

Their theory, rooted in Keynesian economics, is simply that every additional increment of production requires additional labor and workers. Therefore, the "answer" is, obviously, to stimulate production. The tax cut, they reason, will stimulate output by giving business and industry more money to invest in expansion and more incentive to expand because of lower taxes and therefore increased profits. The added dollars in the pockets of American citizens will be thrown into the marketplace for consumer goods, and this increased demand will require business expansion, more workers, etc. The resulting prosperity will yield more than enough added tax dollars to offset those foregone in the tax cut.

There are other ways to stimulate business, of course; John Maynard Keynes once suggested, only half jokingly, that one method would be to have the government stuff dollar bills in bottles, bury them at the bottom of caves and coal mines in the nation, and let free enterprise take over in retrieving them. This would, he theorized, give the economy a vast stimulus and put millions to work developing equipment, manufacturing it, employing it in digging, and so on. The only really questionable parts of the equation would be the scale of the project and the means of sustaining it.

Unfortunately, it is about as likely that the tax cut of 1964 will result in spectacular prosperity and economic growth which will solve our unemployment problems as it is probable that the United States will adopt Keynes' bottled-dollar scheme. In spite of the rosy predictions pronounced over its birth, tax cut is not going to dissolve the unemployment problem. This conclusion is well known to the nation's economists, leading industrialists, financiers, labor leaders, and government officials. The reason is no secret. And it is simply this: The figures don't add up.

According to Dr. Walter W. Heller, the President's top economic adviser, the tax cut "will generate about $30 billion to $40 billion of added output." [7] He estimates that this will result in two to three million additional jobs, which, he believes, will cut Negro unemployment by more than a third.

However, at the beginning of 1964 there were four million unemployed Americans, of whom one million were Negroes. President Johnson reported that last year 1.1 million would-be workers joined the labor force and said there would be as many, if not more, every year from here on. Furthermore, the Labor Department estimates that two million workers will be displaced by technological advances during the year.

Therefore, if Dr. Heller is right in his prediction, there will be 3 million new jobs to be shared out among an existing pool of 4 million unemployed, plus 1.1 million new workers, plus 2 million displaced workers. The equation is: $4 + 1.1 + 2$ equals 7.1 million

[7] New York Post, July 19, 1963, p. 26.

unemployed in 1964, and, using Dr. Heller's figures, 3 million new jobs, for a net total of 4.1 million unemployed at year's end.

Not all economists are so optimistic as Dr. Heller about the ability of the tax cut and business productivity to create new jobs.

According to Professor Ginzberg, from mid 1961 to the end of 1963 our gross national product increased $100 billion. In this same period, two and a half million additional jobs were created in the nation. This indicates that our economy has to add $40 billion in new production, or GNP, in order to create one million additional new jobs. If Professor Ginzberg's reckoning is right, we are likely to end 1964 with unemployment ranging around six million instead of four million. And the long-term prognosis is no better: during the sixties we will have four million young people a year becoming eighteen years of age; more of them are going to enter the job market than we have new jobs to offer. Furthermore, automation and technology will continue to displace millions of workers each year if present trends continue.

This is why I say that our obsession with facing immediate problems in the nonresponsive way of pointing out the much larger aspect—dealing with the rise of mass unemployment, for instance, rather than meeting the breadbasket needs of millions of Negroes now—this evasive technique must go. The immediate need always gets lost in this "balanced" view, in the "overall perspective," in the "consideration of the total picture."

My position is a simple one. I know that we are not going to have full employment under current circumstances; the Secretary of Labor knows it; so does the President and every businessman and labor leader worth his pay. Because of the inroads of technology, the inadequate expansion of the economy and the steadily increasing size of the labor force, we just are not going to have full employment in the foreseeable future. I say, therefore, that it is unfair to tell the Negro to wait for the arrival of an economic condition that no intelligent person even expects to develop.

At one end we are talking about civil rights, and at the other we are talking about weaknesses in the economic system. The Negro should not have to wait until the economic problems of the nation are resolved before he gets his fair share of employment. It has been said by more than one observer that the Negro is reacting more vigorously than the white man to the economic shortcomings of our society because he is in a more exposed position, bearing the brunt of the increased population, of technological, educational, and political shockwaves that are drastically changing the nation. This is true. However, more and more white families are being affected similarly every day as these factors leave increasing numbers of workers or would-be workers jobless. It is, therefore, also in the interests of the entire "underclass," as Gunnar Myrdal calls these unemployed left-outs and cast-offs of our economy, that the Negro drive for a better life succeed. The country certainly cannot help the Negro without helping the poor whites who are living in similar neighborhoods, stranded by similar lacks of skill, and in similar poverty. The problems faced currently by many white citizens living in the Appalachians is a case in point, and it is interesting to note that the federal government is launching a massive aid program for this area with the full understanding and support of the whole nation.

The Negro's increasing political strength and success are crystallizing public opinion in favor of action to meet the nation's pressing problems, and may well be responsible for major social reforms in the whole society. The Negro, therefore, is going to pull up with him other disadvantaged Americans, including the poor whites.

It appears to me that our attitude toward the unemployed must swing about 180°. Instead of viewing the growing group of unemployed Americans as a side-effect of economic progress to be lived with, we should look at them, first, as individuals who have specific needs and capabilities and, second, as people who have positive potential for our society if we will help them contribute to it. Let us consider them as workmen whose tool kits are filled with outmoded and unusable instruments; let us harness the expertise of the psychologists, vocational and adult educators, guidance specialists, labor and demographic statisticians, industrial placement and testing experts and equip the unemployed with the tools, skills, knowledge, and guidance to earn their way.

As we know, there are at present two basic kinds of unemployment in the United States. One is the type caused by the advancing skill requirements and technical efficiency of industry. The second is the type in which the poorly trained and inadequately educated are left behind. Now it should be obvious that we have before us two general approaches to dealing with these: we can develop more jobs which require minimum skills and education, and we can train or retrain workers to fill the increasingly sophisticated demands of industry and business. Without question we must do both.

As to training and retraining, I have some suggestions.

First, the training will be only as successful as it is appropriate for the skill-needs of industry. In this era of rapid technological change, it makes no sense to train scores of thousands for work which is fast disappearing. Even at present the information gap concerning currently needed skills is a severe handicap. We in the Negro leadership organizations are more aware of it, perhaps, than many other groups in the nation, for, as I have indicated, we receive more calls than we can fill for people with specialties that are rare. To deal with this more adequately, the National Urban League has set up a Skills Bank, which operates as a nationwide clearinghouse for employers and job-seekers. We are registering thousands of Negroes and recording their job qualifications so that employers may come to this central source of information for people to fill positions.

But this if-and-when-needed approach on the part of management is clearly inadequate. The only method that will work is a comprehensive, periodic survey-report mechanism that reviews industry's immediate short-term and long-term skill-needs and places this information in the hands of employment bureaus and agencies, vocational counselors, placement people, educators, churches, and personnel men. With such information in the hands of the many groups who can and will act to change the situation, we can refer people to job openings on a rational basis with the national job picture in perspective.

The federal government can accomplish this. It can modify and sharpen its current survey methods, now used to provide employment data by the Bureau of Labor Statistics. These are sampling techniques, wherein not all companies are heard from. Something like a frequent census of industry may be required and, with computerized data processing, would be practical. It is upon such information that we can base sound programs for moving workers from pockets of unemployment to areas of industrial need.

Second, the basic information should be available to design and implement the vast vocational and technical training, retraining, and rehabilitational programs that are needed. This is one area in which government should have no monopoly; industry, labor, and the educational institutions must pitch in. I am not advocating technical training to the exclusion of conventional education—far from it. Statistics prove that broad education is the best insurance against unemployment and that workers with less than an eighth-grade education are increasingly unemployable. Also, we know that industry's educational requirements are moving upward at an accelerating rate. Therefore, I certainly advocate conventional general education and urge literacy training for those who have slipped through the education net and are to be found at the bottom of the employment pool. More on these subjects will be found in the chapter devoted to education.

Counseling and placement have been handmaidens in sustaining the economic disadvantage of the Negro. Counselors, white or black, have more often than not advised Negro youths to take out early work permits as soon as jobs were available, thus cutting off their work-futures at a relatively low level. Most Negro schools and colleges simply have not had counseling or guidance services and have often depended on advice from teachers or others who have no experience in, or knowledge of, the labor market. And so, because status in the Negro community has traditionally stemmed in large measure from membership in the professions, parents and teachers have counseled Negro youth away from manual or technical work. Wages in the skilled trades are usually high; sales and commission work and accounting offer opportunities; yet professional status is the goal of most young Negroes. (As recently as 1963, of thirty Negro colleges checked, not one offered an undergraduate major in accounting.)

Placement activities have proved inept and inadequate. Many placement officers have assumed automatically that industrial recruiters are not interested in interviewing Negroes. And there have been some colossal fiascos when industry has made recruiting visits to Negro colleges because both the firm and the college knew too little about one another.

And when the skilled Negro leaves school he has difficulty finding adequate placement services. Private employment agencies still cater to the employers they serve and make referrals on the basis of race. Hardly a week goes by that the newspapers do not carry a story in New York about another agency that has been found guilty of this practice. Certainly New York is not alone in this.

But one of the most crippling blows has traditionally been inflicted by the U.S. Employment Service. This federal agency, supported by the taxes of Americans of all colors, underwrites 100 percent of the cost of administering the state public employment offices. Yet this agency has for decades been guilty of supporting employment referrals on a racial basis. Thus, discriminatory job orders have traditionally been accepted and filled, and nondiscriminatory orders have been processed on a biased basis. Part of the problem here has been the method of basing federal payments to state employment office budgets on the number of job placements made. Obviously it has been easier and faster to place whites in better jobs and Negroes in menial positions, so that little effort has gone into promoting hiring on merit. Slight improvement has been noticed in recent months because of more aggressive action on the part of the Secretary of Labor, and the fact that states with FEP laws no longer permit discriminatory practices in placement and in receiving job orders.

A discouraging feature has been the practice in many sections of the nation of segregated offices, or segregated facilities in one office. The Employment Service has won no prizes for initiative in developing jobs for Negroes either with its clients or on its own staffs. As of 1963, only five of the Service's eighteen hundred office managers were Negroes. Because they suspect, justifiably, that they will not receive unbiased help, many professional and skilled Negroes have shunned the public employment services.

The U.S. Employment Service is part of the Labor Department and is one example of the historical posture of that Department in accommodating violations of its regulations and policies. Only in recent months has the Department moved to end segregation in local offices of the Employment Service itself. This is something that could have been halted overnight through the Department's purse-string control of these facilities.

In all U.S. Employment Service offices we should establish centers for testing the aptitudes and skills of the unemployed to determine their potential for training for jobs. Acting as a clearinghouse, these centers should direct people to appropriate training facilities in their vicinity, or elsewhere in the state or nation if necessary. Furthermore, these centers could help coordinate vocational training activities in their areas.

One of the deterrents to participation in retraining programs is the low subsistence pay received during training by those in the programs. Since the purpose of the training is to prepare the worker for reemployment, loan funds should be available to him while he trains. With such loans he can support his family. These loans should be repayable after reemployment, should be stretched out over a long term, and should be at low interest rates.

Industry, of course, has the finest facilities for worker training. These it uses to train and upgrade its own workers. In many cases these facilities are not being used to full capacity, if at all. To stimulate industry to make use of them to train workers other than their own employees, the federal government should provide incentives. Obviously the best incentive is one which will increase industry's profits, possibly by providing a tax benefit of, say, 2 percent for training programs which industry would originate, administer, and carry out, after determining that they qualified under this government-sponsored scheme.

Another variation of the same general approach could be a government-sponsored effort to encourage training and retraining by government contractors, especially defense contractors. The contracts could be so written that an additional increment of profit would go to the companies which instituted qualified training programs.

Both of these, the tax relief and the incentive bonus, have been successfully used to promote business expansion in directions that the government considered vital. Navy Secretary James Forrestal in World War II smashed the bottleneck in ship production by the relatively simple expedient of rushing the clearance of amortization certificates. This action stimulated industry to tool up to build the ships and resulted in the greatest fleet the world has ever seen. More recently, fast tax write-offs of industry investments in machinery caused wide investment in new equipment.

This approach has other advantages. The Manpower Retraining Act says that all contracts and all decisions are made between two departments at the state level. These are the state labor and education departments. The labor department determines the manpower needs in the community, finds out what skills are present, and selects the person to be retrained. The education department has the sole decision as to where and how that person shall be retrained.

These two departments also have the authority to select an industry and to subsidize it, but they have seldom if ever done so. Furthermore, the education department too often elects to use its own vocational facilities, to the neglect of industry facilities that are better designed for specific retraining purposes. Incidentally, it doesn't take any great imagination to grasp what happens to Negroes seeking retraining in southern states under this arrangement.

But when all the vocational education, training, and retraining activities are added up, there will still be hundreds of thousands, if not millions of workers untouched and unemployed. To insure that this residue is not predominantly Negro, we must move in at least three broad ways:

First, the basic educational level of *all* Negro workers must be boosted. This is one type of discrimination we would favor: the seeking out and intensive education of Negro workers across the nation to prepare them to enter, participate in, and profit from, the program we have discussed above. Without basic literacy skills they will not qualify for vocational or adult education, training, or retraining. They will increasingly be concentrated in that hard core of unemployed that is the bedrock of the "poverty corps." Most may be slow learners, many will be unmotivated, and a few will be relatively uneducable. But all can play a constructive role in American life if we give them the help they require to do so. One example of a creative effort in helping illiterates through educational TV and night schools acquire minimum literacy is that presently being conducted with limited resources by Raymond Hilliard, Director of the Cook County Department of Public Welfare, in Chicago.

Second, special effort for Negro workers is needed *on an emergency basis,* to offset the generations of deprivation which this nation has inflicted. We have seen how the Negro has been excluded all down the line—from education, from apprenticeship, from union protection, from hiring, training, promotion, from *consideration.* Now his deficiencies in skill and knowledge, his educational, psychological, and motivational handicaps are so vast that only an effort

that is country-to-community-wide and federal-to-precinct-deep—
that will actively seek out and bring Negroes into special programs—
will be even adequate.

As this is written, too many Negroes are being passed over in the
counseling, guidance, technical training, and industrial programs
aimed at aiding the unemployed. They are not qualified; they are not
interested; they are not motivated. These are the arguments. But
America can not afford to accept this superficial assessment. The
challenge is to go beyond the conditions that appear to make these
citizens irredeemable. This society has many layers of scar tissue to
penetrate before it can effectively apply its healing powers to the
Negro.

Third, jobs are needed *now,* to keep Negroes alive, to pull them
out of the urban morass in which they are mired.

The government, as the nation's largest employer and "contractor" can play a key role in putting Negro jobless to work. Through
grants-in-aid to state and local governments, to private nonprofit institutions such as colleges and schools, and to public institutions, the
federal government subsidizes employment throughout the nation.

In 1961 the federal government paid out $7.5 billion in grants-in-
aid through more than sixty different programs. These were administered by the states and localities, sometimes on a matching basis
that multiplied the dollar volume involved.

A catalog of federally funded projects would include airports,
hospitals, public-housing projects, research grants to colleges, milk
and lunch programs for school children, water and sanitation facilities, maternity and child welfare clinics, slum clearance and urban
renewal, building and operating certain local public schools, operation of the U.S. Employment Service, and administration of unemployment compensation and apprenticeship programs.

These various programs are administered by many federal agencies in the Departments of Health, Education and Welfare, Labor,
Defense, Commerce, and Agriculture. There has been no strong,
overall federal policy on equal employment on work created by federal grant-in-aid programs. In the past, the President's Committee
on Government Contract Compliance and Committee on Government Contracts sidestepped the question by interpreting such employment as outside the jurisdiction of the committees because these

projects were not executed under "contracts." This is clearly nit-picking, for the grants are agreements with the federal government and federal money is paid for goods or services delivered.

The heart of this problem is executive courage. It is clear that the powers available to those in the Executive Branch, from the President on down, are greater than are now being used. Often department heads hesitate to enforce nondiscriminatory policies for fear of stirring up matters at the state level. And, of course, they are vulnerable because they are dependent on Congress for appropriations for their operations.

Sometimes an agency head will not take vigorous action because of the hierarchy through which his directives must be transmitted to the community level. This involves regional state, county, and city authorities, each of whom, in turn, may have decidedly less enthusiasm for antibias enforcement on a particular project. And the states are hesitant to take the initiative in locating jobs for Negroes because of the additional work and cost involved and because they simply do not want to tackle segregation—especially in the South.

However, vigorous efforts consistently and continuously applied by the federal government to require unbiased hiring and integrated work forces on jobs paid for with unsegregated American tax money can provide substantial numbers of jobs for Negroes. Back in 1961 the U.S. Commission on Civil Rights reviewed several of the grants-in-aid programs and turned up some interesting conclusions.

Under the Hill-Burton Act, there were 5,390 hospitals and health centers built between 1946 and 1962. The federal dollars spent on these in 1961 alone totaled $154 million. There is no reason, says the commission, why Negroes should not have been employed on these projects. Yet Health, Education and Welfare issued no regulation calling for nondiscriminatory work on these projects.

Federal funds are available to assist communities where large federal establishments have caused hardship, as when the government takes over land for a military base. This removes land from the tax rolls, and the increased federal activity may add to the school load. In 1961 the government spent $181 million to aid schools, and $63.3 million to help build schools in such areas. Again, HEW had not issued nondiscriminatory employment requirements on these impacted area school programs.

91

The grant program administered by the Bureau of Public Roads is the largest in dollar volume. It is used to help the states build highways and amounted to $2.7 billion in federal funds in 1961. The bureau includes a brief nondiscrimination clause in its contracts, but, as the Civil Rights Commission states in its 1961 report:

> The clause is, however, considerably less inclusive, . . . does not require posting . . . nor is it effectively enforced: there are no provisions for enforcement beyond periodic inspection of job sites . . . primarily concerned with . . . the construction and engineering terms of the contract. Since the insertion of the clause in 1941, no inspection has ever revealed discrimination in employment in any program administered by the Bureau and only one unsubstantiated complaint has ever been received.[8]

In urban renewal and low rent housing programs administered by the Housing and Home Finance Agency, Congress intended federal funds to help "alleviate present and recurring unemployment." The HHFA's Urban Renewal Administration had $152.3 million available in 1961, and an additional $148.2 million was committed to the low-rent housing program of HHFA's Public Housing Administration.

The Urban Renewal Administration construes the standard nondiscrimination clause to apply only during site clearance, but not during site improvement or after the site is sold to private developers. Says the commission:

> a nondiscriminatory employment requirement could undoubtedly be imposed to apply to all phases of the grant program. . . . Though there have been complaints of discrimination and inspectors have reported violations, the URA cannot cite any instances in which sanctions have been applied to violators.[9]

Until 1948 the Public Housing Administration had a vigorous enforcement program on its construction projects. At that time it changed its procedure, so that the local public agency sponsoring the project has been made responsible for record keeping. Once the project is completed, the records are forwarded to the PHA regional office and then transferred to a warehouse without inspection. So,

[8] *Op. cit.*, p. 87.
[9] *Ibid.*, p. 89.

without a specific complaint while the project is in progress, it is impossible for PHA to know whether biased hiring is being practiced. I have no doubt that serious, dedicated efforts to make employment opportunities equal on projects supported by federal funds would have immediate, widespread effects on employment of Negroes. And until someone in authority comes up with documented statistics to the contrary I will continue to believe this to be so.

There is no great mystery as to how this fog of bureaucratic inconsistency may be cleared up. First of all, the grants-in-aid should clearly be treated as contracts. A uniform federal policy of nondiscrimination should apply, without a question of doubt. Enforcement of such a policy should be the responsibility of the administrators of the various agencies administering the grants, but all such programs should be reviewed by the new Equal Employment Opportunity Commission which has the power of investigation, counseling, and bringing suit.

The new Civil Rights law has given statutory authority to the former President's Committee on Equal Employment Opportunity which President Kennedy established with an executive order in 1961. The committee was initially set up to "promote and ensure equal opportunity for all qualified persons, without regard to race, creed, color or national origin, employed or seeking employment with the Federal Government and on Government contracts."

The committee had considerable power, with complaint, compliance procedures, and sanctions spelled out, and clear jurisdiction over both unions and employers. Its major effort went into signing up more than 200 giant defense contracting corporations in the "Plans for Progress" program. In this, each signatory agreed to equal opportunity hiring, promotion, and reporting tailored to its own industrial situation. The corporations report on a regular basis the results of their efforts in hiring at various levels and in different categories of work, and their activities in promoting Negro workers. The program had the prestige of direction by President Johnson when he was vice-president, and drew top level businessmen into its administration through working committees on which they served.

Under the new law, the commission will serve as the successor to the old committee, and will be in the position of a Fair Employment Practices Commission, though with broader power and enhanced stature because of the interest of the President and business leaders. The major new areas open to the commission are all business establishments of one hundred or more employees (becoming twenty-five or more from 1967 on), labor unions, and employment agencies affecting interstate commerce. Formerly, the committee was largely confined to defense contractors. The new commission will fall short of requirements, however, if it does not extend its authority to training and recruitment facilities as well. And, as we have seen, it must manifest its interest and concern with the grants-in-aid programs of the federal government.

As to direct federal employment of Negroes, we had, until the past two or three years, given up on civil service. But there has been definite progress on this front. As of June, 1963, 13 percent of the 2,298,808 federal jobs were held by Negroes, up 3 percent from 1962. The administration trumpeted this news to the nation with much fanfare. It boasted of the fact that Negroes hired in jobs paying $6,667 to $10,000 had increased by 19.5 percent, and that the number of Negroes in the $9,475 through $20,000 range had jumped by 38.7 percent.

What gained little space in the papers was the fact that by this reckoning only 3 percent of all the Negroes in federal jobs were in grades GS-9 or above (receiving $6,667 or more). So, though there has been progress, and some of it has been in the higher-paying jobs, Negroes are not dancing in the streets over Uncle Sam's newly liberal hiring practices. There are reports that the U.S. Civil Service Commission is reviewing government hiring and promotion policies in cities in all parts of the nation. This is fine, but the civil service was established in 1883. Let us hope that it will not require eighty more years to act upon its findings.

As recently as March 11, 1964, the *Wall Street Journal* reported that the federal government was reluctant to crack down on its bigoted minions, preferring persuasion. The newspaper said that "the only action taken against uncooperative officials has been a temporary lifting of the Los Angeles and Atlanta postmaster's promotion authority."

In what appears to be a case of bedazzlement by "the old shell game," the *Journal* notes that a 1963 survey found only "tiny numbers [of Negroes] toiling for Uncle Sam in Birmingham, Savannah,

Nashville, Jacksonville, New Orleans and elsewhere [in the South]." As evidence that federal offices in Dixie are "hiring more Negroes, giving them larger responsibilities," the *Journal* reports that in Birmingham, Negro clerks have been shifted to the front counter to deal with the public in Social Security and Internal Revenue Service offices; the Veterans Administration has hired its first Negro stenographer in Jackson, Miss.; the Agriculture Department has installed a Negro clerk in a Mississippi county office for the first time; and the Federal Housing Administration has put Negroes in "semiprofessional" jobs in the South. This is progress, but it serves more to highlight the abysmal situation that exists in federal employment than to give cause for jubilation.

Let us be realistic about current conditions. If the federal government conscientiously adopts a nondiscriminatory hiring and promotion policy in all of its employment, and even if all state governments do likewise, we still face the problem of finding gainful employment for hundreds of thousands of Negro citizens. It is obvious that government hiring is not going to expand sufficiently to solve this problem.

What hope is there for one million Negro unemployed? Education is usually cited as the panacea. But recent evidence[10] indicates that among the better-educated, young Negroes fourteen to twenty-four years of age the unemployment rate is far above the average. Furthermore, according to the Department of Labor "rates of unemployment for young nonwhites, both high school graduates and dropouts, remain relatively high even after they have been out of school several years...."[11] The Negro college graduate's lifetime income is less than that of a white man with an eighth grade education.

It should be clear, therefore, that education takes too long; unless extraordinary changes occur, it is not the answer to putting substantial numbers of Negro citizens to work in a short time.

What can be done? President Johnson's message to Congress calling for a "War on Poverty" promises some answers, if the Economic Opportunity Act of 1964, as it is called, succeeds in getting Congressional approval and appropriations. Of the major elements

[10] *Manpower Report of the President*, U.S. Department of Labor, 1964, p. 195.
[11] *Ibid.*

of the program, those that hold promise are concerned with stimulating communities to tackle their own problems with federal aid and local organization; the enlistment of anti-Poverty Warriors in "domestic Peace Corps" activities; stimulation of industry to hire the unemployed; a work-training program, and a work-study scheme for youth.

Existing programs, such as the Area Redevelopment Act which was designed to aid distressed areas, the Manpower Development Training Act and Vocational Education Act for Youth, do have appropriations and should swing into action in imaginative new applications.

One example is that of community mobilization in South Bend, Indiana, to cope with the pullout of Studebaker Corporation which had been a major employer for 122 years until December, 1963, when it shut down its manufacturing facilities in that city. Under the coordination of the local community chest organization and with the cooperation of the University of Notre Dame, Studebaker, and the United Auto Workers, the community is pitching in. It has developed a "saturation" program drawing on federal, state, and local government as well as on union and management for cooperation. It expects federal approval of its program and aid under the Manpower Automation and Training Act.

With 6,600 persons cast on the job market by the shutdown, the community is offering courses ranging from chef training to computer operation. Forty experienced counselors are guiding workers through retraining and then helping them to find jobs. Since two thousand of the workers are over fifty, a concentrated effort is being made with employers to hire older men. For the first time federal subsidies will be sought for moving-costs of workers who locate jobs in other cities.

Special help is being given to Negro workers who must upgrade their reading, writing, and arithmetic skills. Counseling by professionals from both the UAW's and Studebaker's industrial relations staffs is available on a twenty-four-hour-a-day basis. The project director explains that this is necessary because many of these people have never had the experience of applying for any other job. Without special help, he says, they would be unlikely to accept retraining. Furthermore, older, immigrant workers fear taking and possibly failing tests because they lack education. The counselors are giving such problems special attention.

Efforts are being made to search out all available jobs in the area and region, with all community agencies, both public and private, participating aggressively. Studebaker is contributing facilities worth $70,000 and the federal government is expected to put in $1 million. The program is designed to last fourteen months. The clincher for this effort: without such a program, direct relief payments to these unemployed would cost $2,750,000 per year.

The Secretary of Labor estimates that it costs the community $1,000 per person, per year for the rest of their lives, for every one of the young people who comes into the labor market and finds no work. The average cost of equipping these new job-seekers for work comes to about $3,000 each—a one-time cost. The price of idle hands is becoming too expensive to tolerate.

Opportunities for harnessing the energies of millions of Americans are in our midst. I propose that we concentrate major federal, state, and local government effort, organized and directed at the community level by the best talent we can muster, in a concerted effort to bring our Negro citizens into the mainstream of employment. I recommend that in the twenty-five worst urban ghettos of this nation—the Harlems from New York to Los Angeles—we focus the necessary resources of money, leadership, expertise, and enthusiasm to rejuvenate these areas and to redeem those slum-dwellers now consigned to oblivion.

Think what can be done to the Harlems of this country if we apply ourselves and bring to bear some of the same fantastically effective intelligence that has so successfully harnessed motor power. There are hundreds of millions of man-hours of work needed to make a ghetto such as Harlem truly inhabitable. From the paint to the plumbing, the sidewalks to the sinks, the roads to the roofs, these enclaves need everything. And they have the manpower to do the jobs, if given the leadership and help in applying themselves. Because the needs of the ghetto and its inhabitants are so vast, this community rejuvenation will require a wide range of skills and the application of substantial effort over many months, perhaps even years in the case of some of the worst problems.

But the multiple-city ghetto reclamation program I advocate is not aimed simply at making the slums spic and span concentration camps instead of the miserable, squalid cesspools they are now. Its purpose is not to encourage or institutionalize any further the slum crowding and the segregated life of Negro citizens. Rather, it is to put people to work in constructive ways; to bring to bear the resources of the community and its state and federal partners to make what must be endured by some as livable and healthful as possible under the circumstances, while we continue to move toward open housing. Let no one misread this to believe that either the Negro slum dwellers or I will be satisfied with living in the ghetto after it receives a gilding. It takes more than frosting to make a cake.

For this program we require the application of the best renewal and conservation concepts, carefully worked out in what I choose to call a program of community investment. South Bend and Philadelphia are moving in this direction. Who can doubt that the money and effort used in constructive programs such as these—giving work, counseling, hope, leadership, and self-respect to hundred of thousands—will benefit the larger community? We have choices to make, and the alternatives are very clear. Either we make these people constructive citizens, productive and healthy, or they are going to be destructive dependents. In the latter case, we are going to be forced to spend increasing millions year after year for these people to survive in penury, while we pay the cost of our shortsightedness—our neglect—in outlays to combat crime, fire, disease, and to cover the cost of welfare payments.

I am not calling here for experimental, tentative, and timid attempts to determine what should be done. The torrent of eloquence calling for action is equaled only by the flow of suggestions that committees be appointed, investigations be carried on, and pilot projects be started. These next-week warriors, willing to risk only a token force in the battle, miss the urgency of this war which we are losing at an accelerating rate. I seriously question whether an academically oriented approach is warranted. This country has venerable organizations and citizens who have spent their entire adult lives in dedicated effort to improve the lot of the ghettoized. The expertise required for drafting effective programs is available. What is needed is courage, commitment, and carry-through. For this program will not be cheaply bought; its success will not be easily won; but its victories will be universally shared.

Though no one should believe that I begrudge our Marshall Plan aid, it would be unthinkable for this country to spend $17 billion between 1947 and 1951 to rehabilitate war-torn Europe and to do nothing to rehabilitate our culturally torn and historically deprived Negro citizens. We have given refuge to Hungarians and Cubans fleeing dictatorship; we waived requirements calling for a sponsor and a job before admittance to this country; we permitted these refugees to secure welfare and even declared certain areas emergency regions where there was a heavy influx of migrants.

Yet here, in our Negro citizenry, is a group of people who have expended their skills to build this nation, who have been loyal defenders of democracy, who have deeper roots in this nation in terms of generations in the United States than most of their white contemporaries. I submit that these citizens who happen to be black deserve the concerted effort, the community investment that I have proposed.

The President, in his message to Congress, asked for $960 million to launch the attack on poverty. What I have outlined as a ghetto reclamation program may well require an input of five times that— still less than 1 per cent of our Gross National Product—over a period of five years. The yield on this investment in human resources, however, will include a thriving industry, greater prosperity, and proof to the world that this nation's Negro as well as white citizens can successfully share its abundance.

If, deaf to the voice of the
Zeitgeist, we refuse to use and
develop these men, we risk
poverty and loss.

W. E. B. DuBois,
"Of The Training of Black Men,"
The Souls of Black Folk, 1903.

In the field of public education,
the doctrine of 'separate but
equal' has no place.
The Supreme Court
of the United States,
Ruling, May 17, 1954.

4
Education:
Last, Best
Hope?

F or people desperately seeking answers to the civil rights and other problems that face us today—whether in employment, race relations, or automation—the panacea seems to be education. Both the expert and the man on the street seize on this as the remedy for the difficulties that besiege us.

Acknowledging that there is validity in the overriding value of education, it is particularly appropriate that we face up to the extent to which the Negro citizen has been historically and currently deprived. Statistics reveal that in spite of heralded progress the average Negro youngster receives three and one-half years less schooling than the average white child. When one considers that the bulk of elementary training for the Negro child is received in inferior, segregated, slum schools—North and South—then the real difference is more accurately five years.

Probably the peak of interest in education as "the answer" to race relations problems occurred just prior to, and at the time of, the Supreme Court's unanimous decision calling for integration of the public schools, May 17, 1954. In this ruling, as is well known, the justices of the Supreme Court took into consideration and made one of the determining principles in their decision the fact that even though students might receive equal instruction in equal facilities, they were unavoidably receiving inferior education if they were segregated.

How intelligent human beings, and Americans particularly, could or can countenance the mocking travesty of equality in racially segregated situations of any kind is beyond me. Whether it is a neighborhood, a hospital, a school, park, or business office, segregation per se has a poisonous influence. In the words of the Supreme Court:

> Separate educational facilities are inherently unequal. . . . segregation of children in public schools solely on the basis of race, even though the physical facilities and other 'tangible' factors be equal, deprive the children of the minority group of equal educational opportunities. . . . In these days, it is doubtful that any child may reasonably be expected to succeed in life if he is denied the opportunity of an education. Such an opportunity, where the state has undertaken to provide it, is a right which must be made available to all on equal terms. . . . To separate [Negro children] from others of similar age and qualifications solely because of their race generates a feeling of inferiority as to their status in the community that may affect their hearts and minds in a way unlikely ever to be undone.

It might be interesting to speculate whether or not there would ever have been the current drive for integration if, in fact, truly equal schools and facilities had been developed in the South and throughout the country. More than likely any such serious effort would have collapsed under the weight of the economic strain it imposed. The resources simply were insufficient to provide absolutely equal but separate facilities, as several Southern states proved decisively in the 1950's when they frantically attempted to upgrade the Negro educational systems within their borders. At one stage, when the trend of court decisions was clearly leading up to the big one in 1954, some Southern states were spending more money on education outlays for Negro schools and equipment than for white—and still the inherent inadequacies of the teaching staffs, the books, curricula, guidance, and counseling produced Negroes whose education was inferior, year for year, to that of whites.

After all, segregated schools required teachers who had themselves been brought up in inferior, segregated school systems and this "compounding" flaw was inherent in their teaching. As late as March, 1964, it was estimated by the President, that three-fourths or more of the Negro teachers in one Southern city entered the school system on standards below those required for white teachers. Similar differentials are reported throughout the South.[1]

When the Southern states began upgrading teacher salaries to something like the scale for white educators, some interesting situations began to develop. For the first time the Negro principals and teachers found themselves receiving comfortable wages and working in new or renovated schools with adequate facilities. They were in a dilemma. In such circumstances, did they truly want integration or did they not? For in integrated school systems their own positions would be threatened.

After the Supreme Court's decision in 1954 the South immediately felt that "this was it." There was no reflex reaction of the kind that was expected. People did not immediately organize to circumvent the new decision. By and large most Southerners believed that by the following September the schools would be integrated. I am convinced that at that moment in history the only thing necessary to integrate southern schools would have been statesmanlike leadership by the President. He could so easily have called the governors together and said, "Gentlemen, I didn't bring you here to discuss whether or not you or I like this decision. I have brought you here to say this is the law of the land, and I intend to enforce it."

But this didn't happen. Instead, President Eisenhower maintained an aloof attitude, saying it was strictly a court case and a legal decision right up to the end of his administration. Only recently has he acknowledged the Court's decision was morally right.

Thus, at the critical moment the tremendous persuasive power of the Presidency was not enlisted to bring home to American citizens that this was a moral issue, as well as one of rights and entitlement. During this period President Eisenhower's hands-off attitude

[1] *The Manpower Report of the President*, March, 1964, Supt. of Documents, Washington, D.C., p. 98.

plus the Supreme Court's implementation decision in May, 1955, with its vague call for "all deliberate speed" in integrating the schools and placing this implementation in the hands of the local courts encouraged the segregationists. They decided that the 1954 decision could be delayed, if not completely circumvented.

It was these factors that spawned the resistance movement. Virginia set up its "massive resistance" program; other Southern states tried the hoary "interposition" tactic and nullification of legislation. A variety of legislative subterfuges ranging from crude to ingenious were used at the local level to prevent, delay, or discourage integration. Many of these were designed to make it difficult for Negroes to file suit and force litigation. In addition, intimidation was used on Negro principals, teachers, students, and families, making action virtually impossible.

As these roadblocks sprang up in the absence of executive leadership, it became clear that the Supreme Court's decision in 1954 was, in effect, reduced to apply only to the five specific cases at issue. It became apparent that every other school district was going to be desegregated only through the expensive, laborious process of challenge at the local level by a local person, then movement of the case up through each of the higher courts. Even to this day, this is the way in which school integration is being ever so slowly accomplished.

There are painfully few instances of completely voluntary action in which a local district or state has initiated change without an actual case or threat of a case before it. In fact, according to the New York Times, on the tenth anniversary of the Supreme Court's 1954 decision last May, 98.9 percent of the Negro students in the eleven Southern states were still in all-Negro schools.[2] And Mississippi, says the Times, has not made even token progress. It has not yet taken the first step toward compliance with the court's ruling and its officials "are still committed to a policy of defiant resistance."[3]

Until 1959–1960, the north reacted with moral indignation to the South's various shameful techniques of resistance and to the miserably slow pace of desegregation. There were editorials published about these matters in all the newspapers of the North. Liberals were vastly upset. Liberal leaders and the platforms of the

[2] New York Times, Jan. 16, 1964, p. 73.
[3] Ibid.

political parties berated the South for its evasion and intransigence.

This self-righteous attitude continued until, in many Northern communities, civil rights groups and Negro citizens became aware that, because of housing segregation and some rather odd school district lines, education in the elementary schools of the North was as rigidly segregated as in the South.

Probably the most celebrated example of this was the New Rochelle school case, which clearly revealed that the school board had some time earlier drawn district lines purposely to keep Lincoln an all-Negro school. In this case, Judge Irving Kaufman of the Southern District of New York held on January 24, 1961, that the local board of education had maintained racial segregation through a policy of gerrymandering school boundary lines and permissive transfers. This case, therefore, was not a true test of de facto segregation.

At any rate, it did not touch the fundamental question: that an all-Negro school, regardless of how the district lines are drawn, is innately inferior. But the case did lead to dialogue between civil rights groups and local school boards in Northern communities and brought the term "de facto segregation" into current usage. And, interestingly enough, the phrase "neighborhood school" was not heard until de facto segregation came to light. Then, suddenly, people who had ignored, been indifferent to, or hadn't spoken to their neighbors for years became highly emotional about the neighborhood school.

The neighborhood school became sacrosanct; life couldn't go on without it. This was particularly interesting because many of the parents who began to show cornern for this "little red schoolhouse" concept were the ones who were bussing their children across town to parochial schools or sending their youngsters to prep schools hundreds of miles away.

Obviously, much of the sudden concern about the inviolable character of the neighborhood school was a subterfuge. It didn't really reflect newly regained respect or fondness for the neighbors as much as it seemed to provide a means of preventing integration of suburban schools.

It was New York City that took the first steps to bring about better integration in the city schools after studies had shown the extent of de facto segregation in the city. Actually, Negroes began

106

their fight against discrimination and segregation in public schools of New York state and city in 1857. As a result Grover Cleveland, when Governor of New York in 1884, signed a bill abolishing colored schools and opening all the schools to all the children "without regard to race or color." Teddy Roosevelt, when Governor in 1900, signed a bill repealing the law that permitted separate schools for Negroes. The new law reiterated that no person could be refused admission to, or be excluded from, any public school in the state on account of color or race.

But as Harlem became a Negro community, its schools became de facto segregated schools. In early 1954 the Urban League in New York tackled this by organizing a group to study the schools and urge the Board of Education to adopt an integration policy. The study by noted psychologist and educator, Kenneth Clark, was released in June, 1954; it resulted in further studies and in the establishment of a Commission on Integration by the city's Board of Education. The board set as its goal the attainment of completely integrated schools.

The board has moved to aid integration of its one million pupils in many ways. It inaugurated special programs such as open enrollment, all-day neighborhood schools, reading clinics, Higher Horizons Programs; it installed a human relations unit, added guidance counselors, and instituted many other features. And it built new schools in segregated areas (against the recommendation of its own Commission on Integration) where many schools were and are overcrowded.

These efforts, though well-meant, were too meager. By 1963, the number of public schools with fifty percent or more Negro and Puerto Rican students in New York had tripled since 1954. The imbalance was accelerated by a decline in white enrollment from 70 percent to 60 percent in the years from 1958 to 1963.

In 1955, a study by the Public Education Association in New York revealed that achievement levels of Negro and Puerto Rican pupils decreased the longer they stayed in their segregated schools. In 1955, the eighth graders were almost two and one half grades behind their counterparts in all-white schools. By 1962 things were even worse: the Negro and Puerto Rican children were three and one half grades behind in achievement.

Now it should be noted that these colored students enjoyed the

107

benefits of neighborhood schools—though not of the type usually envisaged when this term is flourished by articulate spokesmen for the status quo. No, the Harlem and Bedford-Stuyvesant youngsters, in their cozy neighborhood schools in 1963, studied under these conditions: far more substitute and inexperienced teachers than in the all-white schools; as many as twenty-six per diem substitutes during a three-month period; faculty turnover at least double that of the all-white schools; 35 percent Negro and Puerto Rican teaching staffs vs. 99 percent white teaching staffs at the all-white schools. The buildings and facilities were an average of 33 percent older than the all-white schools, with less floor and playground space for fewer rooms.[4]

Is it any wonder, therefore, that integration of the schools is such a hot issue in New York? And if I do not cite specifics relating to other major cities of the nation, it is to spare the reader the repetition, not because New York is unique.

In many suburban areas, as in those around New York and New Jersey, school integration has stirred up controversy. I moved to New Rochelle after the matter blew up there. The issue was focused upon the Lincoln School which was all-Negro. There was a concerted effort to break up this situation and to disperse these children, because they were receiving inferior education. Furthermore, it was recognized that the white children in other schools were being handicapped because they did not have opportunities to learn and play with Negro youngsters.

The school board, desirous of raising the standards of Lincoln School pupils, found that the achievement of youngsters in integrated schools was higher than those attending all-Negro schools. It, therefore, proposed to close Lincoln School and permit free transfer of students to other schools in the city.

This became a burning issue in the community, and I was called on to testify at a hearing held after the board announced that Lincoln was to be closed and the children bussed to other schools.

I said then that the rest of the world will conclude, that by whatever refinement of evil, or rationalization that this part of the plan was opposed (and there was some opposition by a few Negro citizens as well as many whites), it could very well be an expression of unconscious or conscious fear of social change that would be painful

[4] *Urban League of Greater New York*, Research Study, Sept. 1963, p. 22.

to some at first, but that must be faced because inevitable. Because my main points apply today to many communities, I include some of this testimony here:

> I have seen these fears operate many times in the past few years, where, under the influence of mob psychology, rational people became irrational, and some of the same people who in other periods had suffered severely because of hate and bigotry became the perpetrators of injustice to others.
>
> I have also seen Negro citizens caught up in this web of fear. Acting with good intent to protect their children they have withdrawn to the seemingly comfortable house of segregation only to do irreparable harm to those children by making them ill-equipped to work and live later with all peoples.
>
> On the other hand I have witnessed great intelligence and courage. I have seen white parents plead for an end to their all-white schools so that their children could develop in a healthier and more secure manner, better prepared for the creative and diverse world in which they are called upon to live. And I have seen brave and courageous Negro parents take their little children by the hand and, in the face of violence and hostility, lead them into an integrated classroom. Can we who live in a city of relative enlightenment do less than this?
>
> But make no mistake about it, the maintaining of Lincoln School as the inferior physical facility that it is now, or the building of a new one which will be ninety percent Negro is wrong for everyone. The closing of Lincoln without providing free transportation would not only be placing an unrealistic burden on the parents who can least afford it, but it would also be a cruel subterfuge, for soon the two nearby schools would be largely all-Negro. The school bus for which we would pay relatively little is not a new innovation to the American scene. At present, I pay sixty dollars a year transportation for our older daughter to the high school.
>
> There are many municipal and special school services provided by my tax dollar which I don't use because I do not need them or am not eligible for them. But surely I do not begrudge anyone those services which might make his life better and our city a healthier place in which to live.
>
> I, too, share the concern of those who are honestly disturbed by the high tax rate we pay here, but, until we show enough civic interest to attract to our own community light industries and department stores which now bring sizable profits to our neighboring communities for whose school systems we pay over

their counters, I'm afraid we will continue to be saddled with this problem. The modern answer for lower taxes is to encourage industry, not to discourage education.

I am asking, therefore, that you do not postpone or delay the inevitable, which you sooner or later must face in the midst of great acrimony. If you do what you know is right you will incur the gratitude of generations yet unborn, and you will make me forever proud of the city we now call our home and its citizens who will truly be our neighbors and friends.

The whole brunt of my talk—and of this book—is that while bussing or redrawing school district lines to assure integrated schools and ethnically balanced student bodies is admittedly artificial, I would remind people that the segregation and discrimination responsible for the situation were also artificial. They were deliberately and consciously planned; they did not just happen.

Now, obviously, with integration Negroes will benefit from a better educational system, better materials, facilities, and teachers. But as I see it, there are precious benefits for both whites and Negroes. I do not believe education can be absolutely first rate without integration. To the extent that people say that integration of the schools has no relationship to the quality of education, they are, in fact, saying that separate but equal education is valid.

Essentially, the issue is that unless youngsters go to school together they are not likely to work and live together naturally later, so that we shall have segregation forever. The question is, therefore, how can we provide white children with the kind of experience that will prepare them for the kind of world in which they will live as adults? White children need this exposure to, and familiarity with, diversity. A paramount function of education is the preparation of individuals to relate themselves comfortably to their fellow men. As long as people existed in a world where they were born, lived, and died in one little hamlet, never venturing more than ten miles from home, this preparation was unnecessary. But today, in an era of great mobility and interchange, of increasing contact with peoples of differing colors, beliefs, and backgrounds, it is imperative to so educate our children. This is the fundamental concept for which I advocate integrated schooling.

In New Rochelle, the closing of Lincoln School resulted in about 180 children being redistributed to other schools in the town.

Soon after, the New York State Commissioner of Education issued a directive to all schools to move toward racial balance. The state also helped by providing funds for the transportation of students to achieve such integration. Thus, the burden on the local school system was reduced, and so also was the force of the argument that taxes to pay for bussing would be prohibitive.

There are, of course, several methods of integrating the schools. The most frequently used are:

1. Redefining districts in order to promote better distribution of the races in the schools. This usually can be accomplished with relative speed by conscientious school authorities.

2. The so-called Princeton Plan. This derives its name from the method initiated at Princeton, New Jersey, in 1948. In this approach, the schools are reclassified so that each handles fewer grades and thus is attended by students from larger geographic areas. Two nearby schools are paired, one covers perhaps the first three, and the other the last three elementary school grades. This "doubling" of the geographic area for each school sometimes is successful in achieving integration if it occurs near the fringes of the ghetto.

3. Sometimes new schools can be built in locations that will facilitate integration, particularly on the fringes of the ghetto.

4. In the ghetto itself, where the population is solidly Negro, the previous three techniques do not scratch the surface. Therefore, shifting Negro students to under-used schools in white neighborhoods is often the only way to break up the homogeneous pattern. Usually this is done by open enrollment, in which the student may decide where he wishes to attend. And free transfer, or public bussing of pupils, is a necessary aspect of such a plan.

5. Establishment of superior schools in the Negro community, partly through the utilization of "educational parks."

A "neighborhood school" by any name is one that serves a certain area and reflects the cultural, social, economic, and racial makeup of that area. Since Negroes in urban communities are packed into ghettos, their "neighborhood schools" are inevitably Jim-Crow institutions. Characteristically, as we have noted in the New York schools, these schools are inferior and so is their product—education. Meanwhile, in other parts of the city there are frequently

111

schools with under-utilized class rooms and staffs, particularly in sections where the population is stable and older.

Now, the emotionalism that many people today are displaying toward the "inviolability" of the neighborhood school is rooted in several myths. We forget that the little yellow school bus is as much an American institution and a tradition in our society as the little red school house. Throughout the country, for four decades we have accepted the concept of consolidating districts and bussing children to centrally located schools in order to give them superior education from better teaching staffs and facilities than could have been afforded otherwise. Nobody became upset over this bussing and consolidating—as long as it was segregated. These precious neighbors didn't become so important until allowing entry to the neighborhood school meant also allowing entry of some Negroes. Some people seriously believe that the standards of the school will be lowered by integration. Others contend that it is unfair to the Negro children because they are less well equipped to compete. The truth is that if integration lowers the standards in the school it proves that something is wrong with the educational system. For it implies that the segregated schools are not keeping up and/or that the system's teachers are largely inadequate to keep up the standards when faced with shifts in student load.

People should realize that not all Negroes are stupid nor all whites geniuses. The facts show that the gap between the slowest-learning white child and the smartest white child in any one school is wider than the gap between the average white child and the average Negro child. This simply means that in any school system you have fast-learners and slow-learners.

It is probably true that at first there will tend to be more Negroes in the slow-learner classes and fewer at the top, but there will be some, at least, at the top. If education has not yet solved the problem of what to do with diverse abilities in a single school system, then it has a much greater problem than integration. Insofar as it has solved this problem, it is not a question of race but of education.

As the President's Manpower Report states, "It should be noted, however, that in schools with a mixed population, the achievement of Negro children tends to be comparable to that of white young-

112

sters of the same socio-economic backgrounds."[5] It is interesting to note also that in those places that have desegregated their schools the experts have been wide of the mark in their predictions of the time it would take the Negro students to close the gap. In Washington, D. C., on the basis of achievement level tests the experts predicted that it would take from five to ten years, depending on the pupil's age, before Negro children would catch up. However, they had not tested, nor can you ever test, such intangibles as motivation, incentive and drive.

The studies showed that on the first day of integrated schools most white parents told their children, "Now go to school, don't start any trouble, and if any starts, come home". The Negro parents, according to the findings, awakened their children early, cleaned them up, slicked down their hair, and told them, "Now you must really study like you never studied before. We've got to show these people what we can do!" So here you had considerable differences in attitude and in motivation to achieve. These had not been and could not be tested. And they proved to be major factors.

It was in 1954 that the schools in the District of Columbia were integrated. At that time the composite test score for Negro and white sixth graders was 2.3 years below the national norm. By 1958 the student population was 84 percent Negro. Even though there had been a substantial increase in the proportion of Negro students in the school system, sixth graders were achieving at a level equal to or above the national norm, according to the 1964 President's Report on Manpower.[6]

The results of aptitude and achievement tests should be viewed with caution and with an effort at understanding the prevailing circumstances. Many Negro children cannot relate the test material to their lives and, taking the tests with their peers in a segregated school means little or nothing. Most of the tests around the country show the segregated Negro child to be behind in achievement at the first grade level by about one to two years. This can be attributed to inferior environment and cultural deprivation even before he starts school. He is not tuned in to the teacher's wave length,

[5] Op. cit., p. 99.
[6] Ibid., p. 99.

because of stunted language facility and development and narrow cultural experience. Often, he never finds the right channel.

When you check this child at the fifth grade he is behind about two years; at the eighth grade, he is doing work at the fifth grade level. And by the time he reaches the twelfth grade, if he is still in school, he is at a level nearly four years behind his white counterparts.

It is difficult to say for sure that Negro children in integrated schools do better. It is true that some Negro youngsters have had no favorable experiences with learning, either at home or at school. When thrust into schools in other neighborhoods, placed in classrooms with children who are not handicapped and, in fact, have a solid grasp of the subject matter, these children are often overwhelmed. They become depressed, anxious, and uneasy. As one school psychiatrist puts it,

> They [Negro children] yearn to learn. They want very much to become accepted in the new setting and yet they feel so hopelessly behind the other youngsters that they begin, almost inevitably, to resort to the only behavior they have learned to use to cope with such distressing feelings.[7]

The Urban League has called for special effort to prepare Negro children so that they will be motivated to achieve and to learn. This means that we expect that extra aid may be needed to assist Negro children who go into these integrated schools. Some of these youngsters will require remedial help; many will require compassion and horizon-broadening stimulation. They must not be allowed to "sit out" or drop out because of discouragement and demoralization. They must be included in the extracurricular activities of the school and in mind-expanding programs that have proven so effective, such as the Higher Horizons program in New York City, the Banneker Group program in St. Louis and the "Great Cities" projects sponsored by the Fund for the Advancement of Education.

Teaching materials that have meaning to Negro children also must be developed. Books, illustrations, audiovisual materials, songs and stories that describe a middle-class, all-white world with trees, flowers, pets, zoos, parks, toys, and comfortable living conditions

[7] I. N. Berlin, "Desegregation Creates Problems, Too," *Saturday Review*, June 15, 1963, p. 66.

are incomprehensible to many Negro youngsters. Not only are the scenes and situations foreign to him, but they continue and reinforce his underevaluation of self, intimidate and disorient him. He must be given materials that allow opportunities for identification and recognition.

These youngsters need and deserve more than just isolation or a teaching attitude that ignores them, in the hope that they will become discouraged and transfer back to their ghetto schools. They deserve help, not "pass-along" treatment in which teaching standards are tossed out the window and children are promoted from grade to grade regardless of their achievement. U.S. Education Commissioner Francis Keppel cites one case in which a record of reading achievement of an eighth grade class in a great Midwestern city showed that more than half of the pupils were rated from fifth grade down to second grade level. In fact, 80 percent had failed to reach eighth grade reading standards, yet all had been passed quietly on.[8] This in our society is intolerable.

The dropout situation has received much attention but not enough action. These youths are often pushouts, rather than dropouts. However, the youngster who quits school does so for a variety of reasons not necessarily associated with his intelligence. Sometimes he drops out when he gets so far behind the class that he cannot stay without suffering great damage to his ego. He gets tired of being left behind, of being unable to understand questions with which he cannot identify, questions beyond his comprehension. He may drop out because the other children tease him about his poor clothes. He may drop out because he continually lacks the money to attend the opera and other activities in which his class is participating. Or sometimes it may be the continual lack of lunch money. The reasons may be infinite; they may be simple or complex; but usually the youngster drops out because he doesn't feel adequate either emotionally or educationally to the situation.

I believe that we oversimplify the case when we single out as the major reason for the dropout's leaving school the necessity for him to earn money for the family. I don't believe this is the primary factor today. And I don't think we have done nearly as much

[8] Francis Keppel, "The 'Pass-Along,' " New York Times, Jan. 16, 1964, p. 73.

as we should to encourage him to continue his schooling in order to have a better chance—one might almost say any chance—for a decent job. Most teachers until recently did not feel much concern about dropouts. They were far from sure that the Negro could find better jobs, even with education. They were not convinced that he was not wasting his time in further education. Therefore, they did not press hard to motivate and interest these students.

Today in progressive communities there are programs aimed at preventing dropouts. But in many cases the schools have taken the passive route and passed the child along until he voluntarily quits. Or there have been efforts to push the child out, particularly in cases where teachers wanted to rid their classrooms of what they considered sources of disorder and confusion.

Here is what the psychiatrist sees in such behavior:

> The only way many of these children have learned to master anxiety, tension, and unease is by loud, boisterous, disturbing behavior, which at least evokes a known and predictable response from authorities. With this in mind, teachers and administrators may be able to anticipate and prepare themselves and the other children to deal with tension and anxiety.[9]

Though the number of Negro high school graduates nearly doubled from 1952 to 1962, 46 percent of Negroes eighteen through twenty-four years of age who had been in high school failed to finish. As the Manpower Report of the President puts it, "the high drop-out rate among non-whites is understandable—an apparently realistic response to the lack of economic incentive. The unemployment rates indicate that by completing high school the average white student can halve the probability that he will be unemployed, but for non-whites, high school graduation reduces the chance of unemployment very little."[10]

Dr. James B. Conant underscored the dropout problem in his book "Slums and Suburbs." Here he described the appalling discrepancy between the education provided in these two areas that are typical of metropolitan regions in our country today.

As he put it, the unemployed, out-of-school youths in our large cities, especially the Negro slums, are building up into "social

[9] Berlin, op. cit., p. 67.
[10] Manpower Report, op. cit., p. 98.

dynamite." From my personal observations of the 32 percent of all students who quit school between the ninth and twelfth grades, the potential danger that they represent to society is more akin to a nuclear explosion. Such explosions in our urban centers would rend our society savagely.

Secretary of Labor Willard Wirtz has spoken of the 350,000 out-of-work boys who have given up looking for work as the "outlaw pack." Mr. Wirtz says these boys will be unemployed the rest of their lives, at a cost in unemployment insurance or institutional care of $1,000 per head per year as long as they live. He estimates that 6,500,000 boys and girls will come into the work force in the 1960's without high school diplomas, will compete with machines for jobs and lose. In this group will be untold unharnessed energy, with potential for eruption.

There have been suggestions by Mr. Wirtz that the legal age for school leaving be moved up to eighteen in order to train better and keep off the job market temporarily some of these youths. Dr. Conant recommends that the schools be responsible for educational and vocational guidance of youths until they reach the age of twenty-one, and that work-study programs for slow students as well as meaningful courses for pupils with less than average ability be instituted.

We know this about the dropout: He is not uneducable, though he tends to score lower on IQ tests. The dropout's major handicap is retarded reading; he is at least two years behind in reading ability when he quits school. Dropouts often come from families where the father is missing, where education is viewed with indifference, distrust, resentment or contempt, and where cultural background is limited by lower socioeconomic status. The average 1961 income for the nonwhite dropout was $2,427, and $4,090 for the white. This contrasted with average income of $3,381 for the Negro high school graduate, and $5,155 for the white.

Since in the cities the dropout problem is also to a considerable extent a Negro problem, it is of great concern to us. Over the years the Urban League has striven mightily to motivate youngsters with a national Vocational Opportunity Campaign (begun in the early thirties), Tomorrow's Scientists and Technicians program, Career Conferences, Back-to-School Campaign, "Success Centers," Career

Clubs, Cultural Enrichment Projects and vocational counseling and placement services. The League's resources in money and staff have unfortunately been inadequate to the dimensions of the problem. But the root inadequacy has been at the local school district level. Here the unprofessional educators, the unperceptive school boards, the unperturbed citizens and the unmotivated and culturally handicapped children have continued to compound the dropout difficulty year after year. The time of reckoning is upon us.

The dropout is the product of a complex of factors, and only a multifaceted approach to aiding him will be effective. Among the avenues that promise improvement are these:

1. Intensive programs to inculcate reading skills, above all, and writing and arithmetic must be inaugurated. These may be initiated at the preschool level, during summer vacation, before or after school, post elementary, and at junior high level. Neighborhood centers, church, voluntary agencies, and recreation centers can help.

2. Counseling centers and services should help the potential dropout when the symptoms develop, rather than when the battle is lost. The National Urban League and Delta Sigma Theta, a Negro college sorority, for example, are training counselors through workshops and launching a nationwide tutoring program for this purpose. College students in many towns are following the lead of the Wesleyan University Tutorial Program. In this activity Negro public school children are helped in specific subjects and in general problems and attitudes. Additional skilled personnel must be added to schools in which dropouts are endemic. Such professionals should have the diagnostic skills necessary to determine what incentives and aids can be used with the pupils who are slipping.

3. Training and employment centers to help develop marketable job skills are necessary, and can harness the voluntary help of industry, labor, vocational advisers, and programs such as Junior Achievement, for instance, where businessmen help youngsters learn small business procedure by actually setting up a company and marketing a product.

4. Programs whose purpose is job skills development, whether apprenticeships (where entrance requirements might be modified) or evening trade schools (where prerequisites might be waived).

5. Cross-agency coordination of efforts to improve education. We know that the metropolitan area school districts have almost

no social and economic cohesion, that the mobility of family units is extraordinarily high, and the consequent problems for the pupil are often severe. As Dr. Conant says, "To a considerable degree what a school should do and can do is determined by the status and ambitions of the families being served." Unless the families are drawn into the community's efforts to educate the children the chances of success are minimal.

Adult education, though useful, is not likely to be of major help in this matter. It requires concerted effort by social welfare, health, and education workers of public and voluntary agencies to bring families of dropouts into the educational process positively—to reverse their negative attitudes toward education, to reading and basic skills, to the opportunities for their children *if they will learn*. The Banneker program in St. Louis, with its "general uplift" approach to the education of low academic level children has scored notable successes. It has motivated principals, teachers, students, and parents. Meetings held with parents to involve them in the education of their children were very important in the excellent results obtained.

6. Meaningful curricula tailored to the employment future, student aptitudes, and training resources of the community, are needed desperately. This is not an area for dilletantes and "crash project" teams to stir about, "settle the problem," and leave. The curriculum lies at the very heart of popular education in this nation and challenges every school board as a matter of central policy.

7. Plans such as Secretary Wirtz's, requiring two years more of schooling geared to vocational needs, and Dr. Conant's, for educational and vocational guidance by the schools of youths until the age of twenty-one, are but two of the possibilities that should be adopted. They aim to increase the preparation of youths and to give them needed help in the job hunt, rather than to dump them, as at present, on the labor market with insufficient skills, inadequately prepared to find suitable positions by themselves.

Dr. Conant's book *Slums and Suburbs* pointed out that it is necessary and urgent that more money be invested in schools in slum areas to bring them up to standard. He also advocated interracial teaching staffs in all schools.

Now the *special-effort* approach calls for making the ghetto schools absolutely top flight. This inevitably requires the most talented administrators, teachers, curriculum specialists, guidance and remedial experts; it demands smaller classes, the best facilities, the most modern teaching aids and equipment; it further requires the assurance of discipline.

Dr. Conant recognized that desegregation of the schools is interlocked with residential desegregation and with the fair and objective districting of school zones. At the time he wrote the book (1961), Dr. Conant believed that these techniques would be the most effective in bringing about integration. His opinions have since been cited in many school integration disputes by those who favored maintaining the Negro schools in the ghetto and by those who sought to "protect" the neighborhood school.

Though he opposed bussing at the time the book was published, during the winter of 1963 Dr. Conant addressed a convention of secondary school principals in Chicago and stated that, "My present view is somewhat different. If I were a school board member in such a city, I would achieve integration . . . in two ways: by redrawing boundaries to provide as many mixed districts as possible; and, for high schools, I would bus students."

Now my position is that open enrollment is mandatory because segregated schools cannot provide adequate education, as the Supreme Court has so eloquently stated. And rezoning alone will not integrate ghetto schools. The schools of a free society such as ours must shoulder their responsibility as engineers of social change to help develop democratic attitudes among all students. All-Negro or all-white schools in our urban centers cannot develop such attitudes vicariously.

Furthermore, Negroes must have the opportunity to select schools of their choice, representative of the total community. The neighborhood school is no boon to slum dwellers. The Negro neighborhood is artificially created. It is deliberately confining, and it effectively blocks the free movement of Negroes in urban areas.

Though there are many dedicated, talented teachers struggling against ferocious odds in the schools of our urban ghettos, too often slum schools are saddled with probational, substitute, or problem educators. Sometimes assignment to the ghetto schools is the educational system's equivalent of sentencing a teacher to Siberia—a disciplinary action rather than a career challenge. Meanwhile, the skilled teachers are to be found in the less-crowded, high-achieve-ment schools and in the suburbs. Here they teach the children who have the advantages. These youngsters come from homes where encyclopedias are commonplace, where there are intelligent dialogue, opportunities for travel and visits to cultural centers and performing arts. Many of these children know how to read before they arrive at school. And their teachers are forced to stay on the ball because at every PTA meeting all the parents turn out and challenge the teachers on modern teaching methods.

My respect has increased for teachers who aspire to educate de-prived children. I believe these are the best people for the teaching profession because they are apparently more concerned about mak-ing a contribution to young people, the metropolitan communities and their country than about status or salary.

The whole profession of education must change its value system so that it will give its rewards, prestige, and status to those teachers who will work in these schools. I would not give outright bonuses to teachers just for assignment to ghetto schools. These better teachers would be called upon to do more in terms of spending longer hours for needed counseling and remedial work, and in some cases for visiting students' families (because Negro families would be unlikely to go to them). Because they would be superior teachers with special duties, they would receive more money. But I believe a shift in attitude by the education profession is imperative. Money alone will not buy good teachers.

But perhaps the winds of change are blowing. U. S. Education Commissioner Keppel last winter told the American Association of School Administrators:

> For years we have talked of the disinterest and apathy of slum parents. We have argued that we can't teach their children because they are not interested in education and because their parents have not taught them to be interested. But now, out of the civil rights movement, we are learning differently. . . . These children need the best. And they need an imaginative change from ways of teaching which do not work, and will not work. . . . It is true that [these children] come from families of low educational attainments, that their homes lack books and other incentives to learning, that they come to school without

121

middle class cultural endowments. But we cannot and dare not use this dreary recital as an excuse for poor schools and ineffective education.

It is not enough to administer the status quo, he told the educators; they should give creative leadership instead.[11] However, the National Education Association, the Parent-Teachers Associations and other organizations of educators and administrators have not generally been conspicuous for their activity in this area. They have not endorsed or worked for fair housing laws, for fair employment practices, for vocational and retraining programs and other measures which would help to make equal opportunity possible and would hasten the day when neighborhood schools would be truly representative of the total community.

Until I see these groups testify in favor of and fight for the adoption of these basic measures, the suspicion will always be present that their concern is more racial than educational.

There is a demoralizing, discouraging quality about segregated schools—both in the attitudes of staff members and of parents. These schools are generally much more autocratic. One gets the feeling that the PTA is run by the principal and the teachers; without parent "interference." One certainly does not have that feeling in the integrated school PTAs.

In the matter of leadership, the Negro teacher can play a key role. She can do wonders to overcome the disadvantages children bring with them, accumulated from their preschool and home experiences. We have learned in recent years, particularly, that the development of potential in Negro youths depends to a large degree on the amount of motivation and stimulation they receive during the formative years. In so many instances there is little, if anything, within the great majority of family groups to stimulate Negro boys and girls to achieve.

The paramount requisite today is a more thorough grasp of the three Rs. Along with this must be developed the ability to think logically and the flexibility to accept change. Most of all, the Negro teacher must demand excellence of her students according to one set of standards, without compromise with or retrogression into the Jim-Crow past. The going will not be easy; criticism can be expected

[11] Francis Keppel, Jet, March 5, 1964, p. 26.

from segments of the Negro community who fear to look reality in the face, for there our own shortcomings, weaknesses, and neglect will be seen. But Negroes must be prepared to participate in the no-holds-barred competition for jobs that will open up as the barriers of discrimination are cleared away.

We must not conclude that what our ghetto schools need is more Negro teachers so that Negro children can identify with them. What these youngsters require is more excellent teachers, whether white or Negro. The old chestnut that Negroes can best teach Negroes and whites best teach whites is not only ridiculous, it is one of those insidious, wish-myths that circulates all too easily and is accepted all too willingly.

It should be clear that integration is not for the student body alone. The ideal should be assignment by skill without regard to race. Certainly more Negro teachers should be assigned to white schools. In New York City, the Public Education Association study revealed that out of 5,424 teachers only 31 Negroes were assigned to schools that were 90 percent white; in contrast, in the schools that were 90 percent Negro, 33 percent of the staff were Negroes. This is neither good staffing nor good sense.

Clearly, more Negroes are needed at the administrative and advisory levels as well as in the teaching slots. Until recently, New York City had only one Negro principal in the whole city—a city with 860 schools in 1962.

The overwhelming need is for first rate teachers of any color who have the heart, skills, ability, and motivation to reach out to Negro youngsters, and say, "Child, you count! You're somebody! I like you, I want you to like me and I'm going to help you go places in this big world!" Such teachers can be tremendously effective. In their way they can be substitute parents. The best of them will be sensitive enough to understand that if a child is withdrawn or hostile he needs more reassurance. A teacher has to extend herself because such a child is seeking attention, affection, and the sense of belonging that most youngsters normally have in their homes. That hostility, that resentment, that clinging, or that dependence has to be viewed with compassion.

A teacher who is having difficulty just keeping up with the subject matter herself is in no shape to bring these other qualities

123

to bear in the classroom. What I am recommending is good teachers, whether white or Negro. And I would prefer any day an experienced, human, patient, understanding white teacher to a Negro who lacks these qualities.

In our concern for education we frequently tend to overlook the vast potential of vocational training. The Marshall Plan *special effort* that we advocate would require an improved, realistic vocational education program to prepare youngsters for the modern work world.

While the states spend more than $200 million per year on vocational education, the federal government distributes more than $50 million in matching grants through the states. Under the National Vocation Education Acts more than four million Americans are taking vocational training in high schools, apprentice training classes, work-study programs, and adult courses.

Since 30 percent of American youngsters never finish high school and 30 percent never go beyond it, vocational training can be of crucial importance. Economic emasculation has been practiced on the Negro with subtlety through the clean-handed route of controlling education and vocational training. Apprenticeships in skilled trades have been off-limits to Negroes. Furthermore, in many parts of the nation, young Negroes have been kept out of programs designed to prepare workers for new industries.

There have been many vocational education programs, stretching as far back as the 1917 Smith-Hughes Act that used $7.2 million a year to help train Americans for jobs, with most of the money going into home economics and agricultural training. The post-World War II effort was centered around the George-Barden Act that added $29 million a year for expanding the program and including special support of postschool work-study programs. This was augmented in 1956 with additional funds for fishery industries and practical nursing.

But it was Sputnik I and the resulting National Defense Education Act that caused a clean break with the past. The Act authorized $15 million per year for four years to train technicians for jobs essential to our national defense. This program was extended to 1964. Then, in the Area Redevelopment Act of 1961 the government officially recognized the threat of unemployment by setting up retraining programs for jobless in depressed areas of the country. In 1962 the Manpower Development and Training Act earmarked $435 million for use across the nation in retraining programs spread over a four-year period.

Some indication of the difficulties is to be seen in the fact that even before the Area Redevelopment Act and the MDTA swung into action there were 3,856,000 Americans enrolled in federally assisted vocational education programs. About half of these were for high school youths; the rest, for adults taking extension courses. But these programs were, in most cases, out of touch with reality. Here were these expensive programs aimed, supposedly, at preparing our citizens for gainful employment, and of the total enrollment fully 2,416,000 as late as 1961 were still taking agricultural or home economics courses!

In other words, two-thirds of all those enrolled were being trained for work on the farm—a field where science, economics, and machines have literally driven workers to the cities in search of jobs—or for matching wits with the mechanical marvels of the modern kitchen and the supermarket's prepared foods.

Another problem that has perhaps been overdramatized, but not overanalyzed or corrected, is that of the *Blackboard Jungle* approach. In all too many cases school boards have treated the vocational education schools as catch basins for those students who couldn't qualify for the academic program, or were otherwise marked for the discard heap. This devaluation of vocational high schools has caused industry to shun them in many cases, and with justification.

Vocational high schools are supposed to equip a beginning worker with basic skills which will help him to become a foreman or craftsman. They are not intended for the incorrigibles, intransigents, ineducables, nor the inept. Their courses are much the same as the academic high schools but for the omission of foreign languages, and generally the curricula meet the prerequisites of technical institutes and many engineering colleges. There are many pupils whose abilities simply do not measure up to these demands, and for them curricula offering basic tool skills, work habits, and reading, writing,

125

and arithmetic are needed. It is in the design of meaningful curricula for the vocational high school that industry can give invaluable counsel and guidance.

The Jim-Crow use of vocational education and training facilities has seriously crippled the Negro wage earner. In general, vocational courses are open to fewer than one-fifth of high school students in the cities. In the north and west, few Negroes are found in vocational and technical high schools because of the traditional lack of job opportunities in fields for which schools prepare students. In the south and midwest de facto segregation excludes Negroes from training for all but menial jobs. Segregated schools do not offer training in skilled trades, because few Negroes have had occupational experience to teach these skills.

A major roadblock to the Negro youngster's vocational training has been a Department of Health, Education and Welfare provision that a student's entrance to vocational courses be dependent on his chance of securing employment in the occupation for which he is to train. Of course this policy helped to freeze the racial employment patterns of the past. And it contributed to the present unemployment problem by training Negroes for the traditionally "Negro jobs," in those fields where there has been speedy and unprecedented growth of surplus labor. Meanwhile, as we know, openings for men qualified in the technical fields have increased.

Here the federal government has held the initiative in its own hands. Through its massive underwriting of vocational education across the nation, it could have called a halt to discrimination in training overnight. This is doubly true in apprenticeship training. Here, not only federal funds but federal accreditation are used. Labor Department regulations require that apprenticeship programs be registered with it and that they be open to all, without regard to race. Registration can be lifted if bias is found, and this means that apprentices in such programs cannot work on government building projects.

There has been considerable optimism over the Manpower Development Training Act, with its annual budget of $70 million. It is true that about 24 percent of the MDTA trainees are Negroes and that most of them are training for professional, managerial, clerical, skilled, and semiskilled positions. But this is a very select group: 90 percent of them have had at least a ninth grade education and 61 percent are high school graduates.

Though this is an encouraging trend, we must not lose sight of one major shortcoming: when the program started, with much fanfare, it was intended to provide "answers" to the hard core unemployment situation. It was to blaze a trail for a full-scale assault on the unemployment problem. Instead, of the hundred thousand that the program was to have trained, only sixty thousand were aided, and, as noted, nine out of ten had some high school background. In other words, the hard core of functional illiterates has not yet been touched. In fact, less than fifteen thousand of the one million Negro unemployed have been affected.

It is reported that Negroes are still being ignored as staff and advisory committee members at both the departmental and community levels in the new Manpower Development and Training program. Too many of the programs require skills that are not easily found among unemployed Negroes, or they provide job training for low-level work that will be out of existence by 1970. Further, because many of these programs are administered at, or related to, the public employment service local office, Negroes continue to lack confidence because of years of negative experience with these facilities.

One project which appears to exemplify the effect the Manpower Development and Training Act can have if well executed is under way in Philadelphia. Paid for by the MDTA, administered by the state's Department of Public Instruction, and put together by business leaders in the city, it aims to train ten thousand unemployed in two years at a cost of about $3 million the first and $5 million the second year.

The Chamber of Commerce unveiled the plan, which had been developed during a year of study and planning. Essentially it will consist of classes to train workers in one hundred categories of jobs to fill skilled labor requirements of business and labor in the area. Top executives of seventy-five of the district's largest business concerns worked together on the project. This will eventually include several hundred concerns in the area.

The classes are supervised by industry and are designed to match known job needs. Therefore, the Chamber expects 100 percent placement of trainees, in contrast to other results under the same Act, which averaged 60 to 70 percent placement. Philadelphia is in an area where hard core unemployment has averaged 118,000 or 6.5 percent. Surveys of companies in the area showed that a minimum of seventy-two thousand workers will be needed by November 1964 in 101 job categories. To make sure the workers will be employable when they complete the courses, the program includes advisory committees made up of experts from business and industry. These specialists will help screen, test, and train in each job category.

Furthermore, the committee has been divided into task forces to spur plans to set up training classes and encourage jobless to register in them. They work with companies to spot job opportunities and encourage on-the-job training and promotions.

The Vocational Education Act of 1963 will quadruple the amount of federal aid to vocational training by 1967. In the year beginning July 1, 1964, $148.5 million will go to the states for expansion and improvement of existing programs, construction of schools, supplies, equipment, materials, teacher training, and salaries. Some experimental vocational "boarding schools" will be built in urban slum areas where the dropout rate is maximum. Further, there will be work-study programs for youngsters who cannot afford to continue in school without some earnings. There will also be research grants for development of programs to aid youths who have academic, economic, or social handicaps.

If it works as expected, the Act will make some real contributions by pioneering new techniques. In addition to doubling facilities, staffs, and classroom space in the next three years, we can expect introduction of new vocational curricula. These courses will be attuned to the needs of today and tomorrow—instrumentation technology, radiography, stenotyping, computer programming, nucleonics, and community service occupations. The work-study program is aimed at the high school dropout between fifteen and twenty-one years of age. Some twenty-five thousand students a year will be paid $45 a month and work in public service jobs while completing their vocational studies.

Another aspect of the Act will be construction of five vocational schools in major cities. At each of these in a campus atmosphere, one thousand students will live and study—receiving room, board and vocational training while working part-time.

Because 20 percent of the unemployed are under the age of twenty-two, all of these efforts promise to be valuable if soundly administered, without bias. But Negroes are justifiably wary of federal programs run by the Labor Department because of its history of accommodating violations of its antibias regulations and policies.

To implement these recommendations, local boards of education must act with speed, sagacity, statesmanship, and steadfastness. This may and probably will require changes in the boards, for most of them are middle- and upper-class oriented and lack labor or minority group representation. The case for including all facets of the community on school boards and the need to seek out Negro candidates for these agencies are self-evident and urgent. Unfortunately, local school board members seldom have backgrounds that qualify them to serve.

In our society people are tremendously mobile. Urbanization is continuing, and automation is going to cause further disruption such as mass migrations from town to city and state to state. There is today no such thing as a local or state citizen, living his insular life in one spot. The whole nation can be affected by the failure of one section of the country to educate its citizens adequately. As long as some states have extremely limited resources, there must be a method for insuring that citizens of that state will receive a certain minimum level of learning to equip them for productive work. As it is now, a state like Mississippi spends 31 percent more on education relative to its resources, than does New York, but is able to give less than 10 percent as much aid per classroom. To reach the national average, Mississippi would have to triple its school taxes. The result is, inevitably, inferior education for whites as well as Negroes in Mississippi: in 1959, only 52 percent of the white and 3 percent of the Negro high schools in the state were accredited.

Now, since youngsters are going to live in other cities hundreds of miles away from their childhood homes, it is in the best interests

129

of the majority of American citizens to establish a floor of educational skills below which no youngster should be held because of local lack of funds for education.

During all the years in which we engaged in philosophical discussion of states rights—"Let the people of the sovereign state of Mississippi take care of their problems in their own infinite wisdom"—what we really were doing was insuring that our cities would be burdened with the ill-equipped, undereducated products of the inferior educational systems so jealously guarded and zealously mismanaged at the local level in these intellectually and economically impoverished states. So in our cities today, much of the freight underwritten by our local taxes consists of the social-work case loads, the costs of crime and unemployment traceable to the inadequacies of the education systems in Southern communities.

All this means to suggest that national standards are needed, and that they should be under the supervision of the federal government or a national board of responsible citizens above reproach and politics. Where such standards could not be met with the existing resources, the federal government should subsidize the school system to insure that no child's education would be dependent on the income level of the family. Every child should be enabled to secure just as much education as his ability and drive will permit, unhindered by lack of money.

There should, therefore, be aid for the school system as well as for the individual who has demonstrated capacity. We have accepted this philosophy in health: we do not let people die because they have no money; instead, we use our public health facilities and hospitals to prevent it. And when the facilities are inadequate we build new hospitals with state and federal funds. We do not cut off the individual's entitlement to use public health facilities at the age of sixteen as we do in most communities with his entitlement to use public educational facilities.

I am calling here for a stronger stance on the part of the federal government in the education of its citizens. For too long it has deferred to "local custom" to set the pattern in education facilities where unquestionably the federal government could and should have been the determining factor.

Until recently, children of military personnel in Southern states were forced to attend segregated off-base schools. In some communities, court orders and voluntary agreements finally opened up school facilities. The "pattern" was completely without logic, to the extent that in one incredible situation a school actually located on a U.S. military base in Texas was desegregated only after Negro plaintiffs filed a lawsuit in federal court. The Department of Defense late in 1963 issued orders to all base commanders to see to it that children of our soldiers and sailors learn in integrated classrooms, even if it requires building such facilities on the bases.

There are other opportunities for federal action to desegregate education. For instance, earlier this year President Johnson signed the Library Services and Construction Act that will pour $25 million in federal funds alone into public libraries. The fifty states will determine how the funds are to be used. But in this law, as in the 1956 Library Services Act, all participating libraries are required to provide free service to *all* residents of the communities they serve. Furthermore, the 1956 law *directs* the U. S. Commissioner of Education to withhold federal money if he finds that any state plan is so administered that it does not comply with the law's requirements. I can take the Commissioner to many libraries so aided in which whites are served but not Negroes, and to others where there are inferior, segregated facilities for Negroes. Here is one area in which immediate executive action can be taken, and is long overdue.

The U.S. Commission on Civil Rights has made some excellent proposals for federal action to bring about integrated public education. The Commission recommends that Congress tighten the purse strings on education grants-in-aid to the states. Only states in which all schools operate in a nondiscriminatory way would receive 100 percent of their grant allocations. Other states would receive a minimum of 50 percent plus that proportion of the remaining half corresponding to the proportion of public school students in integrated classes. This, it seems to me, would be an eminently fair distribution of tax money for education.

One other important proposal by the Commission calls for the President to direct the Attorney General to protect school board members, supervisory officials, teachers and pupils, parents, and persons aiding them in executing plans to integrate schools. The need, a very real and urgent one, is for protection against bodily harm, harassment, intimidation and/or reprisal by public officials or private persons.

Until now we have focussed our attention on the public schools because it is through them that millions of Negroes must be educated and trained. Further, because of the numbers of pupils involved, the broad scope of the public school education problems with integration, and the unconscionable gap in Negro achievement because of inferior education, this sector obviously deserves immediate, far-reaching action.

This does not mean, however, that we are unconcerned with the private schools. Far from it, for, as they are so fond of saying themselves, it is they that are frequently pacesetters in education and are the training grounds of leaders. A few of the private secondary schools, such as Phillips Andover Academy, Phillips Exeter and Mount Hermon have taught Negroes along with whites for nearly a hundred years. Others have enrolled Negroes for more than a decade. And still others, whose charters specified that they were open to all regardless of race, discovered the existence of the Negro only after the Supreme Court's 1954 decision.

Now, many of these very fine, very exclusive, and expensive schools are actively seeking out Negro students. And, as in industry, their recruiters bemoan the "fact" that they have great difficulty locating "qualified" applicants. "Qualifying," like beauty, is in the eye of the beholder. Some of these schools are seeking only the exceptional Negro students—the future Ralph Bunches, the "stars." Others have dropped their racial bias but continue their social prejudice: they prefer to accept the offspring of the Negro elite, but they find the bright youngster from undistinguished parents less appealing.

Because of their leadership traditions and greater facility to move decisively and rapidly, the private schools are doubly challenged. They share with the public schools a two-fold responsibility which demands educational statesmanship: First, they must shape new images and new concepts about the role and worth of individuals, especially nonwhites. Second, they must develop in all students a new appraisal of man's relationship to man. If by education one means simply the acquisition of knowledge to prepare a person for making a living or running a machine, this is an alto-

132

gether too narrow, but perhaps widely accepted interpretation of its function. But if education is to prepare people to live with one another productively and constructively in a modern world that has been reduced by speed of transport and communications to the relative size of a state or province, this is something quite different. For this, one must look beyond narrow and parochial interpretations of education.

There is ferment and forward movement on the private secondary school front. Dartmouth, in an imaginative program, is currently (1964) providing intensive eight-week study courses for about fifty Negro high school students. These youths, from low-income families, are being prepared for entrance to some of the nation's top private schools under a grant from the Rockefeller Foundation and in cooperation with the National Scholarship Service and Fund for Negro Students. More programs reaching out in this manner should be initiated.

At the college level we find that of 4,000,000 students enrolled only 220,000 are Negroes and 90,000 of these are on the campuses of the so-called Negro colleges. I say so-called, because the charters of most of these institutions are purposely nondiscriminatory. Furthermore, at most of these colleges white students and faculty members are to be found.

Many schools of higher education in the South labeled for so long as "Negro colleges" will continue to play a significant role in the education of young people. Many of these schools today represent the major, if not the only, centers of cultural influence existing in some communities for white as well as Negro citizens. This role will expand. In addition, the number of white students and foreign students in these institutions will increase beyond their present enrollment and interracial faculties will become more commonplace. There is a healthy trend toward the development of more cooperative faculty exchange programs with other leading universities as a spur to greater academic growth. It is, therefore, unreasonable to suppose that these institutions will disappear at a time when the nation is faced with a serious shortage of classroom facilities.

There is a vital need for greater financial support of these schools. When one considers, for example, that the $3 million goal of the United Negro College Fund must be distributed among more

133

than thirty-three institutions as compared with the fact that many single institutions in this country receive several million dollars each, the enormous gaps and needs in educational quality come into sharp focus.

Now the 116 "Negro colleges" have their problems—lack of money is the main one—but bias is not generally one of them. It is their sister institutions around the country that deserve comment. I believe, with Cardinal Newman, that "A University is not a school or a group of schools. It is an atmosphere." Anyone who has studied or taught at the college level knows well that the student body of an academic community does create an intellectual atmosphere. It is to make this atmosphere relevant to the twentieth century that integration of Negroes into the teaching and learning groups is necessary.

This is no time for colleges and universities to adopt a posture of fine impartiality and simply announce: "We are now open to Negroes." After these institutions have for scores of years consistently rejected Negroes, extraordinary courage would be required of any Negro youngster who might entertain thoughts of sending in an application. Negroes are not likely to seek out colleges of which they have never heard, at which they are unsure of their reception. Therefore, the institutions that are serious about wanting Negro students must develop techniques of going out, seeking Negroes with potential, preparing them to meet the qualifications, and helping them over the financial hurdles. None of these factors is so mysterious as to defy solution by the aggregations of intelligence we have on campuses in this country. Some notable efforts are already under way. Northeastern University is recruiting promising Negro students with a $150,000 grant from the Fund for Advancement of Education. The program will enroll twenty Negro students for each of the next three years.

The American Council on Education has at last recognized its leadership responsibility in this field. It has decided to help develop projects and studies to speed and expand opportunities for Negroes in higher education. Also, it plans to serve as a national clearinghouse for information about local, state, federal, and private efforts to equalize educational opportunities.

Clearly, with the Negro student certain handicaps are to be expected, recognized, and overcome. The Negro freshman is usually less well prepared than his white counterpart for college life. His achievement level may be at the tenth grade level. He is unfamiliar with taking tests and, as I have stated, the tests are, by their design and content, weighted against him. (The Graduate Record examination in the social sciences, for instance, recently contained no questions about Negroes or Africa.) He may be unaware of the handicap of his inferior high school education, and the full realization may strike him with possibly traumatic effect. He may not realize the standards of excellence he will have to maintain and how these compare nationally with other colleges. He is generally less well informed about the nation and the world than his white counterpart. He will require more counseling and special help in catching up, keeping up, directing himself toward, and preparing himself for, a career.

However, the colleges should keep in mind certain facts. One is that a follow-up study of college records indicates that Negro students are likely to be better achievers than their aptitude tests predict. Such tests tend to reflect not what they can learn but what they have learned. Another fact, and an alarming one, is the high dropout rate for Negro college students. This in large measure is attributable to the problems cited above; it indicates the urgent need for counseling and special effort by the institution.

Mention should be made of teacher needs. It should be clear that I advocate hiring qualified Negro faculty members at now all-white colleges. This simple act effectively places the Negro in a normal, professional relationship with whites and will, therefore, influence attitudes.

In many cases Negro teachers are underqualified. Programs and money to upgrade their education are absolute "musts" on any list. Among the suggestions for aiding them are better in-service training; help in mastering test techniques; association with first-rate colleges during sabbaticals, summer study, or on an exchange basis. Industry also is beginning to recognize that it can play an important part in this area. IBM, for instance, is bringing a number of Negro college faculty members to its facilities as summer employees. Thus these teachers for three months will observe one of the most advanced organizations in the world from the inside. They will view the kinds of jobs being carried out and the qualifications necessary for them. But

135

most of all, the experience will give practical knowledge to these teachers so that they can, perhaps for the first time, begin to prepare their students for business careers.

In summary, this is a call for education and educators to bestir themselves. Education has performed magnificently in helping individuals vault barriers such as race. However, it has yet to show what it can do to clear away the barriers themselves.

More and more we hear discussed the theory that investment in human capital is perhaps as important as, if not more important than, investment in mechanical and technological equipment. Economists Harbison and Myers, in their book *Education, Manpower and Economic Growth*, state that human resource development is a more reliable indicator of national development than any other, including industrial capacity. They, following the lead of Professor Theodore W. Schultz, consider investment in education and training the most promising use of a nation's capital.

Professor Schultz, in his widely quoted presidential address to the American Economic Association in 1960, concluded with these recommendations for investing in human capital in America:

1. Removal of hindrances to free choice of professions, such as racial and religious discrimination.
2. Long-term loans to students.
3. Larger investments in the health and education of disadvantaged Americans.
4. Retraining of workers displaced by technological changes.
5. Encouragement of able youths to invest in themselves, especially through higher education.

Because the Negro intellectual potential has so long been ignored as a field for this kind of investment, I enthusiastically endorse Prof. Schultz's recommendations and urge them on all those who may have opportunities to implement them.

This discussion brings to my mind the following anecdote told by a noted African educator, Dr. James E. K. Aggrey.

A farmer, hunting in the woods one day, came across an eagle chick, recently hatched. He carried the eaglet back to his farm and put it in with the other barnyard fowl. Here it stayed for a year and grew alongside the chickens and geese. One day a passing naturalist saw the eagle among the other fowl and berated the farmer for raising the eagle with the chickens. The farmer, in all innocence, said, "He has been raised with the barnyard fowl. To all intents and purposes he is one and is happy so."

The naturalist offered to prove that this was not true and for several hours coaxed the eagle to fly. However, the eagle reacted as if it were a chicken, hopping to the ground and scratching for food. Finally the naturalist took the eagle to the top of a nearby mountain. Holding the bird high above his head and over the valley below, he spoke to it: "Eagle you are and eagle you will always be. You were born to soar in the skies, not to scratch in the dust. Lift your wings and fly!" At this the eagle trembled as if new life had come into him; the powerful wings beat, tentatively at first, then with strength, and off he flew, disappearing into the horizon, never to return. It *was* an eagle, though it had been raised as a chicken.

I have related this anecdote to audiences of young Negroes and I have concluded it with these words: "Though you have been humiliated and deprived, suggesting you are a nobody, you are *really* somebody. Though you have been segregated and discriminated against, which would imply that you are a second-class citizen, you are *really* a first-class human being. Stretch your minds, lift your sights, and fly."

Yet Harlem is essentially the same as any other Negro ghetto. It exists in the midst of a city where liberal rhetoric is required for election to practically every public office. There is no legal segregation; there are a Fair Employment Practices Law, a State Commission Against Discrimination, a municipal Open Occupancy Law. And yet the white man is still 'way ahead, and in this Harlem is like any community of Negroes in the United States. . . . In this sense Harlem could well be a warning: that after the racist statutes are all struck down, after legal equality has been achieved in the schools and in the courts, there remains the profound institutionalized and abiding wrong that white America has worked on the Negro for so long.
Michael Harrington,
The Other America,
p. 70—

5
Decent
Housing: Whose
Responsibility?

My work takes me to all parts of the United States. I daresay that I have visited nearly every city of twenty-five thousand or more in the country on business for the Urban League or the President's Committee on Equal Opportunity in the Armed Forces. And in those cities where there is a Negro community of any size I have often felt angered and ashamed as I viewed the incredible squalor and degradation in which American citizens have been forced—yes, forced—to exist, not live. Any person of humane sensitivity would react with similar outrage, if not despair. And to many, as to me, the words of Thomas Jefferson might occur: "Indeed, I tremble for my country when I reflect that God is just."

What possible justification exists for confining hundreds of thousands of American citizens to living conditions which were considered deplorable in sixteenth century London? The fact that such

140

quarters are beyond the wildest dreams of the untouchables of Calcutta or the refugee coolie of Hong Kong is not germane. This is no shell game, in which you change the standards more quickly than the eye can discern. In America we judge by American standards, and by this yardstick we find that the Negro lives in incredibly inadequate housing—shabby shelters that are dangerous to mental and physical health and to life itself. The Commission on Race and Housing has an antiseptic way of stating it in its report: "advanced age of the buildings, a large percentage of substandard dwellings, and high frequency of crowding are virtually standard characteristics of the housing of nonwhite residents—north, south and west."

I am angry and ashamed of man's inhumanity, his cruelty and his indifference to the suffering of human beings who are his fellow Americans. Nowhere are men of good will more indelibly indicted than in the slums of our nation. That we should permit, much less subject, citizens to live in hovels and hell holes such as Hogarth depicted two centuries ago is unworthy of this great country. It is a damaging exhibit in our case for leadership of a free and democratic international society.

And who is responsible for housing discrimination?

All of us. Our sin is either that we participated in it actively, or that we passively permitted it. To be specific:

1. The federal government has actively fostered, implemented, and buttressed discrimination in housing, in ghettos, and in the noxious practices of slumlords.

There is a relic of the Reconstruction Era still on the books stating that "All citizens of the United States shall have the same right, in every State and Territory, as is enjoyed by white citizens thereof to inherit, purchase, lease, sell, hold, and convey real and personal property." But the statute has been interpreted so narrowly that its application serves only to limit government action. No other federal laws outlawing discrimination in housing have been passed.

It is a notorious fact that the first federally financed public housing projects constructed under the U.S. Housing Act of 1937 were segregated. The pattern of segregation continues to this day in most of the nation's public housing though no longer sanctioned by law.

But even more far-reaching was the Federal Housing Administration prescription for discrimination which was written into its 1938 operating manual. This promoted the use of racially restrictive covenants through "prohibition of the occupancy of properties except by the race for which they are intended." It also said, "If a mixture of user groups is found to exist, it must be determined whether the mixture will render the neighborhood less desirable to present and prospective occupants."

With these clauses standing in its operating procedures, the FHA until recently absolutely refused to insure nonwhite mortgage applications for property in white neighborhoods.

It is a matter of fact, not fancy, that the FHA through its procedures, the Veterans Administration through its mortgage loans, the Housing and Home Finance Agency, and the Federal Home Loan Bank board have all adhered to policies strengthening segregation, supporting discrimination, continuing the ghetto, constructing and tightening the "white nooses" around the central cities. Their actions in turn buttressed the loan policies and standards of the private lending institutions—the savings banks, commercial banks, insurance companies, and savings and loan associations.

2. *The real estate brokers, realtors, and builders* reacted to a real market or tried to create an artificial one by arousing or appealing to prejudice in establishing neighborhoods and developments on the basis of racial exclusiveness. They made deliberate pitches for snob appeal. Often it was outright, brazen propagandizing against the "dangers" of living in racially inclusive neighborhoods by implying that life was safer and better in the exclusive neighborhood.

3. *The money changers* included most lending institutions and insurance brokers with the Federal Government setting the example, laying out the ground rules, and leading the way. These money men not only swallowed the myth, but most often worked hand-in-hand with the builders and realtors in making the jim-crow housing system firm and airtight.

4. *City planning boards*, on which Negro citizens are rarely if ever represented, are now aided and abetted by urban renewal boards that often lack true citizen participation. These officials sit in strategy sessions, but they are not planning how to open a city for all ethnic groups or even how to eliminate future slums and ghettos. Instead, they are preoccupied with expressways to transport the commuter and shopper quickly to town; with clearance of land, largely inhabited by Negroes, to build new industry; with high rise com-

mercial buildings and high rent luxury apartments to attract the tired and retired commuter back to the city.

Relocation rarely shows imagination or creativity in improving housing or fostering integration. It usually consists of putting the displaced persons in public housing and older homes made vacant by panic-selling white citizens. Otherwise, it results in a development of low-income or middle-income, minimum-standard housing. But usually the nature of the approved site and of the demand cause these few homes to become yet another Negro ghetto.

5. *Mayors, City Councils and Public Housing Authorities* have managed to place practically every public housing project that is to be occupied by Negro citizens either in or on the fringes of the Negro community. And even those built for white occupancy have sometimes been placed close by out of fear that someday the federal government might decide that federal money should not forever continue to support racial segregation.

There are also city officials who create and perpetuate slums by almost universally adopting an unwritten double standard favoring the whites when it comes to city services, zoning considerations, and code enforcement. In some cases, discrimination in housing is even represented as a concession made to the Negro to maintain his housing supply. In reality, it is a concession to wealthy owners of slums and also compensation for the guilty officials who do not move more forcefully to open the entire city for all citizens.

6. Finally, *some Negro citizens* have played a role, though minor, in perpetuating the ghetto. White realtors have no monopoly on blockbusting. They have taught the art to some Negro real estate brokers who have gotten into the act. Some Negro citizens, out of desperation and resignation, have built large and beautiful but segregated developments. Another handful has perpetuated segregation by not capitalizing on the efforts of the few fair housing committees nor fully exploiting the few good laws that exist.

Yes, we can with ample justification point at all these individuals and groups as contributors to jim-crow housing. But they could not have achieved so much if just a few citizens had spoken out for decency.

Without doubt one of our major problems in housing is that we are dealing with real estate boards made up of "realtors." The boards are trade groups not noted for their high ethical standards, as anyone who has shopped for a house or apartment can testify. In the realtors you are dealing with many people who place profit above all else. These men have little sense of social responsibility, are afraid to be challenged and don't trust each other. Here are men who fear that any effort of theirs in the direction of open occupancy housing will be exploited by their competitors.

Real estate boards are usually quite conservative, socially insensitive groups with which to deal. One index of their feeling about Negroes is that in most communities in the nation Negro brokers have difficulty gaining admittance to local real estate boards. Not being members of the boards means that Negroes cannot be "realtors." And if you are not a realtor, then you generally do not participate in multiple listing.

A classical example of the average realtor mentality is the policy laid down in 1917 by the Chicago Real Estate Board: "It is desired in the interest of all that each block shall be filled solidly (with Negroes) and that further expansion shall be confined to contiguous blocks ..." The board denies this policy today, but this set pattern shows no sign of change. Thus no realtor, if he deals with Negroes, will make any attempt to find them housing except in a "Negro block" or one adjacent. Once a sale in an adjacent white block is made to a Negro the area is set for "turning." And when a neighborhood starts changing the realtors show the homes in it only to Negroes. This setup is made to order for the "blockbuster," the real estate agent who specializes in cracking all-white neighborhoods and turning them overnight into Negro communities, making his inflated profits from psychological pressure.

It has been estimated that twenty million American Negroes put $15 billion into rents, mortgage payments and housing expenses every year. But because his choice of housing is limited to the ghettos, and because the Negro population is increasing at a rate 150 percent that of the white population, the shelter shortage for the Negro is not only acute and perennial, but getting increasingly tighter. It automatically forces the Negro to pay a premium for whatever housing he can get.

For instance, most of Chicago's 838,000 Negroes live in a ghetto and pay about $20 more per month per family for housing than their

144

white counterparts in the city. When a Negro finds a house he wishes to buy within this so-called Black Belt, he discovers that three factors govern: the property may be so old or rundown that the money men at the bank or lending institution will not loan to him; the house may be so located that they will turn him down ("We will lend on properties up to three blocks away from colored areas, but not closer," says an executive of a Chicago savings and loan association); the income profile of the Negro family may not fit the "standards" of the leading institutions (the low income of the male is often supplemented by the working wife, but the money lenders consider only the income of the "head of household" in determining whether or not to extend a mortgage).

Cut off from "conventional" sources of financing, the Negro home buyer is often forced to deal with a speculator—an estimated 30 percent of Negro homes are purchased in this way. This means that he must repay the loan on a contract basis over a period of years at an interest rate up to 10 percent, and under conditions by which he can be dispossessed within five days if he defaults on a payment. The speculator can then resell the property again. The comparative FHA interest rate on a twenty-five- or thirty-year mortgage would be 5.25 percent. Under such pressures, is it any wonder that the Negro house buyer often is compelled to bring in tenants to insure against foreclosure? And it is no surprise that the overcrowding that results helps to speed the deterioration of the building concerned.

If he is determined to buy a house, the Negro's most likely avenue will be to find a place in an adjoining white or transition neighborhood. Often he will have to deal with a blockbuster. Typically the blockbuster "cracks" a white block by moving in a Negro family, then pressuring all other home owners in the area to sell immediately —at his cash price—"before the bottom drops out of the market." He buys a $16,000 house from panic-stricken whites for $13,000 cash, then sells it to a Negro family at $18,500. Newspapers and news media promote the process by playing up the panic aspects of the situation as it develops. And since the Negro family usually cannot get conventional financing for the purchase, the blockbuster generously allows them to pay for it on contract until he has actually received perhaps $35,000 for the property. Of course he can peddle the contract to white doctors, lawyers, and other buyers interested in a

145

7 or 8 percent rate of return if he needs cash to continue the process. If it were not for the malicious exploitation involved, one might take certain satisfaction in the blockbuster's actions. His cupidity capitalizes on the ignorance and stupidity of whites who are filled with racial prejudice. He knows what they do not: that property values are not lowered by Negroes moving into a neighborhood. This has been shown over and over again—most recently in independent studies by economists reporting their findings in the *American Economic Review* and by the ten-year study financed by the Fund for the Republic. This latter, published in 1960 by the Commission on Race and Housing, compared thirty-four interracial neighborhoods in Northern cities. The results showed conclusively that the value of houses in nearly nine out of ten cases either showed no significant change or actually increased in value when Negroes purchased. The cases of increase balance out the few cases of decline. A professional appraiser describes the situation in Chicago: "Prices of residences are depressed from 30 to 55 percent when an area is threatened by transition. As soon as transition becomes a fact, prices tend to rise."

So the blockbuster, like the loan shark, provides a needed service at terrific social and economic cost: he makes housing available to people who need it. In the process he gives a practical lesson in the high cost of discrimination to the whites who sell out in preference to living in an integrated neighborhood. Unfortunately, the lesson is more than likely lost on the embittered self-victims.

There will be blockbusters, and panic selling and inflammatory action and disturbing news stories so long as we have exclusion. Exclusion did not just happen. It was planned and carefully designed by the real estate industry to create new, higher-profit markets. It took a good deal of imagination and energy to convince hundreds of thousands of city dwellers that the "good life" was not in town but in the suburbs, and, further, that restrictive covenants to exclude "undesirable elements" would make for a better way of life. What it did, in addition to creating the "white noose" around the central city, was to increase and enforce segregation, widen the distance and create tensions between groups, commit the center of the metropolitan area to industry and slums, and make it a matter of status to move to the exclusive areas.

146

Because methods of racial exclusion have been built deeply into the shelter supply system, it now is necessary to devise positive methods for inclusion rather than exclusion. They range from dedicated effort on the part of individuals, both white and black, to community-wide cooperation designed to make the most of a neighborhood and its residents.

One of the real issues that always arouses me in a discussion of housing is the question of "benevolent" or "benign" quotas. Most Negro leaders have both a public position and a private attitude on benign quotas. Some do not make any statements on this subject, and most would rather not discuss it at all. The Urban League was the first organization to come out as definitely opposed to quotas under any conditions. There is ambivalance about quotas because of the complexity of the housing situation.

Negro leaders are realistic enough to know that there is a tremendous demand by Negroes for decent housing. They have seen the historical pattern of white citizens panicking and moving out of neighborhoods quickly when Negroes move in. And they have been led to think, naturally enough, that any new apartment building, public housing unit, or housing development that is priced within range of Negro buyers will immediately be flooded with, and taken over by, Negroes.

There has been a good deal of serious study of various types of housing and of the reactions of residents to integration. The scholars and theorists have developed an interesting jargon to describe the process. According to them, that point at which an increasing number of nonwhite families in a neighborhood will cause whites to abandon an area is called the "tip point." They admit that they cannot fix on a definite figure for this and that it is inexact. Yet they say that the tip point is passed when a neighborhood, because of the entry of one additional Negro family, has "gone Negro." Or, to put it another equally inexact way, the tip point is reached when the addition of one more Negro family would, "to any observer," make it appear to be a "Negro neighborhood."

In new housing, developers and builders believe that if the proportion of nonwhites goes beyond a certain point the demand from whites will dwindle and the units will be bought almost entirely by Negroes. The critical point, they admit, cannot be defined with precision. In fact, studies have proved that if the site, the price, the features included in the housing, or all three are attractive to a white market, the neighborhood can "tolerate" a higher percentage of Negroes without going completely nonwhite.

A development, apartment, or public housing unit which wishes to achieve racial "balance" finds this extremely difficult under today's artificial conditions of a dual housing supply. Because so little new housing is built for "open occupancy," i.e., for sale or rent to any financially capable person, such shelter necessarily attracts an unusually high degree of interest from Negroes. Lacking the wider market to choose from, to which the white has free access, Negroes tend to flock to any decent shelter within reach of their pocketbooks.

This has been a matter of concern to sponsors of various housing units. In the few cases where they have attempted to promote racial integration they have advocated the benevolent or benign quotas already referred to in order to achieve a "mix" of whites and Negroes and to avoid an all-black development. Sometimes these quotas are not revealed to prospective buyers, and this angers those who are refused. Sponsors report that most of the "rejected" people do not seem to mind when the quota and its purposes are told them frankly.

All too often the owner of an apartment building decides to increase his profit by shifting to low-income minority group occupancy while reducing services and increasing the number of rent-payers in the same space. This is called "turning" the property and has been done time and again in the large cities which have had immigrant waves. Now it is being done in New York with Puerto Ricans and Negroes. Enormous profits result. The technique is time-tested and almost foolproof. The owner moves some minority families into the building and immediately reduces services and maintenance. This serves to drive the whites out. The conversion to a slum property is rapid and profitable.

Now my position is that quotas are *ipso facto* undemocratic and unworkable, whether intended as benevolent or restrictive. If we spent as much time and effort trying to prevent white citizens from panicking and selling or moving as we do in telling Negroes, "Don't too many of you come in," we would be a long way down the road to practical open occupancy. It requires an intensive, unflagging educational job. And we should spend an equal amount of effort seeing

148

to it that every neighborhood is open, so that there will be no privileged sanctuaries. At present the campaign is always aimed at the guy who needs decent housing most—the Negro. He's told to restrain himself. It would be far better to use a little persuasion on the neighborly flee-brains who are so busy putting up FOR SALE signs when the first Negro moves in.

In trying to arrive at my own position on this question I put it on a very personal basis: I moved into a neighborhood in which I am the only Negro. I moved there because I wanted better housing, more space, land, trees, grass, good schools for my children, and decent city services. Within two weeks perhaps I would see another Negro family coming in, for exactly the same reasons. What right would I have to say to this chap who had been thrifty and wanted these same things, "Sorry, this neighborhood is taken. I staked it out. You go and find one for yourself."

Society doesn't make the same demands on whites that it makes on the Negro. The Negro is told not only "You have to find a house that you can afford," but also "You must find a place where there are no other Negroes or else you will turn the area into an all-Negro section." But this "danger" has been overplayed.

Let's face it: Any Negro who can afford to live in the suburbs has to be, by the nature of things, as successful, intelligent or well educated as his white neighbors, if not more so. This is because the Negro makes his money generally through the professions, not through business; whereas the white person living in such a suburb may or may not be a professional. He may have a limited education but be outstanding as an insurance or automobile salesman; or he may run a successful tavern, hardware store or small business. In the suburbs there is no danger of "flooding"—the economics of the current situation makes it impossible.

And as for fears of the neighborhood deteriorating because of different standards of maintenance on the part of the Negro, I can testify from extensive observation as well as personal knowledge that this is no problem. No one is more aggressively devoted to the middle-class mores of property upkeep than the Negro who has just moved into a white neighborhood. Garden centers report that they sell five times more grass seed and fertilizer to Negro customers than to the whites who formerly lived in the same houses. The Negro is out there mowing his lawn, trimming the trees and hedges, putting in flowers and painting, repairing and adding on to his place while his white neighbor is sleeping in a hammock in the back yard. The Negro gets up at dawn and picks up the beer cans and whiskey bottles tossed in his yard by the sons and daughters of his white neighbors the night before, because he can't afford to have passersby think that he might have had a party and littered the place. And, in my own case, my wife won't let me put the trash out until after dark because it's unsightly, even though almost everyone else in the neighborhood puts it out in the evening.

But there is little reason for Negroes to seek out or move into most neighborhoods simply because the RESTRICTED signs have been taken down or the restrictive covenants and "gentlemen's agreements" are no longer in force. The Negro community knows which neighborhoods have historically practiced discrimination, and Negroes assume—perhaps correctly—that you've only taken down the signs because a fair housing law has been passed. They think that you are adhering to the letter of the law, with that same old segregationist spirit underneath.

Furthermore, however much a man may want a decent neighborhood or schools for his children, if he believes that a community is basically hostile to him he won't move into it. Given a history of hostility and attempts to bar Negroes, the white community that decides it wants the Negro has to take the initiative to get the Negro. It has to spread the word through local interracial groups, Urban Leagues, ads in Negro newspapers, and unequivocal information to the real estate men. The community has to do more than say, "We have a house here." It has to say, "We want you, and we will welcome you into the neighborhood."

In the context of the domestic Marshall Plan, special effort of this kind is required to open housing opportunities of all types on the bases of need and ability to buy or rent. It requires reaching out. I know of many instances where white people in a community are extending themselves because they are anxious to bring Negroes into their neighborhood. In some cases where a bank may not be willing to finance a mortgage because the Negro has so little security, a group of people or an organization is willing to put up collateral to make sure that the Negro family is able to move in. The point is that whites now have to go more than halfway—they may have to extend themselves 75 percent of the way or more.

In the central city the problem of housing is, and will remain, acute for years. Urban renewal gave us a wonderful opportunity to move toward balanced neighborhoods and the open city. We had the mandate and the resources to eliminate the slums of the central city where Negroes were, and still are, concentrated. Under the urban renewal laws a city is supposed to apply for federal approval for funds and to present plans for redevelopment of the cleared land as well as for relocation of those dispossessed. Those relocated were to be guaranteed standard housing at a price they could afford to pay, not housing equal to that from which they were evicted, which most often was substandard slum shelter. Furthermore, those dispossessed were supposed to have first choice on public housing or apartments in the redeveloped area. The cost of the housing both in the redeveloped area and that used for relocation was to be in the total plan. Also, in each case there was supposed to be a citizens advisory committee representative of the *total* community. This committee was supposed to advise on every stage of the development. And the plan was supposed to be submitted to public hearings at which time the entire procedure was to be unfolded.

What has happened most often is development of a total plan and inadequate, purposely abbreviated discussion of it in the community affected. Frequently the plan has been explained at a church, or bits and pieces of it have been presented in small gatherings.

With the federal highway program there were none of these safeguards at all. So what invariably happened in cities where highway programs were carried out was that there was no planning for new public housing outside of the ghetto, no building of low-cost private housing; instead, Negroes were simply moved out of the areas affected. They were unable to disperse around the city, so they moved to the first ring around the hub city into older housing which happened to be available. The ghettos were merely transplanted.

Most Americans have no idea whatsoever of the conditions which prevail in the ghettos. To mention one element only, consider the crowding. The Civil Rights Commission in 1959 reported that if all of New York City was as jammed with people as several of the worst blocks in Harlem, *the entire population of the United States could* fit into three of the city's boroughs, with two of them left over for expansion!

At the end of the fifties, one housing expert estimated that there were more Americans living in slums than on farms.

The urban renewal and highway clearance programs of the last ten years have set off spasmodic shifts of people in our cities. The significant fact, though, is that the movement has been *within* the cities, generally with the ultimate effect of increasing crowding and slum conditions in an urban area other than that redeveloped. Since suburban zoning laws keep out low-income housing, the poor are forced to stay in the deteriorating central cities. Slum dwellers are the pawns of the bureaucrats in the urban renewal and highway programs; and as pawns usually are, they are often seen as expendable by the decision-makers.

In the Mill Creek, St. Louis, urban renewal activity, for instance, a Negro slum was cleared and in its place rose a middle-income housing development. What happened to those evicted to make way for this great advance? The majority were forced into housing in what remained of the Negro ghetto; in other words, the crowding was intensified, the conditions of living for these hapless people was worsened by this "progress."

The Comptroller General of the United States reported on the West Side Urban Renewal Project in Chattanooga, Tennessee:

> As of September 27, 1960, at least 267, or about 40%, of the relocated nonwhite families who had occupied project properties at the time they were acquired by the Chattanooga Housing Authority had moved into substandard housing which the Authority had classified as permanent relocation housing. The Authority estimates that, upon completion of the project, over 50% of all nonwhite project families will have been relocated into substandard housing.
>
> Section 105 (c) of the Housing Act of 1949, as amended, provides that contracts for loans and capital grants which are to be made available for slum clearance and urban renewal projects shall require that there be a feasible method for relocating project families. We do not believe that the permanent relocation of a significant number of families from substandard dwellings in a slum area to other substandard dwellings is in conformity with the objective of this provision of the act.

Low-cost housing and public housing projects are attempts to come to grips with the problem of the slums. Yet the results have seldom if ever measured up to advance expectations and most often have created new problems. The fact is that though the old ramshackle tenements are replaced with modern buildings, the mathematics have one major flaw: the number of housing units built does not equal the number wiped out in clearing the site. The situation, instead of improving, is aggravated by this three-steps-forward, one-step-backward approach plus the continued population increase in the central city.

Public housing and urban renewal can be made to serve the needs of all components of the total community, and we must never lose sight of this fact. One of the big mistakes of Negro leadership has been our myopia about the planning functions of the city. We have become excited about who is to be on the city council and the school board, but rarely have we concerned ourselves about the city planning commissions, zoning and appeals boards, and urban renewal committees. Yet our children's children will be living under the conditions decided by these groups. And, as surveys will reveal, very few Negroes are employed in these positions except in the relocation offices. Almost none are at the policy level in urban renewal, and few are even draftsmen or technicians in such projects.

I speak with some personal experience on this subject, having been involved in both Omaha and Atlanta. In a number of cities, including Omaha, urban renewal has never been accomplished even though well designed for the community interests. In Omaha the plan was defeated by a combination of factors, but the primary one was the action of absentee owners of the slums in making deals with some local ministers and other influential Negroes. They told the local residents that urban renewal would mean the destruction of their homes, possible loss of old age and other assistance. They so aroused the people that when hearings were held on the project at City Hall many swarmed into the meeting filled with misinformation, suspicion, and hostility to the project. This reaction occurred because the Negro leadership had not been involved adequately in the interpretation and explanation of the project to the masses of Negroes, who were understandably suspicious because of previous broken promises. The Urban Renewal project was defeated in Omaha.

Too often public housing is seen as merely better shelter for the masses. But in the process of providing it the authorities generally have continued the concentration of the poor in a given section of the city. One expert calls this the "modern poor-farm" approach. Instead of perpetrating this homogeneous poor neighborhood, modern housing specialists believe that it is much more sensible to mix income groups, races, and cultures by interspersing low and middle-income housing units, limited in size. But equally as important, the transition from slum living to public housing is more than a change from fetid rooms to clean, well-designed quarters. As Michael Harrington says in *The Other America:*

"You cannot take people out of an old-fashioned slum, where reality has been giving them a grim, distorted education for years, place them in a project, and expect them to exhibit all kinds of gentle, middle-class virtues. This transition is a crucial moment. If the people are left to themselves, then the chances are that they will import the culture of poverty into the public housing. If they are helped, if there is a real effort to forge neighborhood communities, this need not happen."

The affirmative action to destroy the racial ghetto which is called for in the domestic Marshall Plan necessarily must focus on the slums. And any effort to come to grips with this accretion of ills which we have allowed to build up over decades must have three elements for success: money, sound planning, and unbiased execution.

It was in 1949 that the Congress passed a housing act declaring that the general welfare of the nation required the realization as soon as feasible of the goal that every American and every American family should live in decent, safe, and sanitary housing within a suitable living environment.

Ten years ago one expert estimated that it would cost $125 billion dollars and take twenty-five years to eliminate slums. Another, in 1961 suggested that a serious start could be made through building about two million housing units a year for four years, about half of which would be for lower income families. The Kennedy administration in 1961 proposed that one hundred thousand low-income public housing units be built and about seventy thousand of these have been constructed. President Johnson's message on housing and community development earlier this year recommended sixty thousand units of public housing per year for four years, at a cost of $46 million per year.

In 1960 one out of six nonwhite dwelling units—houses, apartments, duplexes—was dilapidated (i.e., a danger to the health or safety of its occupants), compared with one out of thirty-two white dwellings. Another 29 percent were deteriorating compared with 12 percent for white housing. Because of discrimination and economics only two out of five Negro families own their homes. And half of all Negro rented housing was dilapidated or lacked some plumbing facilities. The situation is worse in the South.

Furthermore, Census Bureau estimates show that the average Negro dwelling is occupied by four persons while the average white dwelling has only three occupants. If the number or size of rooms were considered, the picture of overcrowding would be far more chilling than these raw statistics suggest.

Not only is the Negro confined to a choice of quarters in the ghetto, but he is exploited by landlords who charge him more for this dismal housing than whites pay for decent shelter. With a dual market system which places white and Negro housing into mutually exclusive watertight compartments, as the population in the ghetto builds up the pressure for available quarters and the rents do likewise. This is a proven profit formula for slum landlords, but the time is past when American cities can afford to subsidize such leeches. The rent strikes, court condoning of rent moratoria, and proposed tough slum legislation in New York state are glimmers of light in this murky void.

What about public housing for low income families? The United States has built less than half a million public housing units. Of these, Negroes occupy 47 percent, or 210,000. Many of these institutionalize the ghetto, though most of the high rise apartments at least offer open space and some recreational areas. But the needs are vast and ten times 210,000 units are needed to have real impact on the problem, provided, of course, that principles are followed which will break down rather than build up the ghetto.

With thirty-five million Americans still living in substandard

155

shelter and the population increasing each year, it is clear that we have not yet come to grips with the nation's requirements for decent housing.

Without law and firm, aggressive administrative action nothing much is really likely to happen in housing. Only a handful of states and cities has truly effective fair housing legislation. I am convinced that here again both legislation and administrative action must come from the federal government. In city after city public officials and military base commanders told me that only national legislation and clear directives from Washington would solve the problem.

And have no illusions, Executive Order 11063, Equal Opportunity in Housing, issued by President Kennedy in 1962, is only a feeble first step. It graciously excluded from its provisions all existing housing, except for the small amount operated or repossessed by the government, and it generously exempted the sources of financing. It is significant primarily because nothing had been done before; our praise or condemnation of the President reflected more the sordidness of our past and the sickness of our present society than it did the revolutionary nature of the order itself.

True to its traditions, the National Association of Home Builders struck its colors when the Kennedy housing order was issued. Its spokesman ran up the "abandon ship" banner with a statement that the order would result in a cutback of more than one-third in home construction and a drop of $6 billion in the gross national product. Yet the nation's real estate and housing men swamped the FHA with more housing mortgage applications in 1963 than in any other previous year since 1958! And of course the GNP hit an all time high—$30 billion above 1962.

This accuracy is typical. In spite of dire predictions by the housing industry spokesmen that city or state legislation to bar housing discrimination would cut back home production the record invariably disproves this. In fact, most of the states and cities which have passed such acts have experienced increases in housing output. This has been most noticeable in California, New York, New Jersey, and Connecticut. But real estate men and bankers are still dominated by stereotyped concepts of race. Therefore, they persist in continuing a dual market system according to race, rather than a common market open to all. Uncontaminated by intelligent regard of the facts, they refuse to recognize the successful experiences with integrated housing to be found throughout the nation. These have been documented in the reports of the Commission on Race and Housing and the U.S. Civil Rights Commission, as well as in those of various academic and trade journals.

In this latter half of the twentieth century in America, decent housing for all is one of the keystones to a healthy democracy, assuring each individual the opportunity for reaching his maximum potential. We are all victims of the tragic consequences of turning our backs for generations on this necessity. When the TV and press bannerline the news of school boycotts, rent strikes, delinquency, gang warfare, mugging, murder, and mayhem, keep in mind that the crime of inadequate shelter provides one of the sustaining chords in this modern symphony of discord. For those who doubt this, I merely refer to the plastic overlay charts so dear to the urban renewal exponents. These highlight the high-incidence areas of crime, ill health, poverty, inferior educational attainment, unemployment and descrepit housing: The charts paint a multicolored bullseye on each ghetto-slum area.

I am at a loss to understand how intelligent, enlightened big business continues to stand silently by and observe calmly the occupation of the central city by the lowest income groups. This has not only serious economic implications in terms of its investment and low tax return, but, if this is a homogeneous racial bloc, it also has meaningful political significance. These reasons alone—aside from any humane considerations—should make these businessmen our most articulate spokesmen for open occupancy and racial dispersion.

The future of our cities and the larger community depends in large measure on effective desegregation of neighborhoods and of the shelter supply in general. Until large-scale progress is made, the problems of segregated schools and public accommodations will continue. We need a common market in housing for a healthy national economy just as a common market is necessary for a healthy international economy. Negro families want to bid into such a market without racial restriction. Their needs and interests *as they see them* and their financial capacity should be the only criteria for any Americans to secure decent housing. Segregated shelter is a negative luxury no nation is rich enough nor strong enough to afford.

DECENT HOUSING SPECIFICS

Long-range needs:

1. The Executive Order for Equal Opportunity in Housing must be broadened to close the financing loophole. At present it applies only to situations where builders receive financial aid from the government through FHA and VA mortgages. But builders use "conventional" mortgages extended by banks, insurance companies, and savings and loan associations and the present order's effect is thus largely nullified. The government can bring banks and savings and loan associations into line by withdrawing insurance on their deposits if they loan to builders who discriminate in the sale of shelter.

2. A federal fair housing law applying uniformly in all parts of the Union should be enacted to destroy the dual market in housing. Furthermore, a fair housing law would once and for all make it clear to all Americans that racial, cultural, and ethnic restrictive covenants have no place in this democracy in the rent, purchase, or occupancy of housing.

3. Federal, state, and local housing agencies, the housing industry, and the financial institutions serving them should carry on positive, intensive education programs to foster diversity rather than exclusivity in housing. Voluntary adoption and publication of nondiscriminatory policies by all builders in a given area would be a practical step in this direction, for instance.

4. Realistic depth studies of the housing needs of our citizens are needed to bring market supply more in line with demand.

5. Involvement of intelligent citizens of vision and conscience in matters of community planning is mandatory. Narrow interests have too long dominated the decision-making processes defining our neighborhoods with results from which we all suffer. The entire community must be represented in deliberations affecting the present and future of the total community. This applies particularly to urban renewal, highway, and low-cost housing programs.

6. Low-rent public or private housing must be provided on a massive scale. Some communities have not yet passed enabling legislation to permit such developments. They should act without delay to do so.

Immediate Action Areas:

Housing is one of the component areas of segregation in which a person can change things for the better through his individual action. He can equip himself with the facts about discrimination in housing, the effects of integrating a neighborhood, etc., and stand his ground when wild rumor and the hoarse shrieks of panic assail him and his fellows. He can extend the hand of friendship and cooperation to new neighbors. He can sell or influence others to sell or rent to Negroes who have what it takes. He can join with others to open housing to Negroes, and to see to it that fear and ignorance never have a chance to take over. Here are some of the actions which can help:

1. Local fair housing groups should be formed at the community level. There are now hundreds of such groups in the nation, many of them affiliated with the National Committee Against Discrimination in Housing or the Association of Fair Housing Committees. Their functions are various in the scores of communities in which they operate. In general, they serve as rallying points for good neighborliness or clearing services for information and education.

Some of these groups circulate pledges and petitions supporting open occupancy; others carry on educational campaigns about equal rights and fair housing legislation; some obtain listings of houses available to Negroes and take responsibility for showing available housing to Negroes. Some groups actively "test," by having Negroes approach real estate offices for housing, and having whites follow up later. If the Negroes are told the particular property in question is sold and the broker then shows it to whites, these groups file complaints with the appropriate licensing bodies against the offending real estate men.

In Denver's Park Hill section, whites induced real estate men to boost this integrated area in their ads as an ideal place to live, where all are welcome. They also put out a neighborhood newspaper, delivered free, playing up the positive features of the area and some of its notable residents. They published figures periodically, proving that Negroes are not flooding the area. Park Hill organized neighborhood meetings at the local schools, and here human relations policies of the organization were announced and speakers heard. This was an area in which rumors ran wild when the first Negroes moved in. This was because there was no com-

159

munication between whites and Negroes. Block-communications units were developed and interchange was made easy and natural within the framework of existing organizations.

In the case of northwest Washington, D.C., an interracial group known as Neighbors, Inc., has for several years been active in creating a stable, integrated, vital neighborhood in an increasingly Negro section of the city. Its major efforts have gone into combating rumors spread by real estate brokers that property values will drop, crime will increase, neighborhood standards will deteriorate and older (i.e., white) residents will be pushed out.

In its program, Neighbors, Inc., has traced the rumors, found the facts, and presented them; built community spirit with block meetings; formed special committees to speak to those who may be wavering or have doubts; encouraged responsible real estate men to show homes to all comers; circulated pledge cards and called on community leaders. It also sponsors clean-up campaigns, receptions for resident diplomats, clinics for real estate salesmen, programs to help schools. And it helps responsible citizens to move in, distributes information about real estate values and practices, costs of moving and neighborhood housekeeping. Because some whites feel they will be stigmatized as residents of a "colored neighborhood," Neighbors builds pride of community by noting the superior education, jobs, and economic status of many of the Negroes in its area.

2. Listing services can be economical, efficient avenues to more democratic neighborhoods. The objective is simply to bring together willing buyers or renters with willing sellers or landlords. It is not always as simple as it sounds, because of the extraordinary pressures on both parties. Real estate brokers normally will sell or rent to Negroes only property in or adjacent to minority housing. Therefore the listing service, clearinghouse, housing registry, fair housing committee, or introduction function can be extremely important.

3. Mortgage assurance is a key. In Chicago, a community group has made it easier for Negroes to find housing by enabling them to take over existing mortgages, thus avoiding substantial costs, delays, and other complications.

4. Economic education or legislation for home buyers would aid Negroes and others if it protected the purchaser by registering contracts to buy, required basic information in the contract, and specified a housing inspection before actual sale.

5. Individuals and groups can perform "watchdog" service by determining whether housing being sold on a segregated basis

has been financed with federal money or credit and by taking appropriate action.

6. Churchmen and church groups can and should provide moral and practical leadership in housing on an open occupancy basis. They can be particularly helpful in dealing with the press— writing letters to the editor to refute rumormongers; taking issue with inaccurate facts; issuing press releases or holding press conferences concerning the positive elements of democratic housing, and, most important of all, using the power of the pulpit on behalf of decent housing for all. The press has no difficulty in getting the negative stories, even if they don't always get them straight, and they don't always have the full picture before turning loose their goriest headline writer on an article.

7. In dealing with housing inadequacy, volunteer groups can keep public agencies on their toes. In New York City, a group called Call For Action threaded its way through the maze of interlocking responsibilities in the city structure. It then publicized in the ghetto the appropriate agency to call for handling such problems as:

No water—call the Health Department.

Insufficient water—call Dept. of Water Supply, Gas & Electricity.

No hot water—call Buildings Department.

Leaky water pipes—call Buildings Department.

Large leaks—call Dept. of Water Supply, Gas & Elec.

Water overflow from apartment upstairs—call Police Department.

8. Building codes and code enforcement are so chaotic that serious overhauling is overdue in almost all cities. Citizen action with builders and trade unions is needed to modernize codes; vigorous enforcement is necessary.

9. Dialogue is needed between the housing trade, unions, local government, and informed citizens concerning the critical state of Negro housing needs and the means for doing something about it now.

10. Negroes must be appointed to local urban renewal boards, housing and city planning commissions, now.

11. Missionary work should be conducted on how to purchase properties, how to live a better life in better housing, how to preserve and conserve housing and neighborhoods. Forums, meetings, and discussions featuring local officials, housing, home economics, and other appropriate experts can accomplish this educational program.

12. Citizens with foresight must prevent location of new

schools and/or school district boundary adjustments to perpetuate *de facto* segregated schools. Schools should be so placed as to increase integration of the school community in spite of the residential pattern.

13. Generations of slum living have deadened the interest of some Negroes in moving into better housing. Never having experienced or expected anything better, they cannot picture themselves in quarters where facilities work, floors, walls and windows are unbroken, etc. An educational job must be done with such people to widen their vision perparatory to moving into decent housing.

The functions of social work are of
three kinds: (1) restoration of impaired
capacity; (2) provision of individual
and social resources; (3) prevention of social dysfunction.
Individuals, singly and in groups, on
the one hand, and the social environment
on the other, are seen as components of
an interactional field. Social work as
a profession is viewed as having an
obligation to intervene at any point in this
interactional field, or in any aspect
of the relationship between individuals
and their social environment where, in
the light of an assessment of the individual
and social factors involved, professional
activity will result in improved social
functioning. This professional obligation
is discharged through several methods often
used in combination—casework, group
work, community organization,
administration, and research.
Werner V. Boehm,
*Objectives of the Social Work
Curriculum of the Future*

6
The
Welfare
of All

Probably in no areas of American life are the needs of the Negro less understood, nor is there less appreciation of the full potential of institutions and their services, than in health and welfare. Almost without exception, from the passage of the social security law in 1935, we Americans have treated legitimate Negro needs with palliatives. Our actions have satisfied the larger society that it was not letting people starve to death. We have given people the absolute minimum in relief, and in the case of the Negro we have usually set up double standards.

Many taxpayers are upset over the drain on public funds caused by relief payments. They think that their high taxes are the direct result of high welfare costs, not recognizing that we actually spend today a smaller percentage of our national income on welfare than we did a decade ago. Many people don't understand why in a period of relative prosperity there are increasing welfare costs, because they

164

interpret welfare need only in terms of money and not in terms of increased population, the urban shift, unemployment and underemployment, mental stress, problems with children, and the fact that there is greater mobility and more tension today than yesterday.

About welfare everybody is a self-proclaimed expert. The average citizen can't argue intelligently on how much is needed for the space program or defense or funding the national debt. But everyone feels informed enough to argue that you make people dependent by giving them money. And if the client is colored, this makes it easier to "prove" the point.

Often citizens have curious misconceptions about typical relief recipients and resent paying money to "all those able-bodied men." It should be noted that approximately nine out of every ten persons who receive assistance is either too young or too old to work, is disabled or busy caring for youngsters who are receiving ADC—aid to dependent children. Of the remaining 10 percent, most want real jobs rather than work relief or welfare subsistence.

A major factor in high welfare costs has been hard-core unemployment. Many are unemployed because their skills are no longer needed. Others have been left behind when industry moved out. Others are jobless because of a downswing in the business cycle, or because of discrimination or because they are just between jobs. Still others are out of work because they cannot hold jobs due to serious physical, mental, or emotional inadequacy. Among these are persons for whom work relief programs may be suitable. Though work relief may be necessary, rehabilitative services can prepare many citizens to find and to hold regular employment.

For the most part, social service to members of the community has been approached on the basis that people must be put through a means test to make sure that they are truly in need. And, too often, we insist that a Negro citizen, regardless of his qualifications, must take any job that the social worker happens to find available and considers appropriate. Even if a person is a college graduate, the social worker can decide that since he is a Negro and there is a domestic job available, he should take it. We do not impose similar requirements on whites.

To compound this inequity, the Negro has been forced to go to segregated facilities and settings—and not only in the South. He has often been subjected to the abuse of people who themselves were members of a profession not sure of its status, people who satisfied their own status needs and feelings of inadequacy by being punitive, hostile to, and demanding of, clients. Often, therefore, those needy people refused to subject themselves to a demeaning process of help and rehabilitation.

The philosophical and theoretical concepts of health and welfare services as preventive and rehabilitative measures have necessarily receded into the background as high case loads, inadequate, largely untrained staffs, and political administrators dominated the foreground. Social work was born in an era of social protest and concern. By identifying themselves with the plight of the sweatshop workers, the children exploited in the cities, the socioeconomic health and educational deprivation of large masses of people, our pioneers in social work earned for themselves society's respect and gratitude. For those of us who have followed in their footsteps they created a profession which one could enter and pursue with dignity and pride.

But somewhere along the way several things happened. Many people in social work misinterpreted very useful psychoanalytical knowledge to make a god of "adjustment"—adjustment at any cost became the goal, the major requirement of "normalcy." Adjust to injustice, to rejection, to humiliation, to all kinds of senseless discrimination and deprivation if need be, but for God's sake, adjust. Somewhat later we in social work became sensitive about our status and our roles as "professionals," and this led to an almost fanatical preoccupation with methodology and technique and a frantic avoidance of things controversial, unless they were made respectable for us by the participation of other professional groups such as doctors, lawyers, and teachers.

Hence, we could never project ourselves into aggressive leadership roles for fear of being called presumptuous self-seekers, simply "acting out our latent hostilities." Interestingly enough, during this period our literature will show that we reached great oratorical and rhetorical heights in our speeches and papers about social action— when we were talking to each other. Even in the classrooms our students listened to, and sometimes participated in, spirited discussions of our "role."

Implementation, however, was another matter. For a long while we social workers rationalized and deceived only ourselves by thinking and declaring that after all, everybody knows where social workers stand and what we think. Others argued that we could not afford to jeopardize our services to needy people by possibly alienating those who provide the bulk of the money for those services. Some just said flatly that injustice and social problems were only fringe and extracurricular concerns for social workers. Since leadership is immensely important, we were hindered by some administrators who were frustrated businessmen and in many cases better known for their success at fund raising or their public relations and political skill than their social welfare convictions.

The time for change has overtaken us and what is important now is the future of social work as a profession and social workers as professionals and human beings. Perhaps in spite of social workers, circumstance has provided our profession with a magnificent opportunity to prove that its members are worthy carriers of a great heritage. The Negro revolution cannot succeed without dramatic, aggressive intervention by social workers at all levels. But if social work remains unidentified or just on the fringe, then it will have lost its reason for being and missed its greatest opportunity to establish, for all the world to see, its basic belief in the dignity of all mankind and man's ultimate right to realize freely his greatest potential.

The helping professions should be involved in the Negro revolution for two basic reasons. By the nature of their intellectual commitment they are supposed above all to have understanding and an appreciation of the dignity of man, together with a real awareness of what deprivation, denial, and rejection mean. Furthermore, these professionals see the results of segregation at first hand, unlike the people who avoid the slums, who drive around them or through them without seeing. Bankers and brokers continue to read their *Wall Street Journals* when their commuter train stops at 125th Street in Harlem. They do not "reach" out into those tawdry tenement bedrooms with five kids and three adults crowded together. They do not even look.

Social workers see these things and they see what happens to people. But they have not capitalized on this background because of their middle-class orientation. They aren't really sure that perhaps these victims, their clients, may not be lacking in thrift, initiative, and that old rugged individualism.

It is well for us to recognize that social disorganization among Negro citizens in the middle income group happens to be the same as or even less than the figures for white citizens in the same socioeconomic class. Furthermore, the figures concerning crime, delinquency and broken homes among white citizens in the lower socioeconomic levels are identical to the figures for Negroes in the same levels. A case in point is ADC—aid to dependent children.

Reports state that there are more out-of-wedlock births among Negroes than whites, and that 60 percent of unwed mothers in this country are Negroes. Such figures must be judged against additional facts.

1. According to the Planned Parenthood Federation of America: There were approximately one million abortions in 1960— about 19 percent of all pregnancies. By contrast, there were about 221,000 illegitimate births, and of these, 90 percent never appeared on relief rolls because they were adopted or cared for by the mothers or families involved. In other words, only one out of about fifty-five illegitimate pregnancies results in a claim on the taxpayer.

Out-of-wedlock births among white citizens aren't fully reported because the vast majority are treated by private physicians rather than by public facilities, and, therefore, do not become public statistics. Furthermore, 97 percent of the abortions are to white women. To exist in these circumstances without ADC requires money. Economic incapability forecloses this possibility to Negroes. Therefore, to Negroes ADC is essential.

2. Most unwed mothers are under twenty-five years of age, and the largest group is between fifteen and nineteen. These girls are almost entirely the victims of circumstances and environment, and they produce nearly three-fourths of all recorded illegitimates.

3. Though we social workers are aware of it, it is not generally known or reported that middle-class Negro citizens have less social disorganization than white citizens of the same economic class. Furthermore, Negroes in the middle income range are less dependent, and have fewer out-of-wedlock births than whites in general.

There is no dodging the fact that the number of illegitimate children on public welfare is increasing. But illegitimacy as it confronts our cities has little to do with Southern plantations or sexual habits of particular racial groups. It is the by-product of social and economic conditions. The highest illegitimacy rates tend to be in areas where housing is poor, recreation and health facilities are inadequate, and where children and adults are rejected by the community. Illegitimacy is a growing problem in all segments of society and is a major cause of dependency.

Negro citizens, therefore, resent the suggestion that disproportionate dependency and high rates of illegitimacy stem from inherent moral weakness or flaws. We resent the implication that we are immoral. For a long time, Negroes had a monopoly on being bell hops, hotel maids, and domestic servants. We were the ones who cleaned out the whiskey bottles with the trash in the mornings. We were the ones asked to procure women at night. If anything, we learned immorality from our white masters and employers. Perhaps we did not learn discretion, but then we were not taught to be discreet. Social disorganization even in the ghettos does not reflect attitudes and patterns of behavior in a culture unique to the Negro, such situations are no more acceptable to, or characteristic of, Negroes than of other citizens. Social workers, as I indicated earlier, know better. We have a duty to inform the larger community of the whole truth.

Today social work in America is on trial. Whether we like it or not, and in spite of what we have done, we social workers are still identified by the public with Jane Addams; the health workers, with Florence Nightingale. And if the public fails to see today's professionals as linear descendants of these great and good people, then we will have lost all of the appeal of idealism and emotional involvement. We aren't ever going to attract people to the social service field for money and status alone, because it is a field that will rarely have a satisfied customer who will go out and brag about the product as he would a car or TV set. We are the symbols of the failures of people. We remind them of their dependency.

The bitter truth is that many of the agencies in the helping professions have done as much to perpetuate segregation and feelings of rejection and indifference as any institution and more than most individuals, because they have contentedly followed the pattern, though they knew better. Many family agencies became so obsessed with being little psychiatric clinics that they didn't reach the Negro. They adopted a posture of: "Here we are. We can only help you if you ask for our services." This was their notion of voluntary service.

There was no real reaching out, no recognition by many of these agencies that Negroes would not automatically come to them. Negroes were not aware of their services. Furthermore, seeing nothing but white faces, Negroes were anything but sure they'd be welcome. To many Negroes with a Southern background, all institutions are viewed as "white" and therefore not for their use. Negroes were suspicious; they worried about the fees that many agencies charged. There was also a very real problem with Negro ministers who felt that by letting agencies do the counseling they lost an important role, status in the community, and standing among parishioners. They could not afford these results and, therefore, did not want to refer people to those who were trained to help in practical ways. Meanwhile the agencies just sat there. Happily, the 1960s have seen changes, the Family Service Society of America, the child welfare agencies as well as the group work agencies are now facing up to some of these problems and taking significant steps to ensure improvements in their service.

The first challenge to social service agencies is to reflect the basic concepts of social work in services as well as in administration. Agencies that discriminate on a racial basis in admission policies are not legitimate social work agencies, nor can their staff members qualify as legitimate social workers. In the South, such practices are sometimes forced by law, though more often the root cause is tradition perpetuated by apathetic boards and timid professionals. If baseball and the entertainment field can insist on integration, should social work agencies be far behind?

Agency services must extend and expand to meet the crucial health and social welfare needs of the urban Negro masses. This requires a review of structure to insure that Negro leadership is brought in on the policy-making level, and a review of programs and services to gear these to meet the special needs of urban Negroes.

The value of minority group representation at the policy-making level is so fundamental that I need not dwell on it except to point out that the requirement that each local board must be representative of its total community has not been taken as seriously as the situation warrants. Lack of such representation perpetuates not only the great social distance between policy-maker and client group, but also continues the practice which Negroes deeply resent, of doing for rather than with the Negro citizen.

I am not impressed by agencies that complain that they cannot get reliable, contributing Negro board members or a substantial Negro clientele. In most cases they haven't really tried or don't know how. This again reflects the limited contact with, and knowledge of, the Negro community that most white persons have. And might it be that agency people are really saying that they can't find any Negroes who they believe are "safe" and respectful—who will not challenge their accustomed practices?

On this matter of board representation today, the concerned citizens must make a special, conscious effort. The only Negro citizens who will be useful board members are those who are truly representative in that they have the respect of the Negro community. You can no longer designate or hand-pick Negro leadership from outside. Leadership today is merited, and one of the best ways to kill it is to have people try to "select" it. This kind of "leadership" is of no value anyhow. We have had enough experience with the Negro expert who is on every committee because he's the only Negro the whites know, respect, and trust. He is an expert all right—an expert in agreeing with white people.

Rightly or wrongly, the view of social welfare agencies widely held in far too many Negro communities around the country is of organizations mainly devoted to helping middle-class families solve their problems. Many agencies appear to have a casual or cursory concern for the low-income group. And, of course, it is in this low-income group that three-fifths of Negro families are to be found. Representative boards and staffs must change this impression.

A major determinant of agency practice is the selection and utilization of staff. Obviously, proper qualifications, demonstrated competence, and merit should always be the major criteria in the selection and promotion of staff. However, it is possible within this framework for all agencies to have interracial personnel. This should not be left to chance. Conscious efforts should be made through tangible, visible employment practices to demonstrate democratic

171

beliefs through deed as well as creed. Experience has shown us that, unfortunate as it may be with untrained workers and tragic as it is with social work school graduates, we cannot assume in either case an absence of racial prejudice, the conviction or the ability to encourage good intergroup relations. Neither can we automatically assume that staff members from minority groups have themselves sufficiently mastered their minority status to operate effectively in this area. This not only suggests but makes mandatory administrative decisiveness in selection, orientation, in-service training and continuing supervisory functions.

There is a pervasive feeling in many sections of the Negro community that the social service agency is more concerned with "professionalism" than with reaching out to people with basic needs. Too many social workers are still so sensitive about their professional status that they are fanatically preoccupied with methodology and technique to the exclusion of feeling and commitment.

This explains in part why the disadvantaged Negro citizen and his family shy away from social service agencies. We have come to the point where we need simpler, down-to-earth language and sympathetic personal understanding that relates to the problems of the people being served. Counseling about "marital stability" or suggesting how the client "can get the most out of marriage" doesn't mean much to the Negro mother who carries the family burden. She cannot afford the luxury of thinking about mental health when her family is undergoing great deprivation—when her children are hungry, and her husband is unemployed.

Just as the social worker helps clients express, understand and, hopefully, work through their hostilities toward parents, siblings, spouses, employers, etc., we should also help them to do the same thing with their feelings about race, religion, or nationality. The same justification for assisting clients to a more productive life by enabling them to look more rationally at some of their myths and superstitions—about child rearing, for example—would also apply to their stereotyped notions about various ethnic groups. This type of counseling obviously implies that there be developed on the part of the workers both sound attitudes and knowledge of the nature, causes, and results of prejudice. In addition to the help given to members of the dominant group in this area of intergroup relations, social workers have an equal responsibility to assist minority individuals.

It is my contention here that we have not met the basic goal of social work, which is the enhancement of social functioning, if we make no effort with social service clients to modify their prejudices where they exist. And this can no longer be an adjunct or hit-or-miss service. It is a basic function in helping clients to adjust to modern society.

At least two reasons stand out as compelling social workers to adopt the improvement of intergroup relations as a primary element in their work, if they are to achieve the true goals of social work. The first is the now universally accepted fact that racial prejudice is a product of either gross illiteracy or extreme emotional insecurity. The second is that today, and even more so in the world ten years hence, we have foreclosed to all citizens the choice of exclusiveness. We are all now citizens of the world. Science and technology have made of the world a neighborhood; we must make of it a brotherhood.

The profession of social work is challenged to be an early ally in the movement toward a better world. With clients who are minority group members, social workers are challenged to new heights of imagination and creativeness. The results of a deprived environment are reflected on a group basis in a disproportionately high incidence of social disorganization, i.e., crime, delinquency, illegitimacy, and family instability. The effects are apparent also in poor health and appalling levels of infant mortality.

The challenge to social work practice is first to understand; and secondly, through skillful service, to seek to modify attitudes and to suggest appropriate resources that can further alleviate mens' ills. This is scarcely an easy job. And for optimum effectiveness social workers today, more than ever before, need to view the panorama of Negro family life in its historically correct setting. Almost without exception, Americans, including most social workers, decry the lack of stability in the Negro family, the absence of a strong father figure and the presence of the matriarchal pattern as if they never knew the causes of these conditions.

The Negro family in the United States is one of the few in the history of man that society made a deliberate, conscious—and all too successful—effort to weaken and destroy as a stable institution. Throughout the slave trade era, it was common practice to divide families forcibly and to sell them on the block upon arrival in America. This practice prevailed during slavery days throughout the South, and each time slaves were sold the family unit was deliberately broken up. Furthermore, promiscuous breeding was encouraged as an economic measure. Even after emancipation the Negro male was emasculated economically by the practice of keeping him at low-paying jobs, if any, and subjecting him to gratuitous humiliation to prevent him from getting out of his "place" and attempting to effect change. The composition of the Negro family continued to be such that the father, if identified, had no established role, and the Negro male, his manhood weakened, suffered economically and psychologically.

Another factor is that Negroes, unlike other ethnic groups in the United States, have no national roots. We do not have a national homeland as such and there has been little direct identification with Africa, despite popular beliefs to the contrary. Slave-trade raiding parties captured Negroes in several regions of Africa, and, therefore, among slaves in America there was no common language, history, or cultural heritage.

The matriarchal society stems from this history, and so do many currently pressing problems. For the Negro male, modern economic deprivation is an updated version of his age-old experience of humiliation and abuse. His present high unemployment, low skills, and inadequate earnings tell us more about the conscious and unconscious injustices of the past than they do about the present.

The effect on family functioning and role performance of this historical experience is what you might predict. Both as a husband and as a father the Negro male is made to feel inadequate, not because he is unlovable or unaffectionate, lacks intelligence or even a gray flannel suit. But in a society that measures a man by the size of his pay check, he doesn't stand very tall in comparison with his white counterpart. To this situation he may react with withdrawal, bitterness toward society, aggression both within the family and racial group, self-hatred, or crime. Or he may seek escape through a number of avenues that help him to lose himself in fantasy or to compensate for his low status through a variety of exploits.

174

As for the Negro mother, her role is dictated more by necessity than by choice. As a major—if not the only—breadwinner in the family, she takes on responsibilities and duties far beyond her ability to perform well. But, contrary to what most social scientists conclude, she knows quite well and resents very deeply the forces responsible for her fate.

Her children, too, often suffer from the absence of a strong male figure. The mother is too tired and bitter to give time, supervision and sometimes, though rarely, love. The youngsters experience bitterness and hostility toward a society that mistreats their parents. They also feel humiliation and shame deepened by frustration and hopelessness.

Unquestionably, there is need for programs that will develop strong families; programs that will also reach Negro men. One of the cruelest inversions of welfare is that it weakens the male's role because the money is always given to the woman. This is one more factor that tends to lower the self-respect of the Negro male.

So welfare has perpetuated the matriarchal family in a sense. But beyond this, welfare departments have made it a condition of receiving certain types of aid that the male be absent from the home, that the woman be either divorced or abandoned along with her children. This practice places a premium on "desertion." There are many women who really would have stayed with their husbands or would have returned after a fight, but who couldn't run the risk of trying a reconciliation, losing their welfare aid, and then having the man leave. The woman would then have to go through the whole tedious, slow, and degrading process of applying for welfare again. This situation has driven many people into clandestine relations, and welfare departments have retaliated with dawn raids to smoke out "immoral" recipients of aid.

In this matter of *special effort* in the social welfare field, the social worker, like the teacher and others, must accept the fact that he is working with persons who may show hostility. These clients are likely to be suspicious—not open and warm and easy to communicate with. Professional workers have got to understand why. We have to go that extra step, especially with children. We must let the child know that we like him as a person; we accept him; we appreciate him. This is the extra giving that grows out of the awareness of the deprivations of the past. Special effort takes more than money and high quality of staff. It also requires this extra sensitivity, awareness, and appreciation.

All too often the best social workers go off into private practice and see five people a day or work in an agency that treats mainly the middle class. The least-trained workers often are those in public welfare that reaches the masses of people. It is important that the public agency see its parallel to the medical profession and recognize that its staff members should be the best-trained workers. They ought to receive the most money and have the most experience because they are working with people suffering from the most difficult problems. And again, this requires a change in the value system of the profession, so that the rewards and prestige will go to those who treat the none-too-figurative social plagues, epidemics, and disaster situations in our urban centers.

I want to see all of the services and the very best of services with the very best of personnel in those worst of areas, where the masses of people are. At the same time I want it clearly understood that the Negro citizen will be freely welcomed at any social service agency office anywhere in town. This ought to be shown by the employment of Negroes in the downtown office, the suburban offices, extension activities and so on. This suggestion represents a shift in policy and attitude among Negro leadership, because we know that there is great need for more family and home counseling services to Negro families where they live.

There was a period when the Negro leadership and middle-class Negroes opposed the existence and certainly the establishment of an agency in the Negro community, because it invariably became an all-Negro agency. The belief was that this was a way of keeping Negroes out of the white agencies downtown. And invariably it was an inferior agency, justifying opposition for that reason.

Most agencies have since, after great pressure, finally consolidated and eliminated their Negro branches. But we found that the Negro, either because of economic reasons—no bus fare—or because he didn't feel comfortable, did not go to those consolidated locations. So we had to rethink this. We found in recent years that the Negro masses were not really interested in whether the agency was integrated or not. Theirs was concern with basic welfare, whereas

176

the middle-class Negro's concern was with status through banishing segregation and discrimination.

Large numbers of Negroes on welfare rolls reflect the impact of generations of rejection and discrimination. The lists include old people whose jobs have never been covered by social security and who must turn to assistance rather than to Old Age and Survivors Insurance. Included are people who are unemployed or unemployable for lack of job opportunity, training, or health. Also listed are dependent children whose parents have never had the chance for stability that adequate job opportunity offers. In the absence of opportunities to become self-supporting, these people will have no recourse other than public welfare as long as these problems persist.

Chronic dependency is not inherited, sought, nor enjoyed. It develops when individuals are given too little, too late, and when it is given in a way designed to demoralize and embarrass. Until poverty becomes a crime in this country, people who are the victims of economic changes should be able to secure help in ways which make it possible to retain dignity and self respect.

SOCIAL WELFARE SPECIFICS

The social service needs of the Negro are so vast and all-embracing that they are nearly overwhelming. But there are innumerable opportunities for individual citizens to take the initiative in their local communities to improve conditions. We cannot let the gargantuan dimensions of the needs keep us from action; as the Oriental sage advised, "When faced with eating an elephant, the way to begin is to take the first bite."

A. Long-range Needs:

1. Federally subsidized programs must offer services without racial discrimination. This includes all-important maternity homes, day-care centers, and facilities for the aged.

2. Greater emphasis must be put on programs that will prevent dependency. We must attack causes as well as symptoms.

3. Public assistance workers are overburdened. Their caseloads must be lowered. Perhaps programs parallel to the hospital nurses' aides and "gray ladies" can be instituted in addition to the training and hiring of more and better workers and the provision of greater incentives.

4. We must have more training and work centers to save functionally illiterate adults and teen-agers from the human scrap heap.

5. Residence requirements for public assistance eligibility should be abolished. The fundamental reason for eliminating such requirements rests on the principle of national citizenship. We have, as Supreme Court Justice William O. Douglas has pointed out, the right to move freely from state to state as an element of national citizenship, protected by the privileges and immunities clause of the Fourteenth Amendment to the Constitution. Furthermore, those who have migrated to urban centers have done so to improve their condition, an honored principle in America—not to live royally on the dubious largesse of relief payments.

6. Demonstration projects must be established in communities all over the land to prove the practicality of Negro adoptions and cultural and social improvement of deprived citizens. The Urban League's FAN—Friends and Neighbors—project is such an effort. It brings together the "newcomer" Negro family and an established middle-class urban family in a mutually helpful relationship of the kind that aided migrants of other ethnic groups.

Immediate action is called for to reverse the trends in urban areas, trends that are intensifying dependency. Men of vision and good will should devote special effort to the following:

B. Immediate Action Areas:

1. Matching funds for public welfare programs should be increased, to raise the standard of living of welfare families and to make possible rehabilitation services that are realistic.

2. Day-care centers for children of working mothers at a price the female head-of-family can afford are a necessity. The alternative is a continuation of the trend to ever higher ADC payouts and dependency. Subsidies for this purpose may be necessary, but communities presently are not taking full advantage of the 1962 Public Welfare Law amendments, permitting states to establish day care programs jointly sponsored with Federal aid.

3. "Suitability of home" policies are in most cases incredibly cruel, unreasonable, and far too subjective. Casework services should be mandatory before a child is removed from a home because of the alleged "immorality" of his parent(s). The cost of

institutionalizing a child is many times that of supporting him in a family situation, even with the addition of social service attention in that home.

4. Public assistance staffs must be skilled, experienced, appreciated. There is no economical way to muddle through. With insufficiently trained or inadequate numbers of social workers we cannot reverse the accumulated community neglect of decades. The emphasis has to be on prevention and rehabilitation rather than on "picking up the debris." This means expert staff members going into people's homes with aggressive casework when called for, to reach those who are out of touch.

5. Deprived citizens generally have little information about social resources available to them, such as public assistance, public housing, community health programs, child care, immunization, nursing, recreation, aging and family services.

Realistic, concentrated information centers are needed to make needy families aware of services. Television, radio, printed media, posters and organized avenues of information such as community groups and organizations plus home visits and church projects can and should be employed.

6. Youth should be encouraged to enter social work. We have seen the tremendous appeal to youth of idealistic projects such as the Peace Corps. This idealism can be channeled similarly into lives of community service.

7. Coordinated planning is needed for tackling social problems effectively, rapidly, with a minimum of red tape. This demands representative citizens in the planning process and more volunteer workers.

8. More group work, recreational and leisure time services are needed for citizens in the ghettos.

9. Family planning information must be made available to citizens in the low-income category. Every family has the right to know about birth control and the various approved methods. Freedom of choice should be left to individuals, according to their own values and religious convictions. Tax-supported medical and welfare agencies have a responsibility to make available such information just as they do information about legally established health resources such as polio shots, clinics, and X rays.

10. More family and home counseling services for Negro families are needed.

11. Strong family life programs that will reach Negro men are of prime importance.

179

12. Disturbed families and deserted mothers need services that are either not available now, or are not utilized.

13. Social welfare programming must be developed to meet the persistent problem of illegitimacy.

14. Multiagency projects cooperatively tackling the problems of ghetto families with action programs are urgently called for.

15. Adoption and foster home programs are inadequate for the Negro children who need such care. Efforts to increase the number of adoptive homes for Negro babies have just not done the job. Many more homes could undoubtedly be found if the attitudes and practices of adoption agencies changed and if interracial placements were permitted.

16. Preschool child-care programs are widely needed.

17. Negro aged are made third-class citizens by discrimination, poverty, and age. Domicile and other services are nonexistent or inadequate; nursing homes are segregated. Extensive health and welfare services are needed for indigent senior citizens. It is important also to increase employment opportunities for the aged and to alert them to the existence of community resources.

18. "Port of Entry" services are necessary to integrate newcomers into the community. Whether labeled as such or not, our cities have areas that, because of low rent or other factors, become unofficial ports of entry for rural–urban and interurban migration. They ought to be recognized as such, and necessary services provided in quantity and in depth to serve newcomers and move them onward into the community. Unfortunately, what were historically ports of entry for other migrants—Irish, Italians, Germans, etc.—became permanent residential ghettos for Negroes. Therefore, it is often the case that a Negro living in such an area for many years may still be a "newcomer" in the sense that he has not made the adjustment from rural to urban culture: he has not acquired the necessary education or training, secured the job, stepped up the economic ladder, or been able to find housing elsewhere. He has not successfully used the public or private health and welfare resources to establish roots as a participating citizen in the community.

Healing is a matter of time, but it is sometimes also a matter of opportunity.
Hippocrates, *Precepts,* Chapter I.

The health of the people is really the foundation upon which all their happiness and all their powers as a state depend.
Benjamin Disraeli, July 24, 1877.

7
Poor
Health
in the
Richest
Nation

It was April 1, 1950. The four men in the auto were physicians, driving from Washington, D.C. to a southern college to lead a series of medical education meetings on the campus. They were on the highway near Burlington, North Carolina when the driver swerved to avoid something in the road, and the car skidded and rolled.

When it came to rest, one of the men, Dr. Charles Drew, was severely injured. The other doctors, realizing that Drew was losing blood rapidly, flagged down a passing car and hurried the man to the nearest hospital. But the hospital attendants, seeing that Drew was a Negro, refused to aid or to admit him to the all-white facilities. While Drew's life blood ebbed from him, the attendants told his companions to take him to the nearest Negro hospital. It was only a short distance and did not take long. Just long enough for the man to bleed to death.

182

So ended in banal irony the life of Charles Drew, whose brilliant development of blood plasma theory and of the blood bank have saved numberless millions from the senseless fate which took him. It was Drew's genius that made the blood bank a practical reality, to the lasting benefit of all humankind. Tragic as his death was, the overriding tragedy is that if the identical accident occurred today the results would be the same, for the hospitals in North Carolina are still rigidly segregated.

Many Americans have been touched by Charles Drew's genius—either as blood donors, blood recipients, or as Red Cross and medical workers who have helped in the annual blood bank drives. Few of those who are familiar with the blood bank know the name Charles Drew; fewer still know that he was a Negro. And few, perhaps, know of Dr. Louis T. Wright, the brain surgeon and antibiotics expert who developed the smallpox vaccine that is used today. Few know of Dr. Daniel Hale Williams, the first surgeon to operate successfully on the human heart; or of Dr. Ernest E. Just, who pioneered cell study.

I have mentioned these Negroes because they have made contributions to medicine and health that in other circumstances and times would have ranked them with Pasteur in the public mind. They achieved extraordinarily by any measure. That they did so while burdened with the senseless weight of racial discrimination is not only to their credit but to the everlasting shame and loss of America. The loss, as in Dr. Drew's ignominiously abbreviated life—he died at forty-six years of age—is incalculable, but we can be certain that many thousands of Negro youths of talent, and perhaps many hundreds of true genius, have been lost to the nation forever simply because prejudice stopped them from developing and exercising their intellectual powers. What has prejudice, which demands such an investment of time, effort, and money, yielded in return in the area of health and medicine?

There is a popular myth that Negroes are healthier than whites. Often the person who holds this view substantiates it with references to outstanding Negro athletes—to Floyd Patterson, Willie Mays, Jesse Owens, Althea Gibson, Jackie Robinson. They may even mention that Negroes thrive on hard jobs under difficult conditions—outdoor work in the broiling sun; heavy, "muscle" jobs at steel mills, foundries and warehouses; tough construction tasks.

183

Obviously, goes this talk, Negroes are robust and really cut out for these heavy jobs; they prefer them and seek them out. That is why one so seldom sees Negroes in white collar positions. Negroes are thought to thrive on a diet of "rough" food such as turnip greens, hog maw and chitterlings, as though "soft" foods such as filet mignon and lobster Newburg, pies and crepes suzettes would upset our digestion. Furthermore, continues the myth, because of this "superiority," Negroes have less need of health services, doctors, medicine, and hospital beds. A clear, close look at the facts is in order. Negroes in the United States are not so healthy as whites. Our mortality rate is higher than that for whites until age seventy-five, when, for reasons not yet fully understood, white overtakes Negro mortality, although any Negro in America who can live to age seventy-five must be indestructible. Between thirty and sixty years of age, twice as many Negro Americans as whites die. And total life expectancy for the Negro is seven years less than that of the white American.

The Negro has more diseases and disabilities, more days in bed, and more absence from work as a result. Though there has been great progress in controlling communicable diseases, tuberculosis and venereal diseases afflict the Negro more frequently than the white. In fact, tuberculosis was the number eight killer of Negro males in 1959, and was ten times more prevalent among Negro men aged twenty-five to thirty-four than among white males. Because of the conditions in which the American Negro is forced to live, the disease proves ten time deadlier to him than to the white citizen.

Today antibiotics provide a positive weapon to eradicate syphilis. Yet, because of inadequate knowledge, income, available facilities, and medical care, the Negro suffers a venereal disease rate ten to twenty times that of his white fellow Americans. This is ironic when one considers that the Negro's first exposure to venereal disease came only after his exposure to white civilization.

In susceptibility to other diseases the white American holds no monopoly or preferred position. Negroes are subject to them all, and the only significant point to be made is that proportionately more Negroes are afflicted with them. The National Health Survey showed in 1960 that Negroes lost more days of work per 100 population per year than did whites (160 days vs. 121 days) and spent more days

184

disabled and bedridden per year (87 days per 100 population for Negroes; 62 for whites).

Both infant and maternal mortality rates for Negroes are many times higher than for whites. In 1959, four times as many Negro mothers as whites died in childbirth, and this ratio was constant for more than a decade. Twice as many Negro babies as white infants die before their first birthday; this ratio also has been constant for years.

We can substantiate the conclusion that the health problems of Negro citizens are no different from those of other Americans, all other conditions being equal. But precisely here is the rub; conditions for the Negro are not equal—his living conditions, his working situation, his information about hygiene, his knowledge of health facilities and resources, and his access to medical aid—all of these are unequal.

A recent Howard University study[1] showed how low income families view health. Employment is their primary concern; everything else is secondary. Persons interviewed did not consider themselves in need of medical care unless they were so sick that they couldn't go to work. Asked how they stayed in good health, they cited personal health habits, but few mentioned early diagnosis, quick treatment, or immunization. They saw health as dependent mainly on good habits such as resting and sleeping sufficiently, eating proper foods, living moderately, and avoiding excessive worry.

Furthermore, even though they were aware of such health procedures as physical examinations, they did not necessarily follow them. In some cases, they knew little about certain health measures but used them nevertheless. Many mothers had their children immunized without knowing what diseases were being prevented thereby. Facts alone do not necessarily motivate action (as we have seen in the case of the Surgeon General's report linking cancer and cigarette smoking).

Not surprisingly, the families surveyed knew little about the health facilities open to them. Though some of the voluntary health agencies had been operating in their area for sixty years, their functions and activities were little known. And many of these people thought that the public health department was a policing agency in-

---

[1] *Cultural Considerations in Changing Health Attitudes,* Department of Preventive Medicine and Public Health, Howard University, 1961.

terested in sewage treatment and garbage removal. One of the few health services with which they were familiar was that of the visiting nurse who comes to their neighborhoods and homes. One curious note was the fact that those who were most active in church-related projects turned out to be least informed about health matters.

In addition to their own lack of knowledge about health facilities and procedures, Negro citizens face the complication of discrimination in health facilities and practices in many communities. As an example, there is a type of mental retardation which, if discovered early enough, can be cured. A test called PKU, given to babies within the first week of life can spot the problem at a time when it can be remedied. This test costs about half a dollar and is routine in many hospitals in half the states in the union. Last year our St. Paul Urban League found that a local hospital was not giving the test to Negro babies. The excuse was loose administration and faulty supervision by both the hospital and local public health service. The net result, however, was hundreds of Negro babies untested at a critical stage.

For good health, access to hospitals is of crucial importance.

> Negroes are denied access to or are segregated in many of the medical care facilities which have received federal grants under the Hospital Survey and Construction Act of 1946 [Hill-Burton Act]. Such practices by facilities which have received federal grants constitute denials of equal protection of the laws under the Constitution. More, these practices adversely affect the Nation's health standards and serve to deny medical training to Negro professionals. These conditions are being financed by the nation's taxpayers. . . . The amount spent on medical care facilities reached nearly $2 billion in May 1963. . . . Yet the evidence shows that Negroes do not share equally with white citizens in the use of such facilities. As patients and as medical professionals, they are discriminated against in their access to publicly supported health facilities. Commission investigation also shows that the federal government, by statute and administration, supports racial discrimination in the provision of health facilities.[2]

As of March, 1964, some 7,118 hospitals and health facilities had been built with federal funds under the Hill-Burton Act, according to the U.S. Department of Health, Education and Welfare. Of these, 104 were segregated facilities, 84 of them for whites only and

___

[2] *Report of the U.S. Commission on Civil Rights*, Supt. of Documents, U.S. Govt. Printing Office, p. 129.

20 for Negroes. The act as written authorized "separate but equal" facilities but provided no policing power to determine that the separate facilities were indeed equal.

Physicians and medical educators agree that the single most important element in determining the quality of medical care is continuing education of the doctor through hospital affiliation. From the standpoint of the suffering patient, a hospital bed is available only through his physician, who must be on the staff or have courtesy privileges permitting him to refer patients for admission. A 1963 study of private hospitals in Washington, D.C., indicates the grim nature of the situation:

> In Washington, 54% of the population is Negro and of 2,200 physicians, 300 are Negroes. Of these, 72 are board certified specialists. There are ten private hospitals in the District, yet only 11 Negroes have staff privileges and 90 have courtesy privileges at these hospitals.[3]

The picture is no brighter in other cities. Though the Chicago city council put on the books in 1956 an ordinance to prevent racial discrimination in hospitals, the U.S. Civil Rights Commission found in 1963 that "the situation is especially acute in Chicago." Here, the commission discovered, the public hospital is used both by Negroes able to pay for hospitalization and by those who are indigent. The reason? Simply that Negroes were unable to find sufficient facilities open to them except at Cook County Hospital, though there are sixty-nine other hospitals in the city.

It is true that there are three other hospitals in Chicago with predominantly Negro patient loads. These are accredited and have a total of 329 beds. However, the Illinois Hill-Burton agency officially lists 241 of these beds, or 73 percent, as "unsuitable."[4]

The commission found also that when special hospital facilities for Negroes exist in a community, other health facilities often are denied to Negroes. In Memphis, a city of 398,937 whites and 227,445 Negroes, there is one 128-bed Negro hospital, the only general, accredited health facility available both to paying Negro patients and to Negro physicians. It is city-owned, built partly with federal money.

[3] Report of the Hospital Committee, Urban League, Washington, D.C., 1963.
[4] Civil Rights, op. cit., p. 138.

Though there are in-patient facilities at the city hospital for indigent and part-paying patients and twenty beds at an eye, ear, nose and throat hospital, the only other beds available to Negroes total forty-eight at an unaccredited hospital. Meanwhile, 2,082 beds are to be found in three large, church-related hospitals in the city. These agencies of mercy and healing accept Negroes neither as patients nor as physicians with staff privileges.

The Health, Education and Welfare Department has administered the Hill-Burton Act as though it had no authority to require grant-recipient hospitals not to segregate patients on the basis of race. Also, HEW has considered antidiscrimination regulations to apply only to patients, not to physicians and staff. And where HEW has recognized its responsibility for securing unbiased compliance by hospitals it has financed, it has delegated this authority to the states —with predictable results. Further, HEW requires only that recipient hospitals certify that "essential" services be provided without discrimination. The interpretation of that word essential offers opportunities for a semantic field day.

As the U.S. Civil Rights Commission points out in one example, the North Carolina Hill-Burton agency faithfully reports annually that the number of beds available and planned is proportionate to the Negro and white population of the state. However, it includes in its figures beds in all hospitals, even those unrelated to the Hill-Burton grants. Furthermore, the number of beds does not insure equal quality of service, but this report is all that the act requires.

The U.S. Civil Rights Commission sums up its findings in these words:

> Racially discriminatory policies and practices are found in every region of the nation. They are prevalent to a greater degree in those areas where racial segregation is a basic factor in other aspects of community life. To the extent that such policies and practices limit the provision of medical care to persons in need, the health of the nation is adversely affected.[5]

Another historic milestone on the path to equality of opportunity was reached March 2, 1964, when the Supreme Court affirmed the decision of a lower court that the "separate but equal" provision of the Hill-Burton Act is unconstitutional. The case had been brought

[5] *Ibid.*, p. 142.

by Negro physicians, dentists, and patients against a hospital in Greensboro, N.C. They successfully proved that the hospital pursued "a policy, practice, custom and usage of barring plaintiff physicians and dentists from admission to staff privileges . . . on the grounds of race. . . ." and that "Negro patients cannot enter the . . . [hospitals] on the same terms and conditions as white persons, and, if admitted, cannot be treated by their own physicians or dentists solely on the basis of race. . . ."

The Department of Health, Education and Welfare announced after the Supreme Court action that it would immediately move to bar funds from hospitals that "insist" on segregated facilities. But the remedy, as we found in the aftermath of the Supreme Court's school desegregation decision, may not be speedy. As one instance, the NAACP protested the disgraceful condition in Huntsville, Texas, Memorial Hospital which was built with federal funds. Here, though empty beds are available in the "white" portion of the building, facilities for Negroes are so jammed that patients are forced to use beds in hallways and aisles; no private rooms are available and there is a single bathroom only, for use by both male and female patients. The NAACP asked for an investigation and was assured by the Secretary of HEW in January and again in February, 1964, that the situation would be promptly reviewed. By April, since nothing had changed, the NAACP requested HEW to cut off federal funds to the hospital.

There is no reason in the world for the duplication of facilities and expense caused by segregated hospital accommodations. This is clearly shown by the experience of the Veterans Administration over the past decade. The VA has officially and scrupulously carried out integration policies in its hospitals throughout the country for more than ten years. This includes its hospitals in Birmingham, New Orleans, and Jackson. All over the country, private negotiations, public education, and nonviolent protest have been effective in bringing about desegregation of public and private hospitals in important cities such as Chicago, Washington, Knoxville, and San Francisco.

In this area of inequality of health care, the churches of the country deserve some criticism. With few exceptions, I have found it much more difficult to enter a Negro patient or to obtain staff privileges for a Negro physician in a sectarian hospital than in a public one. When medicine moves in, religion apparently moves out. These institutions seem interested primarily in status and economics rather than the humanitarianism of either the religious or medical calling. Jewish hospitals constitute the exception, particularly in recent years. Member hospitals of the Council of Jewish Federations and Welfare Funds extend services to all patients and hospital privileges to all physicians without discrimination.

The Supreme Court's recent affirmation that segregated facilities supported by federal funds have no place in our country should put spine into responsible private and voluntary hospital boards and administrators. They can end shameful, costly, and degrading segregation and two-class services in their institutions overnight, if they will.

Only a few years ago, seventy-five percent of the hospitals in the United States reported that Negro physicians were neither on their staffs nor allowed courtesy privileges. Because of this situation, their continuing education has been curtailed, and Negroes requiring hospitalization face the agony of trying to find admittance to the few available facilities, which are often Jim Crow, admittedly inferior and unaccredited by the inspecting body of the American Hospital Association.

Even the county or city hospitals that may be open to Negroes have traditionally been staffed with low-qualified, low-paid personnel and part-time physicians. Inadequate funds, cramped quarters, antiquated equipment, discriminatory attitudes by staff members, and lack of understanding of the living conditions of the poverty-stricken —all of these are common features of such institutions. They are generally unattractive if not repellent, and the ailing Negro avoids them if he is able. Usually he has no choice, Anxiety-ridden as to his chance of finding decent hospital facilities and apprehensive of the quality of care he will receive if and when admitted, is it any wonder that the Negro in ill health holds out against hospitalization until the last possible moment?

Yet anybody who has visited a public hospital or clinic in an urban area cannot help but be impressed by the disproportionate number of Negro patients. The same is true for public health clinics and visiting nurse services. One also is struck by the wide variation in the responses of the staff members of these institutions to their patients. There is no place in the world where you have a wider range of response to human suffering than in the hospital. In it you find the height of humaneness so far attained by our society. Yet, in the same building, you also see examples of the depths of human callousness and indifference—attitudes that seem to demand the patient's total sacrifice of human dignity. The Negro is made to feel that to be poor and to have to accept grudging services by the whites is almost despicable. All too often, the fact that there is no alternative provides an opportunity for staff and personnel to take advantage of the patient. Here man's tendency to exert and enjoy superiority is given rich opportunity.

The Negro who enters a hospital usually feels strange, insecure, and frightened. He is told to sit down and wait, and he may wait all day on those hard, wooden benches in which hospitals specialize. In the South, he is addressed as "Boy" or "Girl," and asked pointedly, "What do you want?" as though he is trespassing in forbidden territory.

Once admitted, all patients—whites and black—are in the most dependent human condition: without explanation they must undress, conform to a strange schedule, regimen, and diet, while clad in a shapeless, impersonal getup. They are confined to institutional surroundings designed primarily to promote sanitation and ease of cleaning rather than to give comfort and reassurance to already unsettled human beings.

There is no excuse for treatment of this sort and no reason why it should be corollary to hospitalization. I suspect that it might disappear if we had more Negroes in administrative positions at our hospitals and clinics; more Negroes in county medical societies; more Negroes (one is tempted to say any) on the boards of directors of hospitals, medical facilities, and agencies of all kinds in the health field; and, finally, Negro representation on the state and area agencies administering the disbursement of Hill-Burton Act funds and appointment to responsible positions in state, county, and local public health agencies that regulate and license hospitals and health facilities, schools and physicians.

It would be useful to give intergroup relations courses to the staff members of health facilities. But it seems redundant to have to indoctrinate those who work in the healing professions with information about the worth and dignity of the human being. And it seems to me most unnecessary of all to teach the equality of men to people whose professional training, if adequate, has proved to them that under that layer of epidermis 1/100 of an inch thick we all are the same.

When it comes to improving the health of Negro citizens there is no one, simple solution. In cities around the nation, we have observed that often the greater problem is to educate Negroes to use existing health facilities to the fullest extent rather than to expand existing health agencies to serve the entire community. We must concentrate more on educating the urban Negro and interpreting health information to him. Often the Negro citizen who has migrated to the city, particularly in the North, does not know of the health facilities available, because such facilities either do not exist or are off limits to him in the South.

To promote better health among Negroes, each agency concerned with health must, at the community level and in language that laymen can understand, interpret to the people what can be done, why, and at what cost, by using the facilities that are offered. Only by successfully carrying out such educational campaigns with the trust and cooperation of the Negro community can health agencies hope to eliminate harmful home remedies, superstition, and folk-cures. This implies, of course, that culture, literacy, and socioeconomic factors such as occupation, housing, and sanitation are integral elements in the total health picture. Only if this truth is seen is a program using preventive medicine and health facilities likely to be successful. Furthermore, it points up the necessity for participation in all these areas by those in the health services who are serious about bringing up to standard the level of health of the Negro population. Their serious concern must be demonstrated actively in efforts to improve housing, employment, welfare services and education for Negro citizens in their communities.

The ghetto dwellers are handicapped by inaccurate and incomplete information about medical care, about the types and even the location of health facilities open to them. They lack knowledge of how and when they should make use of such facilities, when or how often they should visit doctors, dentists, and clinics. The less well-educated have grave misgivings about certain simple health techniques. For instance, they are apprehensive about X rays and birth control devices and suspect that these latter affect virility and fertility. Further, they look at health facilities as resources to be used only when at the brink of calamity, not as preventive or health-sustaining facilities. Because the Negro in the population is not able to afford the time off from work for physical checkups, because his experience in hospitals has typically been negative, and because he usually does not have the money to pay for expensive diagnostic and remedial care, he shuns contact with doctors and health institutions until the ultimate, unavoidable moment.

Dr. Paul B. Cornely, head of Howard University's Department of Preventive Medicine and Public Health points out that health education, to be successful, must be brought to people where they live, must be identifiable, and must be delivered to the individuals as dignified human beings. He cites the Visiting Nurse Association as a capital example of this approach: the nurses visit families in their homes, their uniforms are easily identifiable, and patients are dealt with as individuals. Dr. Cornely suggests that health agencies adopt these approaches, and that serious consideration be given to using "practical health educators." These persons, from the same environment as those being served, would be able to talk their language, would be acquainted with community leaders and, thus, be able to motivate them and their peers toward better health habits. They would work under professionally qualified supervisors. He also believes that health educators similar to the "detached social workers" in antijuvenile delinquency programs could be effective. He sees these workers visiting barber shops, pool halls, beauty parlors and store-front churches to carry health information to those who need it. And, because Negro families usually go to clinics for health care rather than to private physicians, Dr. Cornely suggests that such outpatient facilities should be used intensively for health education. Here, he advises, health departments and voluntary health agencies will find people in a situation receptive to health education.

Certainly, much can be done by conscientious agencies that wish to reach Negro citizens. Surely, they can aggressively seek Negro representatives for their boards and committees. They can reach into the Negro community with their programs and, by initiating research-demonstrations of much-needed, high quality family planning, prenatal, infant, child health and aged care programs in ghetto areas, they can enlist community support.

Family planning clinics are an example. We want to strengthen Negro family life and reduce individual and family dependency. Toward this end, positive and realistic programs of family planning can be extremely valuable. Those who have the money, of course, can secure help through their private physician; those of upper educational levels can inform themselves simply through reading. But those in the lower socioeconomic groups are left to the mercy of the resources they can afford, which mean, almost invariably, the public health and welfare institutions.

It is here that tradition, timidity, and fear have operated to deny knowledge to these citizens who need it most. But all of us must share the blame for this curtain of ignorance, for, in the end, the public institutions reflect the policies that the larger public either demands or permits. And up to now it has been easier or more acceptable to the public to threaten unwed mothers with jail sentences, loss of assistance, and compulsory sterilization than to initiate programs of education or to work for improved vocational, play, and shelter environments.

Certainly every family has the right to be informed about all the resources of the community. All should know about birth control and the various approved methods, including rhythm. Our responsibility ends at that point, leaving the individual freedom of choice based on his own values and beliefs.

In my opinion, the responsibility of tax-supported medical and welfare agencies to share this information is equally as pressing as the dissemination of information about any other legally established community resources, such as polio shots, and X rays. To prohibit case workers in public welfare agencies from discussing family planning resources with their clients is a discrimination that denies to welfare recipients one of the principal means of family health and progress commonly used by more affluent couples throughout the nation. These prohibitions limit and to some extent even vitiate the effectiveness of expensive programs to help relief recipients help themselves.

Obviously birth control will not solve all the problems of ghetto

194

dwellers. But programs to rehabilitate relief families can hardly be meaningful if health and welfare workers are forbidden to make family planning referrals. More affluent couples, in the course of family growth, have occasion to ask themselves whether their personal health, stability as a family unit, their ability to remain independent, self-supporting citizens, can support the birth of another child. When the answer is no, they have the opportunity to secure effective family planning guidance consistent with their needs. Welfare families should have similar opportunities.

Negro citizens are often suspicious of the motives of family planners, reluctant to make the programs the sole responsibility of public institutions, and sometimes less than enthusiastic about the program even where the curtain of ignorance has been partially lifted or circumvented. Here is why:

1. The administrators of most public institutions are political appointees. It is rare that a Negro is represented at the policy level, and in some states the top administrators are well-known racists. There is discrimination in hiring; there are segregated facilities and double standards in services and relief grants. Negroes are not yet, therefore, willing to entrust to these institutions alone the responsibility for family planning discussions with clients. For the present, we favor establishment of more clinics, and a crash program of mass education where it is needed most so that low socioeconomic groups may understand the value of family planning methods and resources.

2. Until recently few of the proponents of family planning were prominently active in the fight against the basic problems of discrimination in employment, housing, and education, either as individuals or through established agencies. Many interpreted this single interest in family planning for the Negro as designed more to control population expansion and to reduce taxes than to achieve humane and social goals. Those interested in family planning must be similarly interested in equal opportunity for the Negro in all areas.

3. Though some progress has been made, too often there is conspicuous lack of minority representation at the local policy-making level of family planning agencies. This perpetuates not only a social chasm between policy-maker and client group but also the now deeply resented practice of doing for rather than with the Negro citizen.

It will be clear that many of the comments directed to family planning agencies, as stated above, also apply to other health agencies and their efforts in the ghetto.

Another area that requires urgent attention is that of maternal health, including prenatal care. We know that in 1958, 13 percent (up from 10 percent in 1950) of all Negro babies were premature, compared with 7 percent of white babies. And there is a direct relationship between premature births, lack of prenatal care and the proportion of out-of-wedlock births. Studies indicate that more than half of all unmarried mothers do not receive necessary prenatal care. Furthermore, fewer Negro than white births occur in hospitals. Both of these factors boost mortality rates for Negro babies and mothers. Another pervasive factor is inferior health because of low income levels that deprive families of adequate shelter, clothing, food, and medical services. In addition, Negro mothers bear children at earlier ages, continue later in life, and have larger families than their white counterparts. The mortality rate is higher both for very young and for late-in-life mothers.

Moreover, lack of facilities helps keep the maternal death rate for Negroes four times as high as that for whites. In 1960, 98.8 percent of babies born to white mothers were delivered in hospitals. The figures for Negro mothers were 85 percent hospital and 11.5 percent midwife deliveries. But in actual fact, in five Southern states more than 25 percent of Negro mothers were delivered by midwives. Mississippi had the highest figure, with 43.5 percent delivered by midwives. Clearly, our health facilities are not serving Negro mothers adequately.

The federal government extends money through the Children's Bureau of the Department of Health, Education and Welfare to the health departments of the states in order to improve the health of mothers and children. This includes money for services of doctors, dentists, public health nurses, medical social workers, and nutritionists. Prenatal and child health clinics are maintained and school health services underwritten in order to reach mothers and children. The states have added medical and hospital care for some mothers and children and have initiated programs to aid premature babies and mentally retarded children.

Without question these services are of great significance for

196

Negro mothers. They must depend upon public health agencies to a greater extent than their white counterparts. The persistence of the high mortality rate indicates, however, that much greater effort by voluntary and governmental agencies must be brought to bear on this situation. The aid must be extended, it must be unbiased, and information about its availability must be brought to those who may benefit from it.

Another major area of health need is that which concerns Negro senior citizens—those men and women sixty-five years and over. We know from the 1960 Census that more than half of the Negro aged live in inadequate housing and have incredibly low incomes—less than $1,000 per year. In fact, 80 percent of them manage to subsist on less than $2,000 annually. Data on health is limited, but available information indicates that the aged Negro visits his doctor an average of 4.5 times a year, his dentist less than once. He may go to the hospital 2.5 times during the year, and the chances are two in five that he suffers from some chronic illness. Whites over sixty-five average 594 "restricted-activity days," 138 "bed-disability days," and 202 "work-loss days" per 100 population per year. Negroes had one-third more "restricted-activity days," double the "bed-disability days," and half again as many "work-loss days."

These bloodless statistics hardly hint at the misery of life at the outer rim of subsistence, away from the mainstream of American living. In a society that glorifies youth and is centered around whites, the aged Negro is relegated to the forgotten attic. Nursing-home care and foster-home care are two of the programs for aged citizens that need expansion. In the state of Louisiana, for instance, where 2,212,000 whites and 1,045,307 Negroes reside there were 103 nursing homes serving 3,418 older whites in 1962; at the same time the state had 22 nursing homes serving a total of 488 Negroes.[6]

Negro senior citizens, like most older people, tend to resist change, particularly when it wrenches them from their familiar surroundings and friends. They are not likely to be in the forefront of the integration drive, yet this is no time to urge an expanded program of segregated private homes and programs for older Negroes. There is a pressing need for more and better public and private services to

[6] *Annual Report on Personnel—Nursing Homes,* Louisiana State Department of Hospitals, July, 1962.

the aged, and the times require that the response be open, unsegregated facilities to prevent perpetuation of the segregated patterns of today.

It is significant that the Office of the Aging in the Department of Health, Education and Welfare makes no grants of federal funds. Its functions are to serve as a clearing house of information on programs for the aging and to act as a catalyst to promote services where needed. Apparently, the Office of the Aging believes that social security benefits, community health services, hospitals and clinics operating under the Hill-Burton Act, and provisions of the Housing Act of 1961 are sufficient federal programs for the aging. In the case of the older Negro, this conclusion is manifestly unjustified.

Those willing to consider the evidence will find that the impoverished older Negro is in dire need. He lacks money to buy adequate health care; he generally has worked at jobs that afforded no hospital and medical insurance; in instances where he has been able to qualify for some type of insurance it has usually been "health and accident" policies geared to catastrophic occurrences such as loss of a limb or eye, etc. In those cities where the nonprofit hospital and surgical insurance plans accept individual applicants, Negroes generally are not able to take advantage of the policies. Their relatively modest cost is still beyond the financial reach of most Negroes.

A disturbing trend to change the basis of their membership fees has begun among the nonprofit Blue Cross-Blue Shield agencies. Now in New York they are moving to group their subscribers according to actuarial data, so that various categories of membership will be established according to health. Then the low-health-risk, infrequent users of medical care and hospitals will be assessed a subscription rate lower than that of the plan members who are in the high-health-risk groups. This policy will further handicap the Negro and others.

What this means, of course, is that young, white, upper socioeconomic group members will have preferred rates, and Negroes, older people, and those in lower socioeconomic groups will be hit hardest with insurance premiums for the identical services. Obviously, this will force out of the plans many for whom the fees are already too high, and will foreclose hospital insurance altogether to persons who, by accident of birth and factors such as discrimination, cannot hope to shake off the hazards that cause more illness.

One of the most urgent requirements in the field of health today is to make medical care accessible to the masses. It tends to be the privileged province of those who can bid highest for it. Our society is largely geared to the use of medical aid as an emergency resource. Our view of health is that it is the condition of lack of sickness. We should set our sights on a society in which health means true well-being, the optimum functioning of mind and body. In this context we would gear health services and facilities to preventive medicine, education, and care, and we would make certain that those who suffered illness or accident would have decent attention and treatment.

A word about the mental health of the Negro is in order at this point. There is conflicting evidence as to the Negro citizen's mental illness or health in general. The prevailing view in the past was that the Negro had lower rates of mental illness. We have theorized that the reasons for this belief were that if we could survive being black we could take anything. Also, we were so far out of the main stream in American society that we never absorbed and assimilated the neuroses common to white society. One empirical index that reinforced this conclusion was the fact that suicide is the number eight cause of death for white males and that it does not rate in the top ten for Negroes. However, homicide is the seventh most frequent cause of death among Negro males, so perhaps there is a certain "balance" here.

Some authorities conclude that mental illness seems to be more prevalent among nonwhites: proportionately, there were one-third more Negro than white patients in mental hospitals in the United States in 1950. But a recent study in New York City found that mental illness is most prevalent in low income areas. And the 1958 study of *Social Class and Mental Illness* by Hollingshead and Redlich in New Haven, Conneticut, uncovered a shockingly high relationship between low "social class" and mental illness. This study found that the poor had three times as many cases of "treated psychiatric illness" per 100,000 population as any of the first three socioeconomic groups. Furthermore, 90 percent of the illnesses of the poor were psychoses and only 10 percent were neuroses; among the well-to-do, 65 percent of the cases were neuroses and only 35 percent were psychoses.

It should be emphasized that these figures counted only those who actually were treated by a doctor or a clinic. We know that there are proportionately more poor people than well-to-do who will not or cannot seek treatment. But the salient conclusions from the New York and New Haven studies are that mental illness is more severe and higher in incidence among the poor. Since the number of Negroes who are poor is disproportionately high, we may infer that they constitute more than the average number of mentally ill in the population as a whole. Such a finding would hardly be surprising, considering the circumstances in which Negroes are forced to live.

Returning now to the question of the cost of health, under current conditions the high, unstandardized, and unpredictable charges for medical care can literally devastate the family with average income. The Negro family, of course, has lower income, fewer facilities and doctors accessible, and is in an even more precarious position. Health insurance as it exists today must be viewed realistically. It is, by any objective reckoning, inadequate to the needs of the vast majority of people: first, because it serves only those so privileged as to afford it; second, because it is geared to conditions requiring hospitalization, thereby ruling out preventive care and early treatment; third, because it cuts off at maximums that leave lower income citizens subject to economic disaster when extended care and expensive treatment are required; fourth, it is designed for an elite—the elite that is steadily employed, generally part of a work force covered by a group policy and located in communities that have nonprofit hospital and surgical plans.

We know from various studies that fewer Negroes than whites are covered by health insurance, and those that have it are less well covered. One recent study of hospitalized Negroes revealed that only 42 percent had any insurance that would apply (71 percent of the whites had such insurance), and only 30 percent could expect their insurance to cover 75 percent or more of the bill (53 percent of the whites had this type).

We know also that the price of medical care is high and going higher. In the decade of the 1950s the Consumer Price Index of all items rose 12 percent. Yet medical care costs zoomed up three times as much during the decade, increasing 36 percent. Hospital care, for example, went up 65 percent, and the premiums on hospitalization insurance policies went up 83 percent.

The conclusion is inescapable that some type of broad-gauge medical aid plan—such as is to be found in so many European countries—is called for in the United States. I believe it is inevitable that we must provide basic medical services for our citizens without regard to their income. We know, for example, that the inadequate care now available in the United States on such an uncomprehensive basis costs an average of $114 per person per year. Yet in Britain, complete medical care under its universal health insurance system costs only $50 per person annually. President Kennedy's Medicare Program would have been a substantial improvement over present conditions, though still far short of the needs.

Under Mr. Kennedy's plan, insurance benefits would have been available to all persons sixty-five and over who are eligible for Social Security or Railroad Retirement benefits. For example, these payments would have provided hospital and nursing home services, outpatient clinic diagnostic services for all charges in excess of $20, and community visiting nurse services for a limited time. It did not cover doctors' bills. Medical care for the aged, through the Social Security system, would greatly benefit millions of minority citizens, both in kinds of services and in increasing the dignity and self-respect of each individual by aiding his independence.

There is no use in attempting to frighten Negro citizens with the bugaboo of socialized medicine. After all, most Negroes have been dependent for decades on the meager beneficences of medical care provided by society. They know from experience how bad it can be; they seldom have had an opportunity to discover the superiority of the finest care available through our capitalistic system. And frankly, there seems to be nothing on the horizon that will bring such splendid care within their reach unless a comprehensive medical insurance plan is enacted.

I do not mean to imply that, when needed, the care given under public medical programs may not involve the most expensive specialists, drugs, diagnostic equipment, and remedial attention. But the public clinics to which the majority of Negroes must go are enough

201

to discourage all but the most desperate. Clinics are open only during working hours, so a Negro fortunate enough to have a job must take off perhaps half a day. He then finds that he is one of a horde of people whose ailments run the gamut, all waiting in inadequate quarters for their brief moment with the doctors-in-training. His possibilities of seeing a specialist are small; his chances to see the same doctor on a return visit extremely poor, and the likelihood of follow-up on conditions requiring continuing surveillance and care are almost nonexistent. The survival of so many of our citizens under such inadequate and discouraging circumstances is testimony to the sheer hardihood of the human body and the tenacity of the human spirit.

In the view of the health field from the perspective of the Negro citizen, the one word that epitomizes 1964 conditions is shortage. This word applies across the board, to doctors, nurses, dentists, hospitals, hospital beds, health facilities, public health programs and clinics, health education, medical, dental and nursing schools, medical and dental technicians, and specialists of various types. There also exists a deplorable lack of cooperation and coordination in trying to meet these shortages. Few communities have any logical, comprehensive approach to sizing up their health needs and moving to meet them.

The Negro's access to needed medical care is limited in part by the acute shortage of Negro doctors and dentists. Only 2 percent of the nation's physicians are Negroes, and they are concentrated in urban areas to the neglect of the rural areas where Negroes also live. Of course, by any stretch of logic, humanity, or the Hippocratic oath, a physician is a physician, and he should minister to the sick who need him, regardless of their color or of his. In reality white doctors generally see Negro patients only at clinics. Therefore, since there are only 5,140 Negro physicians, each doctor potentially must serve 3,900 Negro citizens. The comparable ratio for the 252,000 white physicians is 1 to 637 whites. Even these figures do not begin to tell the story. Any white who has concluded on the basis of his own experience that his doctor works long hours and is over-burdened is right; but consider the situation of the Negro doctor in South Carolina where there are 12,500 Negroes who need his help. In Mississippi, the ratio is one doctor per 18,500 Negroes; picture, if you can, fifty-seven Negro doctors trying to give medical care to one million Negro Mississippians. In order to equalize the situation, at least 23,000 additional Negro doctors would be needed in the nation. In dental care, current conditions are even worse. There are 1,800 Negro dentists (there were 1,773 in 1930), so the ratio is about one per 11,000 Negro citizens nationwide. To meet the current population needs reasonably well, at least seven thousand more dentists are needed. No wonder that Negroes average less than half a visit per person to the dentist every year, in contrast to their white counterparts who face the dentist three times as often. With so few dentists to serve them, it is understandable that 45 percent of the visits by Negroes involve extractions vs. 16 percent of those by whites. Actually, a recent National Health Survey showed that 80 percent of Negroes did not visit the dentist during that year and 37 percent had never seen a dentist.

Nurses, of course, are in short supply also. Today about 5,000 more Negro nurses are needed by the nation's hospitals. But here, so far as the Negro is concerned, the picture is more promising. Since 1946 the nursing profession has exerted itself with great success to integrate on every level. In fact, in 1951 the National Association of Colored Graduate Nurses voluntarily dissolved itself, and its members were welcomed into the American Nurses Association. Negroes now serve in the ANA at all levels—staff, members of the board, etc. The organization has taken advanced positions in moving against discrimination both in the ranks of nursing and in the health organizations in which nurses serve.

Evidence like the above statistics indicates to me that the medical and dental profession are lacking in social conscience. How could these professions have allowed the current serious shortages of qualified personnel to develop? Negroes are not being trained in medicine or dentistry in anything like the numbers required—nor are whites. In 1956, only 2.7 percent of the nation's medical students and even fewer dental students were Negroes. From 1956 to 1962 the increase in the number of Negroes studying medicine in the United States was exactly ten students per year. Subsequently, there was a drop of enrollment by Negro students in white medical schools of eighty students per year—more than one-third.

I am not advocating the training of more Negro doctors and

dentists in order to perpetuate Jim-Crow medicine, nor am I endorsing the misguided theory that Negroes should minister to Negroes. Far from it. The need is for more doctors, dentists, and nurses, whatever their color—more real professionals who are sympathetic to all races in their attitudes and orientation. At present, the social framework has largely frozen the pattern of white physicians treating whites and Negroes receiving care from Negro physicians.

This situation must change, and rapidly. For even if a crash program to train Negro doctors and dentists is inaugurated in 1964 and continues until the requirements are filled, it will be a quarter of a century before an appreciable equalization of patient load occurs. For the foreseeable future it is more than likely that there will be enough Negro physicians to care for only 25 percent of the needs of Negroes. No thinking person, no helping profession, no humane government can coldly write off the medical requirements of 75 percent of the Negro population as impossible to meet because of custom, individual whim, professional "ethics" or, in a word, prejudice. We shall be bound, inevitably, to depend heavily upon white doctors, white health workers, "white" health institutions.

I have confidence that the white community will recognize the importance of lifting the general level of health in the urban centers of the nation. It will see with increasing clarity that improving the health, sanitation, living conditions, and education of the ghetto dwellers has a direct effect upon the health and well-being of even those farthest removed from the ghetto. I have never understood how citizens of some of the most advanced cities in the world could countenance the conditions that prevail among slum dwellers. For it is this pool of labor that washes their children, pets, clothing, dishes, homes, rooms and offices, that serves their meals, runs their elevators, drives their cars and cabs, and serves them personally.

Inescapably, the ill health of these "personal service" workers must spread to those whom they serve. We seldom have instances of plagues spreading throughout a city from such sources, fortunately. Yet last year's outbreak of typhoid at the Swiss resort, Zermatt, was just such a case. And public health authorities will verify the general accuracy of the main thesis. Therefore, I fully expect to see a vastly intensified concentration of effort on upgrading the well-being of the ghetto-bound. In this country, as we have noted, Negro health workers are insufficient in numbers to do the job.

Without question, we must bring more youngsters into the medical profession. Not long ago, Negroes were discouraged from entering medical training by the extraordinary burden of its expense, and the near-impossibility of enrolling at first-class "white" medical schools and serving internships at top-ranking "white" hospitals. In addition, the problem of qualifying on the entrance examinations was nearly insuperable. In the first place, they were drawn up for use with offspring of the white urban middle class; and in the second, the inadequate education of Negroes in general effectively minimized the number aspiring to medical careers.

Recent studies show that "white" medical schools could train up to two hundred more Negro students each year. The problem, we learn, is that they cannot find enough Negro youngsters who can pass the standard Medical College Admissions Test. In fact, the mean MCAT scores of Negro youngsters accepted by the medical schools of Howard and Meharry are the same as the mean MCAT scores of applicants rejected by all U.S. medical schools taken as a whole. This serves to point out both the inferior quality of education meted out to Negro students below the medical school level, and, as I have stated earlier, the inadequacy of such standardized tests to provide valid criteria of the intelligence and potential of Negro students. As we have noted, efforts to find and aid youngsters with potential at the high school level are needed to counteract this situation.

Today almost all medical schools have opened their doors. But the problem of entrance for the Negro remains, largely because of inferior educational preparation. There is another factor today, however, and that is disinterest. Not many Negro youths are motivated toward medical careers, and the reasons for this lack of motivation are rooted in discrimination. Too few Negro families have the money to send a child to study medicine at a cost of $2,400 per year or more, for six years. Too few Negro families have the appreciation of education that moves a youngster into an academic career with enthusiasm.

It is not enough simply to open the doors to the medical schools with the assumption that Negroes will now queue up to enter.

There was a time when bright, highly motivated Negro youths could enter only Meharry and Howard medical schools. The rebuffs of half a century are not instantly forgotten, and there are many successful Negroes today whose attitudes toward the "white" medical schools are negative because of some personal experience or the previous rejection of a friend or relative. These attitudes are passed on to their children.

So if the present pattern of indifference to medical careers is to be changed the medical schools must bestir themselves. They must seek, reach out, identify, and aid those who appear to have potential for careers in medicine, dentistry, nursing, and medical technology. And they must start their quest at the high school level or below. They will need to launch a persuasive indoctrination campaign to change the outlook of thousands of Negro youngsters toward medicine. After all, many of them have had experience with doctors perhaps only in school or at the clinic. Again, the economics of Negro family life have made association with doctors something that occurs usually when disaster strikes and death often follows. If they have observed doctors at work, they have probably seen some of the most harried, overworked professional men and women in the nation. It may not be easy to convince them that they should elect to follow an arduous, time-consuming course of education to such an end.

Programs of vocational guidance at the high school level can be useful to orient Negro youths to the positive rewards of health careers. The many opportunities in the health profession, for lab and X-ray technicians, dental assistants, physical and occupational therapists, are attractive and pay well. Along with the encouragement of young people must go attention to the attitudes of their parents. At present parents tend to focus their sights and those of their youngsters on the goals of physician and dentist exclusively. They know too little about the other health occupations and the fact that financial aid is available for those who train to be therapists, technical operatives, nurses, nutritionists, health educators and administrators.

It should be clear that programs to encourage more Negroes to enter the health field as professionals or as skilled or semi-skilled technicians will ultimately be only as successful as the removal of prejudice in hospitals and health agencies is genuine. When it comes to the elimination of discrimination, Negroes are all from Missouri. They want to be shown. After generations of bitter experiences they are understandably skeptical. Therefore the health agency or facility that uses all the right words and phrases and none of the practices to implement them does a disservice to itself and to the entire profession.

Today, unlike a half-dozen years ago, Negro medical graduates have no difficulty finding internships at excellent hospitals. The same is true concerning residencies. The fact is that American hospitals have about five thousand more internships available than there are medical graduates to fill them. Nowadays the Negro physician may intern at any one of a wide range of hospitals. The fact that careers in medicine are beckoning to Negro youths is encouraging. But the health needs of millions of Negro citizens cannot wait. Nor should they.

Because voluntary desegregation of health facilities has been so slow, the need so overwhelming and the experience with desegregation of the schools so agonizing, I see no alternative to pressure from the federal and state authorities to bring about equality of medical treatment in our time. A strong force for improvement should be the Public Health Service of the Department of Health, Education and Welfare. This important agency in the health field has not distinguished itself in the battle to eliminate segregation. Few Negroes have been hired for its uniformed corps or as professional civilian employees. And in its relationships with the health departments of the states this agency could bring its weight to bear in favor of integration by a ban on financing any and all health projects which permit discrimination.

The Public Health Service grants research funds totaling millions of dollars annually to hospitals, clinics, research facilities at universities and other institutions. The time is long since past when American tax dollars should have been assigned with a view to using them only in facilities where segregation is not practiced. Important as medical research is, there are first-rate facilities available in which discrimination is not practiced; and/or such facilities can be built. Prejudice must not be underwritten and extended with public tax money. Through administrative order of the Surgeon

207

General, federal grants for health education, research or service could be restricted to institutions in which discrimination and segregation have no place. The leadership position of the U.S. Public Health Service makes such action vitally important.

The Public Health Service also has funds, projects grants and experts for consultation. It is to this agency that communities may wish to look for aid in improving health conditions in congested areas. This may be done through the local health department, working with the state health department and the regional office of the Public Health Service. Federal money is available to develop community service projects and to train personnel; it may be requested by local, county, and state public health services, private, voluntary, and nonprofit organizations, hospitals, and universities. Too many communities have spent too little effort to initiate programs to deal with existing problems. The federal backstopping indicated here should be investigated and employed wherever possible.

However, this brings up the Public Health Service grant review procedures. These are so complicated and labyrinthine that only those experienced in "grantsmanship" can hope for success in applying for support. An interesting situation, which raises the question of conflict of interest, is to be found in the grant procedure. It happens that the millions paid by the Public Health Service to finance projects every year are concentrated in relatively few universities and state health departments. It also happens that most of the consultants to the panels that pass upon grant applications come from these same organizations. As of this writing, it is safe to say that the Negro population is under-represented on these review panels and among their consultants. Here again, administrative courage can correct this situation with ease and speed.

There are some encouraging signs in the health field. Some communities have set up commissions on human relations or civil rights and have acted to end discrimination in medical institutions. In Detroit and Chicago such agencies have been effective. In Detroit, the advisory committee on hospitals studied all available facilities including schools of medicine and nursing. The committee found no hospital in the area free of biased practices in all of its operations.

To prevent extension of segregation to new facilities, the committee worked out an agreement with the Michigan Office of Hospitals and Construction (the state agency administering Hill-Burton funds) that no hospitals in the state would receive public funds for building any facility unless it could produce evidence that it was operating without racial bias in serving people, or would submit a covenant that it would operate openly. The state office drafted a model resolution of nondiscrimination and this must be adopted by hospitals which expect funds under the Hill-Burton Act.

The committee was also successful in prevailing on the Executive Committee of the Greater Detroit Area Hospital Council to recommend by resolution open policy and practice by member hospitals and adoption by them of the resolution. The council plans and coordinates health activities for seventy member hospitals in metropolitan Detroit.

In 1960 an urban redevelopment plan calling for a medical center to be located on two hundred acres in the heart of Detroit was stalled by controversy. The plan included centers for medical research, education, and services, and at hearings of the Detroit Common Council the plan was endorsed as worthwhile; but three organizations refused to approve it until three of the four hospitals involved in the project eliminated their biased practices. These hospitals, the key elements in the plan, adopted the nondiscrimination policy resolution mentioned above, and this was accepted by all concerned as satisfactory evidence that Jim-Crow practices would be eliminated. The Detroit Council thereupon approved the plan.

There are many other avenues that can be pursued to root out discrimination. Millions of dollars annually are allocated in grants from industry and foundations to institutions which discriminate. Grantors should carefully review their programs with the clear objective of using them to promote integration rather than to continue, endorse, and nourish racial bias. These millions of dollars, dedicated to humanitarian ends, should be used from start to finish in a truly democratic manner. There is no reason why the staffs—administrative, technical, and professional—of recipient institutions should not be hired, employed, promoted, paid, and assigned in a wholly open and nondiscriminatory way. To do less is to turn against the basic teaching that medicine is to help all who need its ministrations.

Another useful approach is that of the state of Illinois, which denies tax exemption to hospitals with discriminatory practices—a move for all states to take. But realistically, since such action is not likely, it would be more expeditious to have the Internal Revenue Service rule out the tax exempt status of all hospitals and medical facilities, teaching and educational institutions that are indulging in racial discrimination. Tax exemption is, in effect, a subsidy from all the people to facilities supposedly of benefit to all citizens. The tax-exempt institution that denies its facilities to any segment of the public deserves no support from that segment. Thus, until some means is found to reduce its tax exemption by some amount proportionate to its exclusion of a portion of the public, the institution should be denied the favored treatment, the subsidy, that tax exemption constitutes.

Representation of Negroes on health committees, boards, and agencies is absolutely mandatory for fair use of health facilities by the Negro population. It is these boards that either establish fair policies or idly sit back and ignore—thereby condoning—practices that are detrimental and discriminatory. The presence of a qualified representative of the Negro minority is not only a constant reminder to committee members of their democratic responsibilities, but, regrettably, in many cases the only way to insure equitable dispensation of services.

The professional associations in the health field have varying records on the matter of discrimination. We have noted the excellent record of the Nurses Association, which has worked to effect integration at both state and local levels. The American Public Health Association has gone on record against discrimination and filed a brief in favor of Negro physicians who brought the historic action against the hospital in Greensboro, N.C. But the APHA is not aggressively moving toward integration.

The American Dental Association a couple of years ago passed a resolution calling upon state and local units of the organization to allow Negro dentists to join them—with unreported results.

The American Medical Association has taken the classical ostrich position, with its head in the sands of status quo and its body exposed to justifiable kicks and barbs. It continues to give tacit approval, by its silence, to barriers against staff appointments for Negroes in hospitals and to exclusion of Negroes from county units

210

of the AMA. The association could be a tremendous force for promoting integration by such action as testifying before Congress in favor of appropriate legislation, it could move hospitals and health agencies toward integration by insisting on antidiscrimination clauses in charters, articles of incorporation, etc. So far it has not done so.

In summary, the health of the Negro in America will be improved most by improvement in his total living conditions: his income, housing, education, and opportunities. His well-being cannot be separated from these determining factors, and changes in them will be basic to any meaningful improvement.

Furthermore, segregation and discrimination in health services, we have found, are generally consistent with, and dependent upon, community patterns—and the courage or timidity of leadership and institutions in the communities. The classical study of *Negroes and Medicine*[7] showed that:

> The highest degree of integration was found in communities with influential individuals who were fighting for integration at crucial points. Even more important . . . in all communities where key persons were actively interested in integration definite progress had been made. In communities lacking these interested persons, no pro-integration changes had occurred.[8]

Certainly this emphatically underlines the importance of individual effort to bring about equal opportunity for health. The world cannot afford the sacrifice of a single Charles Drew on the pyre of prejudice. Why should we permit it?

[7] Dietrich C. Reitzes, *Negroes and Medicine*, Harvard University Press, 1958.

[8] Dietrich C. and H. Reitzes, "Factors which block or facilitate integration in the field of medicine," *Interracial Review*, Sept. 1960, p. 199.

"The greatest crime against man is not to deny him, but to keep him from even wanting."
Leo Tolstoy

8
Leadership: The Responsibilities of Citizenship

In Baltimore, an important Chamber of Commerce official said to me recently, "Negroes will soon have the political majority in this city and will elect public officials without the aid of other voting factions. How can we be sure that they will elect responsible people to office?"

My reply was, "Don't wait! Appoint and elect qualified Negroes to responsible positions now. Give them experience. Because if you wait, you are likely to have a repetition of what happened in Boston when the Irish finally achieved a popular majority. They repeatedly elected James Michael Curley mayor even after he was convicted and sentenced to jail."

This situation is not unique. History has shown that no racial or nationality group has a monopoly on altruism or selfishness. The group that finally makes a political breakthrough after being deprived of participation in self-government is seldom notable for responsibility. Up to now, most cities have only grudgingly given Negroes political positions of consequence. And Negroes generally haven't achieved sufficient sophistication to go after important policy positions. We are generally fighting for posts on the city council or board of education when we ought also to be going after positions on the city planning commission or urban renewal board. These are just two of the dozens of highly significant committees where decisions are made that will affect the community from now on into the twenty-first century.

But Negroes rarely hear of openings on such boards, and because we do not, we are not represented on them. City officials know what committees are important. They know whether Negroes are getting administrative and political experience or not, and they should see to it that Negroes do get such background and do represent their constituents in these important matters.

To put the need for such action in perspective, consider that in just five years, by the time youngsters born in 1964 are starting kindergarten, the Negro population of the United States will be twenty-two million. Eleven million Negroes will be concentrated in fifteen urban areas—cities like Baltimore, Chicago, Detroit, Cleveland, Los Angeles, Houston, and Dallas. With the flight of the white middle class to the suburbs, the central cities will more and more consist of the lower socio-economic groups in which Negroes make up a disproportionately large percentage. Thus the balance of political power in the major cities of the nation will more and more gravitate into the hands of Negroes. So the question of whether we sit and wait for the breakthrough or prepare for it is pressingly pertinent today.

In the urban life in which most Americans are participants, leadership by Negro citizens is urgently required. We must appreciate and encourage those Negroes who move effectively into the overall civic, social, and political life of their communities, carrying broad citizen responsibilities. Gary, Indiana, is one American city that is setting the pace in this regard. Here, with 42 percent of its 190,000 population, Negroes serve as president of the city council, hold one-third of the one hundred appointive positions on twenty municipal boards and commissions, and are represented in the mayor's cabinet. Among the key positions held by Negroes in Gary

215

are those of city engineer, housing commissioner, deputy controller, FEPC director, director of the youth commission, chief of city planning, assistant city attorney, assistant director of general services, city engineer inspector, assistant city electrical inspector and judgeships.

Appointments such as these should be made in cities all over the land. They are in line with the *special effort* we have called for. Qualified Negroes should be sought and named to all public and private boards and commissions and particularly those that shape policy in the areas of employment, housing, education, and health and welfare services—the areas in which the racial differential is greatest, and the need for dramatic change is most urgent.

To achieve this objective, strong leadership within the Negro community must be developed. This leadership then will be ready to step into the vanguard of the teamwork effort demanded in resolving the smoldering problems of the civil rights struggle.

Negro citizens are challenged under the domestic Marshall Plan as never before. They are challenged first to recognize that no Negro, however privileged or economically well-to-do, is permanently secure until the most impoverished Negro in the Harlems of the nation also enjoys economic security and dignity. In other words, a man either rises with his race or he doesn't rise at all on any permanent basis.

Secondly, Negro citizens are challenged to assume the responsibilities of citizenship that go beyond preoccupation with matters of race. Such responsibilities include active participation in community affairs; service in voluntary organizations such as united funds and on boards and committees; running for political offices, and participating in political activity. It means serving at the level of policy making and policy implementation. We have already seen that a law can be passed, but unless we are actually serving in a role to influence its execution, we still are not effectively helped or helping.

Concerning citizenship responsibility, Negroes might have wanted to serve in the past, but the question was how. Community leadership was not in the hands of Negroes but was controlled by the majority group "downtown." This meant that only those

Negroes considered safe and reliable liaison persons were tapped for participation.

In the past, Negro leadership was identified by the white community as those persons whose value systems most closely paralleled their own. In fact, there was clearly an inverse ratio, or Uncle Tom's Law, in white evaluation of Negro behavior: the Negro whose values were closest to their own was the most responsible; the Negro whose values diverged most from their own was the most irresponsible. What they wanted, of course, was someone safe, flexible, not a "troublemaker," preferably someone in a vulnerable position so that he could be managed.

This has changed. Now the majority community is intelligent enough to know that it must deal with Negroes who have earned the respect and leadership of their fellow Negro citizens. The day of using the maid as a reliable liaison person has passed. So too has the use of the corner shoeshine boy or elevator operator or the minister to whose segregated church regular contributions were made.

Today's rapidly changing situation calls for a realignment of values for Negroes as well as for whites. For decades Negroes set their standards by other Negroes. In terms of professional goals, they set out to be a good Negro doctor, a good Negro lawyer or a good Negro teacher. And in this way they pegged their goals much lower than the American norm. They did not continue to learn and study and go to clinics and summer school and read the new books in their fields because their goals were confined within this one compartmentalized group. And the Negro community did not demand more of them. Most often it could not, for it knew no other criteria to apply. All too often the excellence of a professional person was judged by how much business he had, or by the impressiveness of his car or home.

Another important shift is occurring. Unlike the white community where the power structure is built around the business sector, the Negro community had no comparable merchant, trade, or industrial groups. This meant that the Negro's status models necessarily were professional people. So the Negro school principal or doctor or head of a social agency occupied a completely unrealistic position of prestige and was considered a top-status person. More and more the middle-class Negro is readjusting his value system. His status and position in the Negro community are increasingly related to his intervention in and contribution to the civil rights cause as well as to his professional competence.

Another challenge to Negro citizens is in their roles as parents. It isn't enough to duplicate the behavior they have seen as they worked as maids in the homes of white people. The Negro is challenged to be more active in school affairs, in PTAs, in supplementing the school and helping the child at home. He is faced with making necessary sacrifices to provide broadening experiences for the child by travel, camps, books, and encyclopedias; by conscious attempts at discussion and dialogue in the home; by helping the child to read and to participate by serving as a role model. The child learns by example more than by exhortation.

To the extent that Negroes participate in PTA and school board activity will their children get the new facilities, the teachers, the books, and the aid in preparing for vocations and merit examinations which they require. On PTA night at the schools parents and teachers are supposed to discuss students and their school. In New Rochelle we found that at Lincoln School when it was all Negro, the teachers would sit there half the night and not see a parent. But at Davis, an integrated school, the teacher can't give a parent more than five minutes because there are so many waiting. This kind of interest keeps both teacher and parents informed and alert. Interestingly enough, more Negro parents go to PTA meetings in the integrated schools, and they line up just like the white parents to see the teacher.

Still another challenge concerns the need for a diversified approach to civil rights programs. While there will be those who, in the interests of justice and equality, must walk the picket lines in front of restaurants, hotels, theaters, business establishments, and so on, these same persons and others must, with equal zest and determination walk on to the libraries, to the decision-making bodies, to the retraining facilities, to the health and welfare centers, to adult education programs, to the schools and colleges, and to the voter registration booths. And they must take time to serve on policy-making bodies of agencies and institutions.

I am not offering a substitute, or an either/or suggestion. Many approaches are necessary. The real test, therefore, of the sincerity and maturity of all of us now participating in this struggle will be our willingness to labor in the vineyards where we are not televised, interviewed, and photographed and where our contributions may not make popular news copy.

Increasing numbers of Negro women are willing to volunteer a few hours a week to tutor youngsters who bear the scars of generations of deprivation. Thus, they are making a lasting contribution to the struggle which is as important in its ramifications as that made by the gallant heroes who go to jail, or those who protest in the streets.

Negro citizens themselves, adults as well as young people, must maintain and even accelerate the sense of urgency that now characterizes the drive for first-class citizenship. Every opportunity for the acquisition of education and technical skills must be utilized. Every means of strengthening the social and economic fabric of the Negro community must be employed.

Negroes are challenged, therefore, to see that the barriers of yesterday—barriers built by prejudice, fear, and indifference that are now crumbling—are not replaced by new barriers of apathy, of underdeveloped skills or aptitudes or lack of training. If this happens, our gains will be but temporary, our victories hollow.

While it is understandable that Negro citizens are reluctant to run the risk of alienation and isolation in new integrated situations, nevertheless if we are to break the pattern, then more adventurous and confident action must be initiated. A good example of this is for Negroes to capitalize upon housing opportunities as they become available in previously all-white communities. Often the availability of such homes is the result of many weeks and months of hard work by volunteer fair housing committees, and Negroes must respond— with equal energy and enthusiasm—to these efforts.

We have suffered a great deal, and still do, from the notion that there was and had to be a monolithic approach to the problem of race relations. For generations the Negro was shut off from other avenues, or had limited knowledge of alternatives. Religion was viewed as the instrument through which the oppressor would either

219

see the light or be punished. Religion, we were told—and we believed—was the only answer.

Many Negroes still lack sophistication about society and social change and the role of money and how power shifts. This is understandable because we have been excluded from the economic decisions of business, labor, and various levels of government. But a Negro population reflecting increased intelligence and maturity and determined to be free must assess realistically the changed character of its problems and leadership.

There are forces inexorably at work, forces such as automation, urbanization, and many others that on the surface are indifferent to race. Unless these forces are clearly identified and remedial steps are taken, the masses of Negroes five years from today will find themselves with a mouthful of civil rights, living in hovels, with empty stomachs.

We must think today not in terms of individual leaders or the approach, but of levels of leadership involving many people, with a variety of approaches and tactics. The issue must now be not which approach, but how we can intelligently deploy our forces, establish roles, and divide the labor in approaches on all levels.

Negro leaders on several levels have now emerged.

First, there is the older, successful professional or businessman whose role is no longer that of a liaison person appointed by the white power structure. This person is now a symbolic role model, with the potential for substantial financial and moral support of the civil rights movement. He can also be an effective channel of communication if he understands the new climate and is willing to interpret it honestly.

Second, there are those who really make the issues—the "confronters" and "protesters." Included are Rosa Parks in Montgomery; the plaintiffs in the 1954 Supreme Court decision; the students who sit in, the Freedom Riders who go to jail, and those who organize and walk the picket lines. All of these are needed, for without them there would be no court cases to fight, no issues to dramatize the injustices, nothing around which to mobilize public opinion.

Third, we have the strategists, planners, and researchers, sophisticated in the nuances of social change, knowledgeable about the social sciences and economics, aware of community resources and skilled in mobilizing and organizing the community to take advantage of these resources. These are the people who can participate in policy-making and implementation, who read and understand the fine print, not only of a civil rights law, but also of laws covering retraining, public welfare, health, youth employment, vocational education, urban renewal, educational policy, minimum wages, and fiscal policies. They are trained in these fields, and they have chosen to work as paid full-time professionals in race relations or to serve without pay as volunteers.

Obviously the educators, small businessmen, and professional people of the first level of leadership are to be found in every community. The second level we usually think of as represented by the student movements, the Southern Christian Leadership Conference, CORE, the Student Non-Violent Coordinating Committee and, to a greater degree than realized, the NAACP which pioneered many of these techniques before the other groups came on the scene.

The third level of leadership is best represented by the Urban League, although in legislative activity and legal action the NAACP and the NAACP Legal Defense Fund are most effective professionals.

There is another leadership group to which all should aspire, though its members are not technically leaders in race relations. These are the Negro citizens who achieve excellence in their chosen fields and who become role models or Negro heroes. Their participation in the civil rights struggle is a strong plus factor and identifies them as sensitive and intelligent human beings who know that they can never be secure until every individual Negro is secure.

This was pointedly illustrated not long ago when the son of Nobel Prize winner and United Nations Under-secretary Ralph Bunche was rejected by the West Side Tennis Club in Forest Hills, New York, when he sought tennis instruction there. Dr. Bunche himself, while visiting Atlanta in 1962, was denied accommodations at a major hotel while a white man wearing overalls was being registered.

The educationally privileged middle-class Negro will share the horrors and hardships of his more handicapped working-class brother as long as racism exists in our society.

221

The great danger of the emerging Negro middle class is that it will not identify with rank and file Negroes. The economic gap between the two groups is not only great, but it is growing. In the white community the rise from low-income status to upper is marked by various levels between the two extremes. For the Negro there is no in-between status; if he makes the grade, he jumps directly from lower-class to higher, with no way stations. All too often the Negro faces a choice between being a highly skilled technician or professional and being a waiter, porter, or domestic; between a desirable house in the suburbs and a tenement in the slums; between acceptance by heads of government or rejection by callous and indifferent human beings.

For generations in the South an established middle-class Negro leadership group has existed that could identify with the masses they represented. They were subjected to the same pressures as the lower-class Negro group because of skin color. They were both fighting something that neither could escape. They couldn't get into schools, restaurants, theaters, parks, beaches, and so on. The enemy, prejudice, was clearly visible. There were laws. There were signs. Or the whites told you what was off limits so that there was never any doubt about who and where the enemy was. There was easy communication between Negro middle class and rank and file because they had a common cause.

In the North, communication between the Negro masses and the Negro middle class is more difficult because the common cause is not so easily identified. The Negro who has money in the North can go to the shows and schools in many cities, and to the theaters, hotels, and restaurants. He can often escape the slums and move to the suburbs, if he can afford it. The enemy in the North is rarely visible and overt. Discrimination is subtle, not by Jim-Crow signs. It is more frustrating, therefore, in the North because the enemy is not tangible. We still suffer from inadequate housing, clothing, food, health, and income—and from fear. At the same time, most public officials talk like Frederick Douglass, the Negro abolitionist, and so do the other politicians. White people are nice, and they smile and speak to us and all the laws guaranteeing equality of treatment are on the books. Yet we're hurting just as much—that's the frustrating, maddening thing. For the Negro citizen who has looked to the North as his last hope, who takes all he can in the South and finally comes to the "land of freedom" to escape discrimination, this experience with amorphous prejudice is the final blow. He has the feeling of utter hopelessness, as though he has reached the end of a gangplank over the side of a ship: he will either turn and fight or jump off into extremism or anti-social conduct.

Then, too, there is grave danger of alienation of middle-class Negroes from the masses. This alienation works both ways. The middle-class Negro often (sometimes unconsciously) disassociates himself from the Negro rank and file, not because of personal dislike, but because the masses symbolize a phase of history that he wants to forget. To the middle-class Negro, the black ghetto means discrimination, embarrassment, humiliation, second-class citizenship, and inferiority. He withdraws from this not so much to escape the Negro rank and file as to escape the trappings and status of that way of life.

But the Negro masses see the flight of the middle-class Negro from their neighborhoods as a desire to turn his back on his fellows. And this, of course, causes tension between the two groups. This is a matter of increasing concern, for the middle-class Negro's flight often results in a loss of leadership that is needed to inspire and uplift the group that cannot afford escape. Yet, those middle-class Negroes who do maintain their interest are suspect. "Why do you get involved in my problem?" ask the rank and file, "you're not really affected by it." And these suspicions are fanned by the demagogue who deliberately plays on fears to strengthen his own position, thus keeping competent leaders from challenging him.

Today, almost without exception, the leadership of the Negro's civil rights struggle is drawn from the middle-class group. But because of the widening alienation of the classes, there is a danger that each class may at times be working toward different goals. For instance, rank and file Negroes often favor building new schools and public housing projects in or near their ghetto districts. As a result, they clash with middle-class Negroes who may oppose locating such buildings near the ghetto because they regard this as strengthening segregation instead of weakening it. The Negro masses are focusing on the tangible benefits of such facilities, regardless of where they may be built.

223

On the other hand, middle-class Negroes have symbolic or status goals to which the rank and file may be completely indifferent. The opening to Negro use of a segregated rest room in a Southern airport may be meaningful to middle-class Negroes primarily because of its symbolic importance. The masses may be completely indifferent to the victory, because they are concerned with reality or welfare goals.

I have found that the best way to bring Negroes of all levels to appreciate and understand the need for a diversified approach to civil rights progress is to speak frankly. We now know that we are not going to solve all of our problems through protest alone. Five years from now the Negroes' adversaries won't need the signs and laws and restrictions that segregate. If we let things take the course they are taking now, we shall hear: "Sure, you can move into this neighborhood—if you can pay for the house; sure, you can come into this hotel, or restaurant, or golf course—if you've got the money; sure, you're welcome in this factory—if you've got the skills; sure, your child can go to the college—if he makes the grades and passes the college entrance exams." And there will be one or two Negroes in all these places to "prove" that there is no discrimination.

At that point the conventional methods of protest will be useless. No legal action, no sit-ins, no picketing will help, because nobody will be stopping us on the basis that we are Negroes. But Negroes are intelligent enough to see this happening; we now know that we have to do something more than just protest. We have to make sure that when our adversaries are finally willing to serve us a cup of coffee we *will* be able to pay for it.

Give the Negroes credit for being as aware as the men in the labor unions. They fought just as we have: they boycotted, they picketed, and some of them died. Finally they won 'their rights.' They got the Wagner Act, and the companies recognized the unions. But labor was still losing because it was sending to the bargaining table people whose basic qualifications were that they had been in a union many years and had come up from the rank and file. They were bargaining and trying to negotiate with management's Harvard-trained lawyers on technical economic matters.

224

Finally, labor hired competent representatives. The steel workers, for example, hired Arthur Goldberg who had a law degree from Northwestern, and was a Phi Beta Kappa. Though he had never seen the inside of a steel plant, he immediately became a top negotiator. When management started talking about gross national product and accelerated depreciation, he and others like him knew exactly what they were talking about, and the balance began to shift.

Negroes know they have to follow suit. No longer does a black face and a loud voice qualify one for leadership, any more than does a white face and a kind heart. Nowadays, basic decisions are being made, and where they are made something other than these superficial qualities is called for. In conferences when a statistic is cited, there are immediate questions as to the size of the sample, how representative was the population from which the sample was taken, what was the research design, and so on.

Today it isn't a case of the Urban League or the NAACP or CORE; it's the Urban League and. Negro citizens these days are sophisticated and mature enough to know that we need direct-action groups for protests, and the Urban League to see to it that our children stay in school and are prepared for real careers.

In this connection, the masses of Negro citizens are being presented a choice as to the most practical and effective methods for achieving full freedom and equal opportunity with all other American citizens. One method is to seek the solution within the framework of Negro society itself. The other is through cooperative effort with others committed to our objectives.

The first point of view has been identified with the Black Nationalists. It says that the problem of discrimination can be solved if the Negro will simply withdraw from any association with non-Negro citizens, especially if the non-Negro is in a controlling or equal relationship with Negroes. It goes farther and declares that we should not even accept non-Negro money, for money carries along with it control.

This approach indicts all non-Negroes as evil and implies that honesty and virtue are qualities possessed only by Negroes. It is interesting that this approach does not suggest resigning from all

225

jobs not controlled by Negroes, or vacating homes not owned by Negroes, or even severing relationships with the United States Congress or certain political parties that are hardly controlled by Negroes.

If it were not for the crucial problems immediately facing the masses of Negro citizens and for the forces at work that go beyond overt discrimination and prejudice, we could easily dismiss and ignore this approach as the ranting of demagogues and malcontents. These attitudes could be attributed to little people, frustrated in their attempts to gain national power or respect, who strike out wildly and irresponsibly, using any device to achieve their selfish ends.

But these are not normal times. The Negro today is at a most critical point in relation to his economic future. Without money, decent housing and even education become unfulfilled, unattainable dreams. In this situation, millions of people are suffering, and the reasons are not easily explained to them. They are easy prey for the demagogues preaching simple hate against the white man, just as the Southern poor whites are always easy marks for the demagogues preaching hate against the Negro.

But suppose we separated Negro resources from white. Suppose we decided to work for no organization or institution that we do not control financially or managerially. Suppose we chose to live only in housing controlled by Negro citizens or to educate our children only in such institutions, or to use only health and welfare resources which we command. I don't need to cite the figures on our economic inability to follow such a course in order to point up the monumental folly of such schemes.

Every great institution in our society has benefited from the contribution of Negro Americans. We are an integral part of the fabric of this nation. Our blood, sweat, and tears have gone into the wars to save this country and into the business, educational, and cultural life that have made it great. We cannot give up what our forefathers helped to develop. Our problem today will not be solved by such escape techniques as withdrawal and demagoguery, but rather by intelligent and multifaceted intervention and participation to make the system work for us.

The Negro's destiny in this country is not to identify himself as a bloc against all white citizens. It is rather to ally himself with decent people of good will of every race, color, and creed in a coalition against evil and prejudiced people of whatever race. Our power and leverage rest not in the isolation of our 11 percent of the national population, but in using that 11 percent politically, economically, and morally in such a way as to affect the balance of power in the normal decision-making that goes on in our society.

From time to time the use of the boycott by Negroes is questioned. I have often heard leaders of boycotts accused of demagoguery and irresponsibility by those who do not understand them thoroughly. We have seen boycotts and the threats of boycotts used against school systems to bring about reforms; we have seen boycotts used against public transportation, against merchants, businesses, products and stores. I fail to see how one can make a blanket statement that boycotts are good or bad. They can be used irresponsibly; it is to the credit of Negro leaders and clear evidence of the maturity of the Negro masses that the boycott has generally been used with great responsibility.

The boycott is not used by the Negro as a punitive measure, it is a matter of being morally selective. I do not patronize places that I believe are unclean, whether they are just plain dirty or are selling pornographic literature. And to me a place that doesn't hire Negroes and doesn't give them an equal chance is immoral, undemocratic, and un-American. I refuse to be a party to this practice or to contribute to its continuance. The burden of responsibility is not on the Negro in boycotting such a place, but rather on the management of the store, factory, or industry. I feel perfectly justified in concluding that if a man doesn't change his employment practices he obviously doesn't want my business.

When I tell the merchant the conditions under which I will consider him morally appealing and he in effect says, "To hell with you" by ignoring my statements, then he certainly does not want my business, and I would be offending him and my conscience to trade there. Fortunately, boycotts for moral reasons such as those cited bring participation by hundreds and thousands of whites as well as Negroes. They offer splendid avenues for those who have some feelings of guilt to participate without running any risk. A boycott provides an opportunity for easy exercise of a moral com-

227

mitment and makes the participant feel that he is doing his part in protesting against injustice.

We have found many times, even in the South in cities such as Nashville and Atlanta, that thousands of white people stay away from stores that are being boycotted because they discriminate. These white people might never "witness"—that is take a stand—in any other way. The boycott places action within easy reach, and they willingly participate in it. So we have observed that the employer or merchant must consider that any boycott will include many more people than those of the Negro community alone.

I am convinced that the complex field of social engineering will be the crucial area of the Negro's struggle for equality in the years ahead. The Negro's leaders in this sector must possess emotional stability, healthy motives, and professional training necessary to understand and cope with the complex psychological, social, and economic factors in our society that create poverty, ignorance, prejudice, and deprivation.

Though the bulk of the Negro leadership today has come from the middle class, this does not mean that only this class is capable of producing leaders. No revolution was ever successfully won by the masses alone, yet no revolution was ever successful unless its middle-class leaders had the understanding and support of the rank and file. And the fact of having been born and raised in a Negro community does not automatically qualify a person to lead. Many white people of real dedication are contributing in an important way to the Negro's battle to gain his rights. Here it is a question not of skin color or social background but of ability and personal conviction.

Now that there are Negro leaders who have earned their spurs by proving their dedication to the Negro cause, leaders who are not dependent and who make no concessions to whites in demanding equal rights, whites often bring up the question of responsibility. The leaders of the sit-ins, the Freedom Rides, the kneel-ins, study-ins and boycotts are radical and irresponsible, they say. And in wishful self-delusion they try to convince themselves and the outside world that these problems are all caused by Negro leaders from outside the community stirring up the people. Actually, as observation has proved, the leaders have been providing direction for justified demands.

With great skill, the leaders of the action efforts have managed to keep Negro protests peaceful, loyal, and legal. It has not always been easy, in the face of provocations that would try a saint. In this respect, one of the most encouraging developments has been the scheduling of regular meetings by national leaders of established organizations, including Roy Wilkins, Executive Secretary of the NAACP; Dorothy Height, President of the National Council of Negro Women; James Farmer, Executive Director of CORE; Jack Greenberg, Director of the NAACP Legal Defense Fund; Martin Luther King, Jr., President of the Southern Christian Leadership Conference; James Foreman, Executive Secretary of SNCC; and myself.

The matter of credit for achievement has posed problems. It is a tough matter to resolve when constituency and public support are considered. Some protest groups have refused to stop a demonstration action even though the injustice had been corrected, because the offending party dealt with another organization to resolve the problem. Sometimes we lose sight of the goal in our concern for a leadership image. Such elementary realities as face-saving for the opposition are lost in the concern for tomorrow's headline, next week's fund-raising rally or next month's election. These difficulties rarely pose a problem at the national level, but often do at the local level, particularly when dealing with newer, younger groups whose claim on leadership is less secure because of organizational instability, less training or experience.

Some problems, such as financing, are natural. Until Negroes and liberals generally are willing to match their convictions with their dollars, fund raising will always be a necessary irritant and a possible source of conflict between civil rights organizations.

It is vital that government, philanthropic foundations, business, industry, and labor reassess the extent of their financial support of established organizations committed to securing equal opportunity for Negro citizens to share in the fundamental privileges and rights of American democracy. It is imperative that all of these major sources of financial support substantially increase their contribu-

229

tions to the preventive programs carried on by established, responsible Negro leadership organizations.

Our destiny, if not our survival, depends on our understanding and appreciation of the need and value of the many different levels of leadership. To insist on uniformity would be tragic. To continue the foolish habit of labeling leaders as "militant" or "conservative" is naïve and divisive. Our enemies never make such fine distinctions. We are separately but equally hated by them. There are pitfalls and difficulties enough facing these levels of leadership without the followers attempting to divide them further. It is not always easy to arrive at a meeting of the minds when the minds are those of a minister, an economist, and a lawyer.

The matter of trust depends heavily on maturity and responsibility. The followers of Negro leaders on the various levels are called on to evidence new maturity in this matter. Liberals who happen to be white must accept the fact that the Negro can no longer be dealt with other than on a peer relationship with mutual respect and, when warranted, the Negro in charge. The day of "missionary work," or helping the Negro on condition that he accept and be obedient, is past. The white liberal must trust the Negro leader to have both the desire for a better destiny and a pretty good idea of how to achieve it.

Furthermore, the Negro community must also trust the leadership that they themselves have selected. Negroes learned through bitter experience to suspect the leader who was too popular with the white power structure. But several changes have occurred to modify that earlier situation: today those who really wield power realize they must have the truth; Negroes in positions of policy- and decision-making are not so dependent nor so vulnerable as they once were; any intelligent Negro leader knows he cannot sell out his constituency and get away with it; and he could not live with himself if he did.

*"Until justice is blind to color, until
education is unaware of race, until opportunity
is unconcerned with the color of men's skins,
emancipation will be a proclamation
but not a fact. To the extent that the
proclamation of emancipation is not fulfilled in
fact . . . we shall have fallen short of
assuring freedom to the free."*
Lyndon B. Johnson,
Address at Gettysburg,
May 30, 1963.

*None is watched so suspiciously
as the one who is rising. None has
so little license, needs all his
virtues so much as the leader. And
America for its own security cannot
retreat from leadership.*
Gunnar Myrdal,
An American Dilemma

9
The Social
Revolution
and the
American
Dream

As Americans, we share mixed feelings of pride and anxiety—pride in the magnificent progress that this country has made in a relatively short time, as exemplified, for instance, by the fact that our national standard of living is the highest ever achieved, and that, as a country, we have developed into a major military power. Part of our anxiety stems from a recognition that our military superiority has been open to question. And we are now gravely challenged to make this standard of living universal for all Americans, as well as to share it with the less-developed countries of the world.

As Americans who are largely the products of this last half century, we have participated in two world wars and several smaller military encounters in our devotion to the stated goal of freedom for human beings everywhere. But today we find our motives questioned and our old alliances interpreted as proof of colonial intent.

As Americans we find ourselves, even with our rich resources, and high prosperity, unable to understand the chronic unemployment that still besets us, the need for greater education, health, and welfare services, and the fact that there do exist islands of poverty in our sea of affluence.

We are all challenged in this situation. We are challenged, and we are on trial as Americans to show that all of the freedoms that have been written into our Bill of Rights, all of the freedoms that have been guaranteed in the Constitution, yes, and all of the slogans that we toss around, such as the beautiful inscription on the Statue of Liberty—"Give me your tired, your poor, your huddled masses, yearning to breathe free . . ." that all of these do, in fact, have life and meaning in our society. All of these commitments must now be honored, or we must frankly admit that America is not really guided by ideological concepts of democracy in practice.

Dreams are no novelty for any age, nor are they the unique possession of any individual. Historians may record that our great tragedy was not that our age dreamed, but that our individual dreams were mainly self-centered. We dream of health, wealth, romance, happiness, and other treasures for ourselves, but not for others. Only when the alternatives for us mean higher taxes and personal involvement in war, or when our own interests are threatened, do we consider sharing these dreams with others.

We begin to suspect that our claim to distinction and world leadership may be based on false standards. We have worshipped the gods of science and material advancement until now we see ourselves as almost trapped by the monstrous creations we have devised. Our ability to create has outreached our ability to use wisely the products of our invention. We are learned in the art of war; we are ignorant in the art of peace. We are proficient in the art of killing; we are unskilled in the art of living. We probe and grasp the mystery of atomic fission; we reject the Golden Rule and the Sermon on the Mount.

Inevitably, we are coming to appreciate that there must be a place in our scheme of things for those great intagible human values that cannot be represented on graphs or ledgers. We can no longer gauge our progress solely by the output of machines or the inflow of profits. We have learned that, important as efficiency is in the factory, the happiness and well-being of its workers are even more important.

No standard of living is high when jobs become drudgery and hours dreary; when rancor and bitterness exist between management and labor; when young men and women can't afford a family; when children in slums are walled off by brick from sod and sky; when there is no equality of educational opportunity for every boy and girl; when decent health conditions are not afforded to all of our people. No standard of living is high when we do not fulfill our obligations to the needy, the aged, the crippled, the blind, the dependent and neglected children; when we fail in our duty to the mentally ill; when we deny equal rights to our people because of race, creed, color, or nationality.

With increasing clarity we recognize that our standard of living is an all pervasive condition that all of us share; in whose excesses or deficiencies, glories or abominations, promises or restrictions all of us are participants in one way or another. This is the opposite extreme from wealth that is the store of personal riches excluded from others in society. A standard of living is experienced by all; it cannot be hoarded by one, nor successfully denied to another. Helping any of our citizens serves to advance our own standard of living. This is particularly true in health, welfare, and education—those sister services that liberate and make whole. The special effort we favor to improve materially the living conditions for America's Negroes will inevitably raise the standard of living that all citizens enjoy.

Our progress, technologically, is the marvel of the age and a tribute to our way of life, but the test of our real and lasting greatness will be our willingness now to invest equal vigor, intelligence, and a substantial portion of our treasure in the solution of the economic, social, and cultural problems that our material advances have created.

In spite of great advances in our gross national product, in our overall per capita income, our means of communication, our gadgets, and even in our health and welfare resources, we have not yet assured opportunities for the most creative life for our youth and adults. Indeed, unless these advances are accompanied by other changes in values and a larger sense of responsibility, we may find that we have regressed.

Creative community living becomes a reality only when each individual in that community, from birth to death, has an opportunity to achieve his maximum potential. *What then are some of the barriers that stand in the way of this realization in most of our communities today?* Let me list a few that I consider important:

(1) *Our society is reluctant to face up to certain facts and realities of modern life as they relate to the family:* the changing role of parent-child relationship; the role of women; the increased responsibility of the community in rearing children; the importance of family planning; and the contemporary responsibility and role of religion. Any one of these could be discussed at book length. But the basic point I would make is the futility of the wishful thinking that would solve our present day problems by a return to the "good old days."

It would be much more productive if we spent our time not in trying to turn the clock back, but in improving the quality of parental relationships with children; and in enriching the supplementary community resources that inevitably exercise increased responsibility in training our youth. This would include not just the schools—the formal resources for education—but also such informal resources as the leisure-time agencies where trained staffs with dedicated volunteers provide the kinds of experience whereby values are learned. These agencies can do much to meet the child's normal needs for belonging, for a sense of identity and self-respect.

The day has long since passed when we viewed social agencies as resources only for the socially, economically, and emotionally deprived. Today we know these services to be vital and helpful to all, regardless of socioeconomic class. So our participation and support is no longer a gesture of humanitarian concern, but rather of enlightened self-interest. Coupled with this is a more intelligent approach to family planning. In our time, having children who are wanted, and who can be cared for and given opportunities, need not be an accident. I look forward to the day when our society matures enough to use all the knowledge now available to assure responsible family planning and to make this publicly accessible to everyone both here and abroad.

(2) *A second barrier to a more creative life in our communities is the existence of moral relativism,* or as one writer has put it, "a type of utilitarian ethic," which seems to pervade our whole society. It began very early to afflict the lives of our children and youth. We have seen it described in books such as *The Organization Man, The Lonely Crowd,* or *The Status Seekers.* These carry the strong indictment that our society is overwhelmingly populated by people who are more outer-directed than inner-directed; that behavior is related more to group consensus and represents a Gallup-like poll of majority opinion. As one youngster put it at a White House Conference, "The mores are the right ways, and what we really have is not a survival of the fittest but a survival of the slickest."

Increasingly, the most important commandment seems to be that which states, "Thou shalt not get caught." We create an environment where it is all right to hate, to steal, to cheat, and to lie if we dress it up with symbols of respectability, dignity, and love. Our children reflect what they perceive to be the values in the adult community.

The most significant point to remember is that values are taught in the home and in the community, and are taught more by example than by precept. Forcing a child to lie when a parent does not want to talk to an unwelcome caller; evasion of, and cheating on, income taxes; avoiding responsibility to contribute to community causes; acceptance of unethical and dishonest behavior on the part of politicians; acts of racial or religious intolerance—these are what our young people see in their homes and communities; these are chiefly responsible for the values we see in children and deplore so strongly.

(3) *A third barrier to a more creative life in our communities is that erected by prejudice against other human beings because of their race, religion, nationality, or social class.*

The cost of discrimination is not a simple problem in accounting. Rather, it is like calculating the cost of war, or of ignorance, for it involves not only the tangible factors that can be related in dollars and cents, but also the real values of human beings that have an indeterminable order of magnitude. What is the dollar value lost in the frustration or the stunting of a human personality? How do you

236

measure the bitterness of an eight-year-old Negro girl in 1945, who, when asked by her teacher, "What would be the worst punishment for Hitler?" replied, "Paint him black and make him live in the United States." The fact that segregation places the badge of inferiority on young Negro children is tragic, but almost equally tragic is the fact that it gives the young white child a false impression of being superior to another human being simply because of the accident of birth.

The unhealthy gap between what we preach in America and what we often practice creates a moral dry rot that eats at the very foundations of our democratic ideals and values. What are we doing to the white children of Prince Edward County, Virginia, or of some of the northern suburbs, when we parrot certain clichés in church about Christianity, and in schools about democracy, and then permit them to live a life that negates the brotherly love and belief in equality that we profess?

Furthermore, our stake internationally is overwhelming and frightening. There are twenty-five billion people in this world: one-third of them are committed to communism; one-third to the West; and one-third are uncommitted: a majority of the uncommitted are nonwhite. I believe that these people, some of whom are well trained and sensitive to what is going on in the world, would very much like to ally themselves with America. Unfortunately, they are often disillusioned and made skeptical because of the treatment of the Negro in this country, and because we seem to give first loyalty to old alliances rather than to people.

What we are dealing with here and now is the American Dream. The founding fathers and their generation had a rendezvous with destiny; the mission of today's generation is to open the American Dream to all. This is a time for soul-searching, for a radical change of inner attitudes and outer behavior.

The Negro has viewed the American Dream from the standpoint of his exclusion. Horatio Alger, the chronicler of the classical rags-to-riches success of the American Dream, wrote of and for whites only. Had the hero been a poor Negro ragamuffin who started in the stock room of the Great Man's business firm, applied himself diligently, and worked long hours and weekends, the realistic ending would have been very different. After fifty years of such devotion to duty,

237

instead of finding himself at the head of the company in the typical Alger fashion, he would be lucky to receive retirement instead of dismissal from his position as head of the stock room (now enlarged to three employees). Chances for upward movement into the management of the firm would have been limited by inadequate education, the impossibility of using the golf course with the boss, and as for marrying the boss' daughter...!

Opportunities for upward mobility for Negroes have traditionally been confined to the "footlight professions": music, boxing, sports, entertainment, and other pursuits in which genius can emerge despite limited education.

We shall never know just how prodigal we have been as a nation with Negro brainpower and talent. Almost invariably after I deliver a talk, someone from the audience will corner me and ask, "Well, wouldn't integration be easier to accept if there were some proof that Negroes can achieve, can benefit from education and the special effort you advocate?" With all the restraint I can muster I usually reply that the questioner has been victimized by the lack of information in our schools, books, and communications media about the great historic contributions of individual Negroes to this country.

Consider the fact that the number of Negroes in college has increased from 40,000 in 1940 to 250,000 in 1960. The Negro population has almost doubled in spite of oppression, exploitation, barriers, inconceivably poor conditions of health, welfare, housing, and economic opportunity. In spite of these negative factors, there have been many Negroes of genius who have made outstanding contributions to our nation.

When I think of some of these individual Negroes and their achievements, I quietly compile an illustrious roster of outstanding Americans:

Crispus Attucks, the first casualty of our American revolution, killed in the Boston Massacre of 1770; Denmark Vesey, an American Negro revolutionary, who led a slave rebellion in 1822; Blanche K. Bruce, the first Negro to serve a full term in the U.S. Senate; Matthew Henson, the first American to reach the North Pole; Benjamin Banneker, inventor of the first American clock; Granville T. Woods, whose 150 inventions rivaled Edison's; Charles H. Houston, called one of the great Constitutional lawyers; Judge William

Hastie, Thurgood Marshall; Percy Julian, the chemist; Paul Williams, the architect; educators John Hope Franklin, Abram Harris, Alain Locke, Kenneth Clark; sociologist Charles S. Johnson; abolitionist Frederick Douglass; Walter White; poet Phillis Wheatley; Bishop James A. Healy, Howard Thurman, dean of the chapel of Boston University. And many, many more . . .

The objective of the current social revolution is to broaden the application of the American Dream to our Negro citizens, at long last. Every major city in the United States has felt some manifestation of the unrest and burning desire of its Negro citizens for equality of opportunity—now! And hundreds of smaller communities have reflected the discontent that has been latent, the protest that has spread like wildfire and has illuminated the land with the flames of a modern revolution.

This revolution bears little similarity, however, to the American Revolution or to the French Revolution or to the Russian Revolution. There is no attempt here to overthrow a government. This is a revolution against historic injustice, against an oppressed way of life, against persons who maintain that the measure of achievement of a man is determined by, and related to, the color of skin. This is a revolution peculiarly characterized by a heroic drive and a courageous fight to gain the rights and respect that should be synonymous with the word "American." It is a revolution not by black people against white people, but by people who are right against those who are wrong.

This revolution is unlike others, also, in that, after three hundred years of deprivation, the deprived seek redress for their grievances in an expression of faith in a nation that has done very little to deserve and nurture such faith. Their demands are simple and elemental, and those who would describe them as difficult and complicated do a disservice to America and to Americans.

For the Negro citizen, therefore, his acts bear witness to his faith in democracy by peaceful nonviolent demonstration, and by channeling into constructive ways justified resentments and pent-up, frustrated emotions born of age-old abuses and contemptuous indignities.

For the white citizen the nonviolent revolution means that he must bear witness to the fact that democracy is more than a convenient institution through which privileges and material products flow to him and his.

For both white and Negro citizens, democracy is a way of life, in which the rewards as well as the responsibilities must be shared by all. Indeed, without this concept, democracy has no meaning and no permanence.

Let me be blunt: *Life*—in terms of human well-being—and human relations—*cannot be measured* by the disappearance of tension and conflict, nor simply by the appearance of a new vocabulary. It can, in the final analysis, be measured only by the extent to which all citizens have an opportunity to enjoy equally the benefits of democracy, by the extent to which their children receive adequate education and are able to qualify for good jobs that will enable them to purchase decent shelter so that they, in turn, may provide their children with a beneficial social, cultural and educational environment. To measure progress in race relations by any other criteria would be fallacious, for it would imply what we have historically disavowed—that there should be any difference in the status of American citizens.

Good race relations—race harmony—is more than the absence of conflict, tension, or even war. *It is the presence of justice.* Nothing is more immoral than the suggestion that people adjust to injustice or that we make a god of "timing." The time is always ripe to do right. It is not time for therapy alone, for the covering of cancer sores with Band-aids, or for rehabilitation to salvage what we can. This is the hour for preventive action as well—to assure a really changed future. The leadership of every community is challenged—both white and Negro—for the day is past when the mantle of leadership or expertness can be given to Negroes simply because they are Negroes, or to whites simply because they are committed to these causes. Now such conviction cannot be assumed; it must be proved, for professional leadership roles today pay good salaries and provide status and contacts that many individuals could not otherwise secure.

The programs we need to meet the explosive conditions of our time are not games to be played by self-serving politicians, opportunists, or sanctimonious do-gooders. The challenge must be met—and met now—by professionals, social scientists and practitioners, backed up by every thoughtful volunteer who can be mustered for the battle. Race relations is no longer a hobby for the well-intentioned, the idle, or the status-seeking. We can no longer play by ear in intergroup relations. We have advanced far enough in social science research so that intelligent, scientific planning can and must replace hit-or-miss action.

The Negro citizen today is unimpressed by arguments that he may be going too fast in the matter of civil rights, that he will have to wait, or that he will alienate some of his "white friends." The Negro resents people who use these arguments, because this reasoning suggests that civil rights can be negotiated. The assumption is that one human being has the right to limit another human being in the enjoyment of rights that are God-given and Constitutionally decreed for all.

As both Presidents Kennedy and Johnson have noted, civil rights demonstrations would be minimized, if not eliminated, if there were as much concern and indignation about the injustices and the discrimination against Negro citizens as there is about the demonstrations themselves. John F. Kennedy once said—when speaking about the Alliance for Progress—"If peaceful revolution is impossible, then violent revolution is inevitable." It would be wise for all Americans to apply these words to our own domestic crisis.

Let us consider this matter of responsibility a moment. The world was shocked last November by the assassination of President Kennedy in Dallas. Yet the trail to that excruciating event is traceable back through the earlier physical attacks on Ambassador Stevenson and the spitting and cursing at the then Vice-President and Mrs. Johnson in Dallas. The trail also leads back through Birmingham and September 16, 1963, when at 10:25 A.M. a blast ended the lives of four tiny Negro girls and wrecked the Sixteenth Street Baptist Church. This was the sixtieth bombing in a dozen years; it was followed by the police shooting of a teen-age Negro youth, and the killing of a Negro boy by two white Eagle Scouts.

The trail includes the ambush murder of Medgar Evers in Jackson, the killing of William Moore on his freedom walk and the many, many other instances of violence with community sanction. The doctrine of dissent by destruction had achieved a degree of unspoken acceptance and approbation over the years. The community, the state, the nation nurtured a climate that made these outrages possible every time psychopathic hatred lashed out without punishment, without prosecution, without even an attempt to locate the guilty.

In the Birmingham tragedy, three men were arrested by state police in connection with the bombing and were convicted of possessing dynamite without a permit—a misdemeanor. The two Eagle Scouts, who shot and killed young Virgil Ware were convicted of manslaughter, received seven months sentences, and were released to serve their terms on probation. Negro teen-ager Louvert Hill, who hurt a white boy with a brick that same day, was convicted of assault and sentenced to six months at hard labor by a Birmingham judge.

Clearly, these events indicated a decline in respect for law and order, and an increase in "personal justice"—to the point where any individual, given enough bitterness and hate plus a psychopathic personality, was encouraged—and even felt justified—in taking the law into his own hands. Given this climate, from the long view of the total community the specific victim is not important: the strong suffer with the weak; no one is safe. When once one person's freedom is violated, no one is free.

In our own time we have witnessed in Italy, Russia, Germany, and Japan the pattern of takeover that starts with the rotting and then the routing of legal justice. As Rabbi Joachim Prinz said in his "March on Washington" speech at the Lincoln Memorial:

> When I was the rabbi of the Jewish community in Berlin under the Hitler regime, I learned . . . that bigotry and hatred are not the most urgent problem. The most urgent, the most disgraceful, the most shameful and the most tragic problem is silence. A great people which had created a great civilization had become a nation of silent onlookers. They remained silent in the face of hate, in the face of brutality and in the face of mass murder.

Though I hope that we shall eliminate hate, we must not stand silent when hatred is manifested. It is absolutely necessary that people refrain or be prevented from acting out antisocial feelings. People in our land may disagree or dislike, but when dislike translates itself into aggressive, destructive action toward another human being such action must not be tolerated. President Kennedy, the six children in Birmingham, Medgar Evers, William Moore and so many others have been victims of a climate of apathy that is increasingly permissive of violence. Though Lee Oswald sighted the gun, all of us who were silent in the face of previous acts of violence, who expressed no indignation, took no action to punish, or reacted with only passing concern—all of us played a part in squeezing the trigger. President Kennedy's death, therefore, becomes a symbol of our silence, our inaction, our lack of courage.

But let us make no mistake. In every community there are leaders, there is a power structure, there are the articulators of conscience and arbiters of mores. On them, because of their privileged positions —privileged in that they manipulate the levers of power—the weight of responsibility weighs sevenfold. How have they acquitted their responsibilities?

Take Birmingham. A *New York Times* editorial stated on September 22, 1963:

> The most basic need—and the one still most glaringly unmet— is a clear acceptance of responsibility by Birmingham's white civic leaders for enforcing the law and making real the elementary pledges of equal opportunity and equal treatment contained in the biracial compact they negotiated last spring. The bestial murder of Negro Sunday-school pupils has shamed and shocked Birmingham, but thus far it has brought no crusading upsurge of community resolve to protect its Negro citizens in the only way that will guarantee genuine protection—by giving them the same rights and the same treatment that every white citizen enjoys.

In the adjoining column, James Reston told *Times* readers:

> the real power structure of the city—the older men who run the industries, banks and insurance companies that in turn influence the stores and big law firms—are not leading the peace effort. . . . There is general agreement here that these men [whom Reston named], working together with the leaders of the local clergy of both races, could do more to produce a compromise in a month than Federal troops, Federal officials and all the national Negro organizations put together could in years.

Was this responsibility shouldered?

Six months later, *Jet* magazine reported:

> Negroes are still not policemen. Negroes are not employed in high paying city or county government jobs. Private employers have made only token moves toward job equality and merit hiring.

243

Was this the touchstone of responsible action?

And what of the clergy? *The New York Times* reported, on March 16, 1964:

> A number of white liberals who disagreed with the city's racial policies have left. Most of these were ministers. One Protestant pastor left after an unsuccessful effort to admit Negroes to worship. In suburban Mountain Brook another Protestant minister resigned after his congregation insisted that his assistant was too liberal on the race issue. Other churches, however, have adjusted to the change. Ushers in a downtown church received notices that they were to seat visitors of 'any creed or color.'

And in his book *A Time to Speak*, Birmingham lawyer Charles Morgan tells how he was driven out of town for speaking out at the Birmingham Young Businessmen's Club against the citizens' guilt in the bomb slaughter of the four Negro girls at Sunday school.

Wherein responsibility here?

So much for Birmingham. On a larger stage, we may see the regional rejection of legal form in the South's defiance of the United States Supreme Court decision of 1954. This rejection, this militant, blatant, notorious opposition encouraged by such documents as the Southern Manifesto, convinced millions of Negro Americans that the vaunted processes of law and order could not be trusted—they were negated by wilful design of those in control of the communities of the South and their elected and appointed representatives.

Having fought the issue to the highest court in the land and seen the decision given in their favor, Negroes then experienced the most shameless perversion of justice. In state after state and school district after school district, human ingenuity was employed to defy the clear statement of the court. And where elusive action failed to nullify the court decision, violence, intimidation, legislative evasion, and even assassination were employed.

Where was responsibility in this?

The night after Mississippi NAACP secretary Medgar Evers was shot and killed at his front door I will never forget seeing the mass meeting at which his wife asked to speak. It was twenty-four hours after the murder and she stood there—a woman whose husband had been slaughtered for peaceful, legal protest of illegal, community sanctioned denials of Constitutional rights. Her children had been made fatherless; she had been widowed; she had no way of knowing what the uncertain future held for her or her family. She had every reason to be bitter and to hate.

But she stood before this highly charged audience and pleaded with these people not to hate but to love, not to be violent but to persist in the nonviolent way that her husband had counseled. Here were thousands of people who had known and loved Medgar Evers and who themselves had every reason to be incensed, to hate, and to seek vengeance. Yet when she finished they stood up and spontaneously sang "My Country 'tis of Thee, Sweet Land of Liberty. ..." Here was an outpouring of simple, deeply felt faith in a country by a people who have had so little reason to keep alive such belief. They said to America, "We believe in you."

Wherein responsibility here? It seems to me time for America to say to Negro citizens, "We believe in you."

Last August more than two hundred thousand Americans, black and white, witnessed, in the religious sense, their conviction that civil rights legislation for "complete equality in citizenship of the Negro minority" is overdue.

When we were planning the March on Washington, we heard many frightening predictions from people who did not want any kind of personal witnessing. They used scare forecasts about the possible outbreak of violence during the March. Mark my words: if the Negro were really a violent human being, he would have been violent long before now, or else he possesses the longest time-fuse ever known!

Actually, when people foresaw violence in connection with the March, they were really saying, "If I were a Negro, I would be violent." They were projecting their own feelings. The only violence that we were really afraid of was that which might have been perpetrated by the American Nazis and extreme right-wing individuals.

After we had taken elaborate precautions and given reassurances that there would be no violence, the prophets then predicted that we might make Congress react in a negative way, that Congress might resent this attempt at pressure. And we thought about the fact that nothing had happened in favor of the Negro all of these years when there had been no pressure. We thought also about the fact that the National Association of Manufacturers, the American Medical

Association, and the National Association of Real Estate Boards certainly were not in Washington merely to watch the Washington Senators play baseball. They were and are there to bring pressure. You can be sure that the people who are opposed to our cause are bringing pressure all the time.

So the March brought a quarter of a million American citizens from every part of the nation to affirm their belief in the strength of public petition in a democracy. They came and they went in a demonstration of peaceful assembly unparalleled in American history.

They asked enactment of the Civil Rights Bill; desegregation of all school districts, withholding of federal funds from discriminatory programs, enforcement of the Fourteenth Amendment, broader Fair Labor Standards Act and federal FEP law; a national minimum wage, an effective executive order banning discrimination in all federally supported housing, a massive federal retraining program and authority for the Attorney General to institute suits when constitutional rights are violated.

Wherein responsibility here?

Back in 1910 several small agencies banded together in New York to form the National League on Urban Conditions Among Negroes to improve social and economic conditions of Negro citizens through interracial teamwork. Initially, the League sought jobs for Negroes. It was at a time when jobs of any kind were needed, and the League did its work effectively, though hampered then as at all times during its history by lack of money and staff. The League worked for housing, health and welfare services, and education—then as well as now. Because of the halfhearted approaches to Negro needs by existing agencies, the League was forced to be the direct service organization to which Negroes came, whatever their problems. In return for taking over this catch-all responsibility, guilt-compensating token financial support was given the League and its affiliates.

An increasing number of Americans knows now what the League knew and has tried to tell the nation's citizens for fifty-four years: that segregation is not only inherently bad, but produces even greater problems. Segregated jobs may reserve better jobs for non-Negro citizens, but they deny to society excellent talents and skills; they destroy incentives for Negroes. Segregated housing may make some realtors wealthy through the carefully nurtured myth of exclusive neighborhoods, but it breeds slums, crime, de facto segregation in schools; it multiplies health and welfare costs. For too long, custom had referred all Negro problems to a single agency—the League—bypassing the numerous specialized, all-white services. This practice was not only unfair, but made it humanly impossible for the League to handle Negro problems adequately, to say nothing of executing its far more important job of social engineering. It was, as Lester Granger, past executive director of the League put it, "like bailing out a sinking ship with a teaspoon."

Nevertheless, the basic soundness of the League's efforts, the intense need for its services, and the solid record of achievement in more than sixty urban centers have won respect, recognition, and, at last, moderate financial support. With five hundred professional staff members and more than six thousand board members, both white and Negro, the League has proved that understanding and teamwork do make for community progress. The incredible element in the League story has been the dedication of its staff, who, as recently as 1950 were existing on average salaries of $3,500 and operating League programs in crucial urban areas on an average of $21,000 per year—scarcely enough to run a second-rate cigar store.

Wherein responsibility here?

The League as an organization has proposed a special effort, domestic Marshall Plan deliberately, to recall America's action in rehabilitating war-torn Europe. Our nation also has helped to rehabilitate and given asylum to Cuban and Hungarian refugees. If America is serious and honest about closing the discrimination gap that exists in our society between white and Negro citizens, we must do something equally special.

Neither the Negro nor the Urban League is asking for three hundred years of preferential treatment such as white citizens have had. We are asking for only a decade of dedicated special effort.

Who can call this irresponsibility?

At this point when the scales of justice are so grossly unbalanced, it is impossible to balance them by simply applying equal weight. What we are really talking about is correcting the injustices of the past and moving toward a situation where equal opportunity is a meaning-full word, and not a meaning-less word. We hope that people will not rationalize and say, "Well, I'm against any form of preference." People, who all of these years have never said anything about zero percent quotas of Negroes and one hundred percent quotas of white people, now suddenly become upset when in the transitional and negotiating stages we have to talk about numbers. We do so because employers and real estate men will hire or rent to one or two people and say, "Oh, we don't discriminate. We've got some Negroes." Yet people will cite the use of quotas as their excuse for maintaining the status quo.

We find such people in the churches of this nation—in the pulpits as well as the pews. Religion, instead of being an asset, has been a liability in this entire struggle for social reform. The church, until recently, anesthetized one of the major forces of social change: the American conscience. It provided people with a place where they could congregate regularly in a beautiful setting, hear pious platitudes, mouth meaningless clichés and then turned them loose to discriminate against their fellowmen the other six and nine-tenths days of the week. Eleven to twelve A.M. on Sundays has been the most segregated hour in America, and it has been easier to integrate the chorus line of a burlesque show than to integrate a choir in most of our churches.

The church must decide what it is going to do and what it is going to be. Is it a physical plant or is it a social institution? Is the ministry a profession where practitioners are more concerned about the facial expressions of their largest contributors than about helping their congregations to live up to the teachings found in the scriptures? Will they only reflect the congregation, will they merely mirror the prejudices of the congregation, or will they mold and lead their congregation?

The church's responsibility does not and cannot end with acceptance of Negroes as communicants. Negro children must be tutored and provided with educational material and extra help so that they will be prepared for the opportunity to be equal. Ministers must stand up and say no to injustice in their communities and in their own institutions. And they can start with the church-run hospitals, with the dollars they spend for building and expansion, with the actions of the church as employer, purchaser, contractor, investor, landlord, and administrator of funds. The church can relate its educational programs for both young and old to current social and ethical problems.

Furthermore, the church must do more than set up its own civil rights groups. It should also support with cooperation, volunteers, and financial aid, the established agencies that have a record of achievement in this field.

Even the President of the United States thought it important to tell leaders of the Southern Baptist Convention, "No group of Chrisians has more responsibility in civil rights than the Southern Baptists," because the power structure of the South attends their churches, and is represented on their boards. Because the beliefs of community leaders are confirmed or changed by the sermons they preach as well as the examples they set, President Johnson urged the clergymen to take a progressive position on civil rights.

The church will have no appeal for young people if it is merely a social society. The church must be a place at which we gather on Sunday to reaffirm our moral commitment. It must be a place where we revitalize ourselves for the moral witnessing that we experience throughout the week.

For the church and its membership, this is a time for demonstrating that piety rests not in affirming a creed but in confirmation by deed. This is the time to bear witness with acts, not with words.

For the public official—whether city, state, or federal—witnessing means implementation of broad, democratic promises and human rights, rather than preoccupation with technical, constitutional details and states' rights.

For the private sector of our society—whether business, labor, health, welfare, education, or philanthropy—witnessing means proving that the free enterprise system works equally well for all American citizens.

For the Negro citizen—responsible civil rights demonstrations are acts bearing witness to his faith in democracy through peaceful, nonviolent action and by channeling in constructive ways justified resentment and pent-up, frustrated emotions spawned by age-old abuses and contemptuous indignities.

For the white citizen—bearing witness means proving that democracy is an institution through which privileges and material benefits flow to all its citizens.

For both Negro and white citizens, democracy is a way of life, an ideal in which all share rewards as well as responsibilities. Indeed, without this concept, democracy has no meaning and certainly no permanence.

The sharing that I foresee is to be welcomed by white as well as black Americans. There are people who seem to think that every advance the Negro makes is at the expense of whites, that the Negro only progresses as the white gives up his freedoms. My concept of integration is not one of either the white or the Negro giving up all that he is used to. After honest examination of the positive and negative elements in each of the two cultures, we will retain the best in each. Responsible white leadership and the mass media must, with honesty and sincerity, promote and teach the idea that integration is an opportunity for all Americans rather than an irritating and uncomfortable problem.

For the Negro, obviously it means a better opportunity for decent housing and education, jobs and living. But it is not a matter of Negroes giving up all that has been part of their community, their background and their culture and adopting all that is white. Out of the years of suffering and deprivation the Negro has developed certain qualities—humaneness, compassion, patience, and endurance— and certain values that should be useful to whites either as individuals or in organizations such as General Motors or the Bank of America.

It was these qualities of perseverance, patience, resilience, of ability to adjust and adapt that were the sustaining pillars of Negro life; they have made possible his survival in spite of everything. These qualities are important to this nation which finds itself in a situation of leadership that is severely challenged, one in which it must make compromises and must adapt. In the United Nations we are finding that in order to lead we must recognize the rights of others.

So, though there are many qualities stemming from segregation that the Negro wants to eliminate and should, the same is also true of white society. The white culture, as a result of a period of dominance and privilege, has developed certain unhealthy qualities—indifference to others, for one, and a tendency toward a sense of superiority and exclusiveness for another.

I believe the time is near when people will apologize for sameness. When somebody asks if you have any Negroes in your neighborhood, and the answer is no, their response will be, "That's too bad; you're out of step." People are beginning to boast of the diversity of their neighborhoods, their business staffs and their schools. Top business corporations, exclusive suburbs and the truly leading schools are clamoring for Negroes. This is where *special effort* is coming into play. Business is sending recruiting teams in unprecedented numbers to Negro colleges and is calling on the Urban League for help in locating qualified Negroes. Citizen groups in the formerly most exclusive residential towns in the nation are writing the Urban League for help in locating Negroes interested in moving to their neighborhoods. And a few of the sincere, enlightened prep schools and colleges in the United States are re-evaluating certain requirements, taking into consideration the fact that the reading level may not be as high for a Negro because of his cultural background, and setting up scholarships because of the Negroes' economic disadvantages.

Integration is an opportunity for white citizens to show to the whole world their maturity and their security. It is time for them consciously to proclaim the creative possibilities in that diversity from which they have unconsciously benefitted. People do not grow through similarity to one another. One grows from the stimulus of people who are different, people whose cultural backgrounds are heterogeneous. One contributes to the other. In my own case, I moved into a neighborhood where there are no other Negroes. Until then, my children had never had an opportunity to light Hannukah candles and until then many of my neighbors' children had never had a chance to decorate a Christmas tree. These children grew and learned simply by knowing each other.

When you surround yourself with people who drive the same cars and have the same skin color and go to the same churches, clubs and parties and read the same books all you do is perpetuate a type of homogenized mediocrity. Probably no nation owes so much to diversity as does ours. We have benefited in myriad ways from the vast variety of contributions to our way of life by people of all manner of backgrounds. Think of the foods, stemming from different cultures, that we enjoy every day; look at the art, dance, clothing, toys and games, music, even the words in our American language that derive from other countries—all of these make life in this nation zestful. In centuries past, the county fair was the annual occasion that introduced to an area the exotic and stimulating features of faraway places. In the United States, with our mobility and our communications media, ours is a 24-hour-a-day, 365-days-a-year interchange with the rest of the world. And how much more we enjoy and absorb from life when we open our senses to the manifold varieties of "otherness" available to us. Men grow to the extent that they are the beneficiaries of diverse ideas, not through the process of having their ideas reflected and reinforced by people whose backgrounds and cultures are identical.

We are, through integration, seeking to help all our citizens realize their true, creative potentials and to move toward a new type of society that is not a replica of any past culture or any single group, but is a culture that has absorbed the best from each.

What can be done to hasten integration? We have considered many avenues in this book. Here is a general checklist for citizens and communities who resolve to bring about change:

1. Face the fact that your community does discriminate.

2. Make right, justice and democratic process your objectives. Do not set your goals merely to be better than Mississippi, Georgia and South Africa.

3. Understand what the Negro citizen wants; but even more important, realize that as an American citizen, his rights are both God-given and Constitutionally guaranteed.

4. Do not use the tragic results of inequality to justify continuing it. This is not only cruel but illogical. George Bernard Shaw once said "America makes the Negro a bootblack, then condemns him because he is one."

5. Understand that words like *gradualism* and *moderation* are phantom terms—meaningless. These are results from, not methods of working. You either hire a man or you do not. You either let him live in a neighborhood or you do not. You either let him join your church or club or use your parks, libraries, public facilities and hospitals or you do not.

6. Do not become patronizing or condescending. The persecutor

suffers almost as much as the persecuted in this business of human relations.

7. Finally, and most important, work for the adoption of a domestic *special effort* program in all areas of our society, such as has been described in this book, so that along with equal opportunity will go the opportunity to be equal.

Time is not our ally in this struggle, and if we fail to grasp the urgency of the moment and to seize imaginatively upon the opportunities that are ours, we shall incur—and justly so—not only the wrath of this generation of young people but the disdain of generations yet unborn.

For Negro citizens more is at stake than personal security, which at best can be but temporary until every other man of color enjoys equally the same security and the same opportunity, whatsoever his present station in life.

For white citizens the same might be said—and even more—for at stake is also the issue of whether they can rise above the moral decadence of their ancestors as the "superior" possessors of special privileges and learn to share equally in what would be a much more creative world of equal reward and equal responsibility.

I am asking Americans to heed Horace Mann, who said, "Be ashamed to die until you achieve some victory for mankind." Do this not just because it is the thing to do, or because you will be rendering good to somebody else. Do it because it gives meaning to your own life; do it so that one day your children won't have to apologize for us and wonder how we could have fought so hard and so long over segregation—a principle that was so basically wrong. Do this because it is only when an individual identifies himself with something that transcends self and family that his life has real meaning.

And whenever you begin to feel helpless, I would like you to think about an experience that I had at Soldier's Field in Chicago at the music festival one August. As we filed into that vast arena, everybody was given a match, and at a certain point in the program all the lights were turned out and one hundred thousand people were in darkness. Each person was asked to strike his match. I am certain each one of us thought, "What can I do with this little match?" But we all went along with the request and struck our tiny matches. And because one hundred thousand matches were struck, the place became as light as brightest day. This we can do as individuals. Each can strike his match. We can't just sit and wait for somebody else. We must go ahead—alone, if necessary, but together in the end.

At stake are people—their hopes and their aspirations for themselves and their loved ones as they witness all around them great social and technological changes that could not only threaten their dreams of a better tomorrow, but make uncertain even the sordid existence that is theirs today.

The Negro is a barometer of all America's institutions and values. He is a test of whether or not the free enterprise system really works. For, as Franklin D. Roosevelt said, "The test of our society is not whether we give more to those who already have enough, but whether we give enough to those who have too little."

The drive to be equal is a crusade for justice, for decency, for morality, honesty, and frankness. It is a crusade to put into operational framework on a day-to-day, person-to-person basis the American creed and the American Dream. As Americans, ours is an obligation most immediately to the Negro citizen, but in the final analysis it is a responsibility to all our citizens as America faces its greatest domestic challenge. By meeting this responsibility America will emerge at last—unified, strengthened, and triumphant.

AFTERWORD FOR THE PAPERBACK EDITION

To Be Equal was first published in 1964, just as the battle for basic civil rights legislation was reaching its climax.

Its purpose was to alert concerned Americans to the need for special effort to change the cancerous conditions afflicting the majority of Negro citizens. By and large, the conditions deforming them were—and are still—a cancerous element in the body politic. Their ills, their poverty, their inadequacies, and their bitterness and hatred were, and are spreading and increasing, in comparative terms, like the abnormal growth of human body cells out of control. As with cancer, treatment of the conditions affecting American Negroes requires all-out, crash-program special effort. In this book I have attempted to describe why such effort is needed and suggest some of the avenues that should be pursued.

The nation has changed and grown in two years. Economically it is in its greatest period of prosperity, ever. The Civil Rights, Economic Opportunity and Voting Rights acts are now on the books. We have a new Department of Housing and Urban Development. The government has, under the constructive leadership of the present administration, provided answers to some of the problems of Negro citizens. Now the prestige and impetus of the federal establishment are officially enlisted in aiding and enforcing the rights of citizens. Previously the government was a bystander and sometime referee.

Many states and cities have acted to improve conditions of Negroes and others in slums and ghettoes. The agencies that have for decades helped Negro citizens are now better-financed and staffed than ever before and consequently able to do a better job for more needy citizens than in the past. Business and industry, the voluntary agencies, the educational institutions have awakened to the situation. The alert, the dedicated, the significant and leading organizations in these fields have applied resourcefulness to the huge tasks of bringing Negro citizens into the mid-twentieth century. The rest, the majority of organizations in these fields, have yet to bestir themselves adequately.

These positive factors have affected the conclusions that seemed valid in 1964 and the projections you will find in this book. They have affected them, but not negated them.

For instance, the great prosperity of today has cut unemployment to the bone—but not for the Negro population. As an example, the unemployment rate for whites, nationwide, dropped from 5% in 1960 to 4.1% in 1965—nearly 20%. In Watts, the stagnating, riot-ripped ghetto of Los Angeles, the rate changed too: from 14.2% in 1960 to 13.2% in 1965—hardly a scratch.

Another instance: Family income in the U.S. reached a new all-time high in 1965. Nationwide, U.S. white family income went from $5,835 in 1960 to $6,858 in 1965. For people living in Watts, as an example, it went from $3,879 in 1960 to $3,803 in 1965.

So, though the particulars may have changed, the over-all situation for the majority of Negro Americans in 1966, is still fundamentally as described herein. The real question for this generation of Americans is whether they will tire and lose interest. Will they turn their backs on implementation of the laws, pronouncements and superhuman efforts that have brought such progress as we have so far enjoyed? Another generation of Americans shrugged their shoulders and washed their hands of such involvement in the 1870's, to the detriment of our nation.

As a nation, as citizens, as human beings, we cannot afford a repeat performance.

Whitney M. Young, Jr.
April 1966